Praise for Light behind

Since the first edition was published in 2(reviews and feedback. Here are just a few of the comments from readers:

I got the book 6 days after it was ordered. As I unwrapped the book I knew I was going to want a sequel.. First glance and I was hooked! The cover picture reached out and grabbed me, the title pulled me in, and the chapter names are so intriguing, I felt like I won the lottery! I have been unable to put this book down, at the same time dreading when I will finish it. I don't want it to end!! This book needs a prequel And a sequel ... Firefly, USA

The book is beyond amazing, and your writing captivating. I have noticed several things in the book that we share in common, allowing me to better understand and accept. Big Thank You for this. You have reached out across the miles and guided me without realizing it. If Light Behind The Angels was mandatory reading for everyone, Earth would be in a better place!!

I received this book in the post and started reading it the moment I got home from work - I could not put it down, it was riveting. Love, passion, intrigue, broken hearts, past lives and an ancient curse - just how was it all going to turn out? Would Lauren find fulfilling love & her perfect life with her 'Twin Flame' or would the High Priest break the curse & win her heart? Not a work of fiction, but a true story and I actually knew how it ended before opening to the first page, but it didn't stop me from being captivated. The ending? Well, you will have to find out for yourself... Crystal Dragon, UK

I have finished your book... one word Amazing! I love your writing style; whilst reading I felt I was getting to know an old friend. Your journey is (and was!) wonderful, it was great to see how your life has been shaped by experiences and that you have your guides etc to help you. I know it has been a tough one for you and I send a hug across the miles...
...It was a genuine pleasure to read and I felt a little sad at the end as I wanted more!! Truly inspirational. James, Kenya

A very deep book told in an easy to read way, which I didn't expect from a "new age" book. Amazing story which taught me and helped me a lot in my own life. I was also touched by Lauren D'Silva's honesty towards writing her feelings which a lot of authors would have disguised or dismissed in their own books. Much respect.

A wonderful and enlightening book to read. It should come with a warning as I could not put it down!! Easy to read as it was written as only a natural writer can - it kept me intrigued until the end BUT then I wanted more!! Can't wait for Lauren's next book.

Light behind the Angels
A past life journey to enlightenment

Lauren D'Silva

Lauren D'Silva © Copyright 2010
All rights reserved
No parts of this publication may be reproduced, stored in a retrieval system, or transmitted in any form or by any means, electronic, mechanical, photocopying, recording or otherwise without the prior permission of the author.

ISBN 978-1-291-08960-8

Cover illustration ©iStockphoto.com/Oleg Prikhodko
Internal photographic images ©Lauren D'Silva
All rights reserved

The names of individuals in this book have been changed, where applicable, to protect people's privacy.

Light behind the Angels

'Our deepest fear is not that we are inadequate, our deepest fear is that we are powerful beyond measure. It is our light, not our darkness that most frightens us. We ask ourselves, "Who am I to be brilliant, gorgeous, talented and fabulous?" Actually who are we not to be?

You are a child of God. Your playing small doesn't serve the world. There is nothing enlightened about shrinking so that other people won't feel insecure around you. We were born to manifest the glory of God that is within us. It is not just in some of us, it is in everyone and as we let our light shine, we unconsciously give other people permission to do the same. As we are liberated from our own fear our presence automatically liberates others.'

Marianne Williamson, A Return to Love: Reflections on the Principles of a Course in Miracles.

Acknowledgements

My thanks to all those souls who have met me on my path and guided me, challenged me, goaded me or held me. Whether you were motivated by love, kindness, cruelty or indifference, knowingly or unknowingly you have shaped my life and played your part.

To my Moon Goddesses, Selina and Semele, you have listened to me when I have been in the depths of despair, forgiven me when I have been unreasonable and joined me in my celebrations. Thank you for demonstrating true and constant friendship.

Grateful thanks to Lyn Webster-Wilde and to all those who encouraged and cajoled me to get my story written and out there.

To Lynne Lauren. You gave me the title for the book years before it was written in a reading, "You are going to be writing a book. It is very spiritual, there's a lot of Light behind it." I miss you.

To my helpers in Spirit for your gentle and not so gentle guidance. Thank you for being there for me all of the time whether I am paying attention or not.

And last, but not least, my especial gratitude to Steve. You have tested me close to destruction more than once, but without you the truth would never have emerged.

Prologue

This is my journey from fear to empowerment. It follows the process of uncovering the light at my core, which often challenged my beliefs about myself and my assumptions about the world we live in.

I have literally been re-member-ing myself. In my quest for freedom I have followed the clues and been led to find pieces of my psyche scattered in distant lands and across time. I have healed ancient wounds, released curses and dissolved shame and in doing so freed myself from the past and made myself whole.

There has been no need to embroider what happened, I haven't needed to fictionalise my story; it is my Truth. The biggest resistance in me has been to publicly own those elements that seem sensational and otherworldly.

Life is a magical and rich experience if you are ready to see beyond the surface and explore your true self. When you truly open your eyes you'll see new layers of existence that have always been there, hidden in plain sight.

Reflections 2013

Had I but known how incendiary this book was to be when it was first published in 2010 my courage might have faltered. The repercussions have been far reaching, bringing me tears and great heartache. I am now the 'black sheep' in my parents' eyes, a persona non grata, however through their rejection I have found greater personal strength and self reliance. I am truly sorry for any hurt caused to anyone in telling my story, however I know I have remained true to my Self and that Truth is not up for negotiation, however much it costs.

From the feedback of readers I know this book has helped many others along their path and I have been bowled over by the warmth and enthusiasm for my writing. I've lost count of the number of people who said they read late into the night, or finished reading the book only to immediately begin it again!

So, would I publish my story if I had the benefit of hindsight? I would.

Light behind the Angels

Moving Times

*'Life is full and overflowing with the new. But it is necessary
to empty out the old to make room for the new to enter.'*
Eileen Caddy, Footprints on the Path

I had all the accoutrements of a successful life. I had a good husband, children, pets, our own house, my dream job. I had all the outer trappings that we are conditioned to strive for in Western society. So why wasn't I content? What was I missing? What was wrong with me?

Perhaps it was living in the suburbs of a busy city? I had long nurtured a dream to move away. By now my nerves felt frazzled by the hectic pace of life and congested traffic. Every time we went on holiday I would lead the conversation round to how much better life would be if we lived 'somewhere like this' whether 'this' was the Norfolk coast, the Welsh hills, the Malvern hills or Derbyshire. Anywhere with less congestion and open countryside felt so much better; soothing to my soul.

It seemed like my fantasy of living in the countryside would stay a dream. We never got around to doing anything concrete about it. Life was a bit too comfortable and the impetus to uproot just wasn't strong enough to make the move a reality. Then one day it was announced my whole team was moving workplace, the journey time would be much longer. There was no negotiation, the decision had been made. I tried the new routine for six months, but my dream job had lost its lustre and I wanted out.

I went to see the manager and found I was weeping with stress and frustration in his office, letting him know that I would have to resign if I couldn't move back. Emotionless he looked at me with eyes like cold poached eggs and said no exceptions would be made. Sometimes you need a big push to pursue your dreams and this cold blooded official propelled me along my path in a way that a kind man would never have done. With no job to hold me in place this seemed a good opportunity to stop dreaming and go for the big move. Thankfully my husband agreed.

Over the years I had surfed the internet for properties in other areas, feeding my dream of an escape to the country. I'd fantasised about what our money could buy in more remote areas of the UK. Having trained and qualified as a crystal therapist, which I loved, I had an idea that I might run a New Age shop full of incense, crystals and candles with a healing room above.

I remembered a huge four storey Victorian property on the market a year before with a shop on the ground floor. It was the same price as a small terraced house in the city and I'd spent a fair bit of time drooling over the details. It was situated next door to a vegetarian café in a little Welsh town I'd never heard of before, Llandrindod Wells.

By the time we made our decision to move the shop had been sold, fortunately for us as things transpired, you'll find out why later. I browsed the internet to see what else was available nearby. Property in this small Welsh Spa town was substantially cheaper than the city and there were a good number of the high ceilinged, spacious, Victorian houses we both liked. I fancied the sound of a huge rectory that came with its own church hall and had fun visualising running courses there. There was a vast hotel on the edge of town just within our reach. Residential courses maybe? Before I could get too carried away my husband pointed out that he didn't really want other people in his living space and anywhere that cheap would need a lot of money spent on renovation. I reset my search criteria to a fair sized family home.

The more I researched Llandrindod the more auspicious the town seemed to me. I found out that the whole town owed its very existence to its spring waters and was dedicated to the goddess of healing Hygeia. Prosperous in the Victorian era it had fallen on hard times after the First World War, when the fashion for taking the waters became just a memory.

We visited and as soon as we arrived I felt at home. Exploring Llandrindod's Rock Park, tasting the cold blood tang of the free running Chalybeate Spring, walking through tree lined paths to the whispering River Ithon, eating ice cream at the lake, all of these things easily won us over.

The air was clean, the pace of life was unhurried and I felt relaxed in a way I'd never done in the city. Living here would be like a permanent holiday.

On our first visit I fell in love with one of the houses we viewed. An airy semi-detached Edwardian property on three floors, with seven bedrooms and three large receptions. It was stretching our budget, but simply magnificent and I loved it as soon as I stepped through the front door into a black and white tiled entrance hall spacious enough to hold a party in.

Back in the City I was teaching Crystal Therapy with a friend and we decided to run a Healing Arts Festival together. We had a psychic reader there and I chose to have a reading with him. Clive turned out to be a true clairvoyant and he gave me a more detailed and specific reading than I'd ever had before. He taped it and I listened to it in the car many times. I'm not sure what happened to that recording,

Light behind the Angels

but I can still remember the key details. He picked up on our move straight away, "I'm seeing Wales, not North or South Wales, Mid Wales, somewhere near the Wye valley. That's funny; we are looking in that area too. I like New Radnor."

Wow, spot on! Llandrindod Wells is in Mid Wales and not far from the River Wye which runs through our neighbouring town of Builth Wells. Clive's reading continued with a description of the house, however this didn't match our intended Edwardian property at all. "An old place, quite small with something a bit wonky about the roof. There are flag stones and a big step to the kitchen, a big inglenook fireplace too. I can see a stream no wider than this table and there are badgers. Your man is outside chopping wood. When you get this place the relationship will just flourish. At the moment it isn't so good but this will suit you both. He's working at something outdoors."

It was true that our marriage didn't feel emotionally fulfilling, but it was an efficient working partnership. We got on well enough, didn't argue and loved our two children. There wasn't much spark; after so many years together maybe that was natural? Perhaps the move would change things?

Clive's picture of a cottage style property seemed rather unlikely. Year on year I would rent a cosy holiday cottage, a style I personally love, and annually my tall husband would bang his head on low beams and swear loudly. Once he nearly knocked himself out. As for chopping firewood and working outdoors? He'd always done office jobs. Gifted with intelligence he was a policy writer, a meeting organiser. This was a very different version of him.

There was a warning for me that didn't make sense until much later, "Men see your power and they try to nick it." Clive moved on, "You do know you are a healer don't you?" I nodded. "You'll both do healing but he'll heal in his way and you'll heal in your way."

My husband had always been supportive of my healing and been a long suffering guinea pig while I'd been training as a crystal therapist, but despite his own natural psychic ability he didn't show a great desire to join in. Perhaps that would all change too?

Clive and I swapped phone numbers and agreed to keep in touch with each other. It was interesting that he was particularly drawn to the pretty little village of New Radnor, with its main street supported by a huge castle mound that rises behind like an upturned jelly mould. It's only new in the sense that it isn't as ancient as Old Radnor. In a search to find the happiest place to live in the UK New Radnor topped the poll.

Over the next few months we visited Llandrindod and viewed more properties, including return visits to the Edwardian house. It was the start of the second Gulf War and it made me smile to see our prospective neighbours were protesting NO WAR in huge whitewashed letters on all of their windows. I'd been active in the Green Party years before and I'd joined a CND candlelit vigil on the eve of the first Gulf War. The press photographer singled me out for a portrait photograph on the front page of the local paper at that time much to the irritation of the woman who'd organised the vigil and to the amusement of all the school children I taught. Peace protesters would be fine as neighbours.

We'd been staying at a welcoming Arts and Crafts style B&B where the proprietor was always friendly, helpful and the font of knowledge on all things local. I asked him about the shop I'd seen on the internet before and enquired where the vegetarian café had gone. He pointed out of his window to a little run of shops opposite. They'd been there, but the shop had sold a while back and the café was closed now. I told him about the house I'd set my heart on and a strange piece of synchronicity emerged. The former proprietors of the café lived in the house next door. They were the peace protesters. It seemed that they really were destined to be our next door neighbours. It felt so right and so guided, despite Clive's picture of a cosy cottage.

Back home we put our house on the market and got a pleasant surprise. House prices had moved rapidly upwards and the dream house was more affordable than we'd thought. Our house sold quickly and within a few months we'd moved.

We had an interesting introduction to the town. Our moving date was set right in the middle of Llandrindod's annual Victorian Festival and so our first impression as new residents was decidedly quirky. Gentlemen in top hats and frock coats walked arm in arm with ladies wearing enormous bustles carrying parasols. Perhaps this was an early sign of the bizarre twists of fate that life would present over the coming years?

The children arrived a few days later, brought to the town by my parents. They turned up just in time for the grand finale of Victorian week, a dazzling fireworks display over the town's lake. I felt it was a fitting welcome for the pair of them.

Our new house was wonderful. It had been neglected over the years and needed someone to love it. At one point it had been a nursing home and it still had the old stair lift and washbasins in every bedroom. The bathroom was tiny and claustrophobic, decked out in a cracked plastic 70's avocado suite. Many of the windowpanes were broken and had been 'mended' with sellotape. I felt it made the house look like it was wearing broken National Health specs. There was

Light behind the Angels

plenty of scope for improvement and we threw ourselves into renovation with gusto.

The beautiful black and white checkerboard tiles in the hall disappeared under a grotty grey carpet in the inner lobby and emerged again in a vestibule on the other side. Out first action had to be to pull up the carpet and find out whether the tiles extended right though. They did! We hired an obliging handyman who went around repairing windows and chopping out rot from window frames, turning his hand to just about anything that didn't involve going up ladders. We converted one of the larger bedrooms into a palatial bathroom fitted with a clean white bathroom suite. It was such a grand space that Clive enquired, "Does that bathroom have its own postcode?" on his first visit.

Gradually the house responded to our care and started to feel loved again. Our neighbours were just as welcoming as we'd hoped and we found we had plenty in common. Their little granddaughter visited often and struck up a friendship with my son. We were honoured that they re-opened the 'window' in the hedge which they'd allowed to grow over whilst the previous owners had been in residence. Now we could share a chat over coffee and hand small children through the gap to play together. It was a lot of fun.

My husband and I both loved the house and the area, but he found it difficult to find work and in those early days I was obliged to travel all over England to carry out the education consultancy work I'd secured. I felt like I'd moved to Wales only to have to leave time and time again. Leaving did underline how at home I felt here. There was a huge sense of relief and a feeling of homecoming whenever I drove back over the border and saw 'my hills'.

As I type, Canada geese have flown past my window in a V-shaped skein honking softly to each other. I'm looking out upon fields, trees and distant hills. Six years on I still adore this area and give thanks for the courage and impetus that we both needed to make the move.

Journeying to Other Realms

'When fairy tales and legends old
Tell the true history of the world'
Novalis

I'd been introduced to a lovely aromatherapist, Marie, who combined her talents as a contemporary artist with her holistic therapies. I'd seen her before. She cut an eccentric, but striking dash around Mid Wales, wearing layers of bright and sparkly clothing, standing out like an exotic bird in this muted landscape populated with welly wearing hill farmers. Her flat was no less striking and incongruous; you stepped from a gloomy Victorian landing into a bohemian palace, with walls daubed in bright colours, every nook adorned with fairy lights, feathers, pictures and ornaments. I loved to visit this magical place and she was always a delightful host.

Marie introduced me to a shamanic healer, Patricia. We got on well together and on Marie's recommendation I decided to do her Introduction to Shamanism course. That was a life transforming decision. I'd been aware of my guides working with me for some years, feeling them around me, sensing their hands over mine when I was healing and knowing that they were helping me, but I didn't know any names or have a picture of them in my mind. All I knew was that their energy felt supportive and I could trust them.

There were just two other participants on the day. One was a rather ample lady who was into angels and crystals, the other a shy young man. He was a Buddhist who had just left a job as a copywriter producing junk mail, which he hated. He was there to try and break through his writer's block and get into more positive and life enhancing creative writing.

We began. Patricia called in the powers of the four directions through rattling and chanting. We then moved through some energy sensing activities and Patricia explained that we'd be exploring the three realms of the shaman, the Lower World of animal spirit helpers, the Upper World of our spirit guides and the Middle World which is essentially overlying the world we live in and is the place where elemental energies can be contacted.

Soon we were on our first shamanic journey. We lay covered by blankets and blindfolded on Patricia's floor. I'd never journeyed before and wondered if it would even work for me. I tried not to let performance anxiety get the better of me and to just allow whatever was to come.

Light behind the Angels

Our first trip was to visit the Lower World to find our power animal. I visualised myself standing by a huge tree with a mossy trunk which had a hollow like a doorway at the bottom. As Patricia started to drum for us I stepped in and found myself in a dark tunnel leading vertically down through the Earth. I didn't feel I was falling, just gliding down it as if riding in an invisible lift.

Arriving at the bottom I found myself in a very dark cave. I could make out glittering quartz crystals in the walls. Although it was dark I could just see creatures. A mouse scuttled past and a bat flew over my head. Suddenly, right up close to me a large black crow-like bird appeared. I asked if it was my power animal and turned a quarter turn away as I'd been instructed. Quick as a flash there it was again right up against my face. I turned to ask in each of the directions and it was there eye to eye with me before I could get any words out.

The drum beat changed to the call back, time to leave. I asked my bird if he would return with me and he spread his wings and flew up the tunnel alongside me.

I was intrigued. I had expected a bird of prey, perhaps an owl, as I have always had an affinity with them. This large black crow was not what I'd imagined and its behaviour was less than subtle. I knew this wasn't just my imagination.

We shared our experiences in the group. The Buddhist had travelled to a dry desert landscape, but had seen no animals; though he had a feeling he was being watched. The other lady had a glamorous white tiger with a magnificent jewel set in its forehead. My crow seemed a bit drab in comparison.

Our next journey was to the Upper World. After my Lower World journey I felt more confident that I could do this. We were to meet our spirit guide and if we had our power animal we were advised it might want to come along too.

The drumming started. I saw the same tree, but this time climbed to the topmost branches where my crow was waiting. I realised he was willing to fly up with me. We flew together through the sky and out of Earth's atmosphere into space, out of our solar system and into the stars. I felt we'd gone as far as we possibly could when I sensed a slight pressure and came through into a land, of sorts.

I was standing in a pure white landscape, snowy in appearance, although I didn't feel cold. In the distance was a picture book range of white mountains. My spirit guide was already waiting for me. Gosh, he was exceptionally handsome. He stood dressed as a Celtic warrior with a thick red cloak, fastened at the throat with a Celtic patterned brooch. He carried a sword and a golden shield.

Neatly bearded with longish wavy brown hair he wore a thin gold crown with a single jewel at the front. Despite his heroic appearance he seemed familiar to me and looking into his eyes I felt I had known him for a very long time. As we stood looking at each other my big crow was hopping between our shoulders in excitement.

We stepped forward and embraced. My guide kissed me on the forehead and I was aware that my appearance was altered. I was slimmer and wearing a medieval style red velvet dress. My hair was similar, but longer and curly reddish brown. I was a ravishing 'Mills and Boon' version of myself!

I asked my Guide for his name and he replied, "Bran." I thought I'd misheard him. Next I asked if he had anything to give me and he presented me with the golden brooch from his cloak. The design was of an even armed cross with a clear red jewel in the centre. I received this gift with thanks. We embraced once again and the drum beat changed. It was time to say our farewells and return.

The Buddhist had only managed to fly a short way before he'd got tired out, so he stopped at a comfortable looking cloud and lay down to rest. The other lady had met with no less than five assorted female guides. I talked about my warrior, but omitted his name as I wasn't convinced I'd really heard it.

It was time for lunch and Patricia went to warm up some soup she was providing. She left us with a pile of reference books to look up our power animals. I flicked through the 'Druid Animal Oracle' by Philip and Stephanie Carr-Gomm. There was no Crow, but there was an entry for Raven. I was astounded to see that directly under the title 'Raven' was the word *'Bran'*. Talk about instant confirmation! My big black bird wasn't a crow, it was a raven and my guide really was called Bran. Here he was listed as one of the heroes of Celtic mythology and 'Bran' means 'raven' in Welsh. No wonder my big crow had been so excited to introduce me to him, we shared our Raven ally.

I felt shy about claiming such an important figure as my main spirit guide. I'd maintained a healthy scepticism when people claimed they were working with famous spirit guides. Suddenly here I was with a superhuman figure from Celtic legend. Why would a Celtic King be guiding me and why did he seem so very familiar?

After a great lunch, we went journeying for each other. I paired up with the other lady whilst Patricia worked with the Buddhist to help him connect with his power animal. I asked for advice on developing my healing. We were told to journey, ask the question and simply report back whatever we were shown. When my partner returned she said she'd been told I'd be a leader of the New Age. This seemed somewhat ambitious, but I noted it down dutifully.

Light behind the Angels

My partner wanted advice on bringing romance into her life. I met up with Bran again. He held out his cupped hands and gold glittered, overflowing them, falling and swirling into a large bronze cauldron. I reported these symbolic images back, unsure of what they meant. I think she was a little disappointed that I hadn't come up with something more concrete, like the name and address of an available man!

We went outside for a medicine walk in Nature. We were to bring back an object. Patricia was living in a farmhouse on a lonely Welsh hillside. I picked my way across a small stream to a copse of twisted oak trees. It felt very peaceful and old. I found myself a comfortable moss covered rock and sat down. I was glad of the solitude and I shed a few tears. For some years I had secretly been yearning for the heart connection of a true soul mate and now I had felt that deep connection with Bran.

On our return to the house we went on a healing journey for ourselves. I travelled around my body and came to my left hip which had been sore. I could see what looked like a spiky metal ball wedged there and with the help of Bran I removed it. Afterwards the physical pain was gone. Shamanism was impressive stuff!

I had often asked clients to go to an area of discomfort in their bodies and imagine what they could see there. I hadn't been taught this; it had just evolved as part of the way I work. On one memorable occasion the client had been due to have gall bladder surgery. When she went to the area of pain she found she was swimming through a lake of horrible black liquid that was blocked from draining by boulders. As I poured healing energy into the site she imagined breaking up the stones until they were small enough to flush away and then the liquid began to drain off.

Next day she rang me. She'd been vomiting vile black stuff and had bouts of black diarrhoea overnight. She thought she was okay and was convinced she was having a major clear out, but wanted to check with me. I felt she was going to be alright, however I went on the net and the only references I could find to black stools indicated internal bleeding. I sent her straight off to the GP to get it all checked out. To his credit he didn't question her when she told him what she'd done and she was not only found to be fine, she no longer needed an operation. I now realise I had been using shamanic-style techniques without knowing it.

Returning home at the end of the course I told my husband about it, going easy on the heart connection between my guide and myself. He seemed unimpressed and rather dismissive even of the amazing Bran/Raven synchronicity and I felt slightly deflated.

Later I went onto the internet to look up Raven and Bran. I realised Raven was a powerful magical ally and was linked both to healing and psychic work. Bran was from a pre Arthurian era and he appears in the Welsh epic, the Mabinogion, as well as being remembered in many Welsh place names. He is also named Bran the Blessed, so maybe this was why I'd received an even armed cross as a gift.

Reading further I found out that the ravens kept to this day at the Tower of London are there because Bran's head was supposed to have been buried on Tower Hill to watch over his kingdom. The legend goes that if the ravens leave the Tower the kingdom will fall and so the birds have their wings clipped, cheating a little perhaps! In the Second World War bombing of London the ravens escaped and Winston Churchill ordered more to be brought from Scotland and Wales, just showing how steeped in myth these Isles are.

Bran had possessed a magical cauldron that brought dead warriors back to life. I'd seen this cauldron on my journey for the angel lady without knowing about the myth. Everything was so closely interwoven that I knew this was a real contact.

Stepping Further into Myth and Legend

> *'The moment one begins dreaming-awake, a world of enticing, unexpected possibilities opens up. A world where the ultimate audacity becomes a reality. Where the unexpected is expected. That's the time man's definitive adventure begins.'*
> Florinda Donner

Clive and I got our heads together and decided to run small psychic fairs. It seemed a good way to get his name known and promote my crystal therapy business in a new area and we planned a series of events up and down the borders and around Mid Wales. Some were great, like our first one in Offa's Dyke Centre in Knighton, some were overwhelming, like the one held in Llandrindod where we had at least three times more customers than capacity, at other times we spent the evening doing readings for each other because there were only a handful of visitors.

Overall the fairs were a good way to meet new people and to get familiar with the small towns around the area. Running these events I realised I was being introduced to a network of people on my wavelength and the psychic and healing world was firing me up in a way that education could never compete with.

I took on a morning a week working in the Celtic shop in town. As well as selling tourist pleasing lovespoons and Celtic design jewellery there were Mind, Body, Spirit books and card packs, essential oils, candles and essences. It wasn't quite the shop I'd envisaged I might run, but it was along the right lines and a pleasant place to be. Again I met new people and was able to publicise my healing and courses. It also cured me of 'wanting a little shop' as spending half a day a week behind a shop counter was more than enough for me and I realised I'd be terribly bored and restricted if I had a place of my own. Nevertheless it provided me with a little oasis of serenity once a week for the next five years.

It took me just a year after moving to assemble my first group of crystal therapy students in Wales. Looking back that really wasn't bad going, but it seemed a long time when I was anxious to start teaching again. This first group were all very capable and mature healers. They gelled quickly and teaching them was a real treat. Sometimes I would offer myself as 'a body' for certain techniques.

One day I was lying on the couch while a sweet and very spiritual lady carried out the healing technique I'd demonstrated.

Holding crystals around my head her clairvoyance kicked in. First she saw sparkling golden rays coming out from all around my head, "Like a picture of the Virgin Mary," she said. She began to receive clairvoyant pictures, telling me what she was seeing. The observing student scribbled down the vision. She saw me at the time of King Arthur's court, as Guinevere. My face was different but I had the same long wavy red brown hair. I was wearing a long blue velvet gown and standing beside a lake with Merlin. We were to find something in the woods. Merlin sent my raven to look. When he returned it was with a shining orb. Merlin was holding his staff with the orb at the top and he said he would be helping me.

I didn't know what to make of this message. It was rather fanciful and yet something was resonating for me. I went round to see my psychic friend Semele and told her someone had seen me as a famous female figure from history. She paused for a moment and I expected her to start guessing. Instead she asked straight out, "Were you Guinevere?" That made me sit up!

It seemed for a while that every time I turned on the television or looked at a book the Arthurian legends would crop up. I'm used to my guides giving me confirmation like this, but I struggled to identify myself with a famous figure. I kept fairly quiet only mentioning it to people when I got a strong 'nudge' to do so.

On a Tree Spirit Healing course in the Midlands I'd been invited to stay with the host's family. I had met Fiona a couple of times before on other courses and got on with her, although I didn't know her well. I did know she communicated with Merlin as her main spirit guide and decided to open up to her whilst we were relaxing in the evening. When I told her what was going on she got very excited and said Merlin told her that she'd been one of my ladies-in-waiting. From then on she earnestly addressed me as 'my Lady', something I wasn't quite ready for!

I had a most peculiar experience staying in her parents' house. In the morning there was a gentle knock on the bedroom door and instead of leaving a cup of tea outside her father walked straight in and handed it to me whilst I was in bed. Rather than feeling jumpy about the invasion of my privacy I felt nurtured and grateful. I'd felt oddly close to him since the evening before when I'd met him briefly. His energy was familiar and kind. Later, it came through to Fiona that he had been a father to both of us in another lifetime and we'd been sisters then. When I found out he'd died a year later I shed tears and felt saddened that I wouldn't meet him again this side of the veil. Typing these words I find I have tears in my eyes again.

Light behind the Angels

Fiona pressed a hematite necklace with a crucifix into my hand as I was leaving, saying Merlin had advised I should have it. It looked rather like a rosary. I didn't know what to do with it, not being Christian, but I kept it with thanks and tucked it away safely. It was to play its part in my story a few years later.

Some of the psychics that regularly joined us at the fairs became good friends. Lynne Lauren was one of the clearest channels I had ever come across. One day I gave her a healing. As she relaxed she found she was looking into my life as Guinevere. She said, "I can see what Arthur saw in you." I was a beautiful young woman of only 13 or 14 when he first saw me and fell in love. I was the youngest child, with older brothers and I was my father's pet. She saw me threading flowers into my hair. Arthur took me a horse as a gift. As she spoke I could see it in my mind's eye, a small horse, light dappled grey with a flowing silvery mane and tail. My description matched her vision. He married me when I was a little older, but I was too headstrong for Arthur, too much of a handful. "You were mischievous, he couldn't handle you. I can see you dancing and laughing. There was great heat between you and Lancelot. You were all over each other, it was a big passion, yet you were frustrated by your lack of privacy. I can hear you complaining about all of the eyes on you all of the time."

She moved forward in time and said, "You never lost your looks, you were faerie-like. You could have the same physique again if you chose it."

I wondered about that. I have struggled with my weight, and carry a few stones more than I would consciously choose. However I have mused that I might get into more trouble if I was slim. Whenever I have been lighter I have felt very attractive and so I think I protect myself with the extra weight.

I realised there had been several significant links in my life to the Arthurian legends. My first independent holiday with a boyfriend had been taken in Tintagel. We stayed in a hotel we chose at random on our arrival. It boasted a huge round plaque on the wall depicting the Knights of the Round Table and our room overlooked the Tintagel Castle ruins.

Later as a drama teacher, the first play I ever directed for a public audience was part of a larger schools' production. It was entitled 'King Arthur'. I hadn't chosen the subject matter, it had been given. I made a collage of pictures from the performance which lived on the wall of my study for years.

Most of the time I put all of the strangeness to the back of my mind and simply got on with my life. I know I'm not the only person to have had recollections of a lifetime as Guinevere. A few years later I attended a weekend on Faery run by Caitlin and John Matthews with Brian and Wendy Froud. In the introductory session John mentioned a book entitled, 'I was Guinevere'. I suppressed a strong urge to jump up and declare, "Oh no she wasn't, I was Guinevere!" It would have been a moment of pure Monty Python farce.

I wonder if these mythic figures connect with us when our lives fall into alignment with their stories? Perhaps it really was my life, or maybe the Arthurian legends are alive in the collective consciousness of the Land and are easy to activate by those individuals in resonance with them? Whatever the explanation I found it easy to connect with Guinevere's energy and if I ever felt nervous entering a room full of strangers I could put on the mantle of Guinevere and become poised and confident.

Looking for Answers

*'Most of us are dragged toward wholeness...
We cling to the familiar, refuse to make necessary sacrifices,
refuse to give up habitual lives, resist our growth.'*
Marion Woodman

Despite the general atmosphere of co-operation and our shared love of our children, the new home and location, I felt my relationship with my husband was still lacking in the vitality and warmth that I yearned for. I longed to love someone wholeheartedly. Looking back it sounds so silly, but I would sigh and think to myself, "Perhaps I'll have real love in my next life."

I got on well with shamanism and Patricia and I met to swap therapies. I admitted to her that my marriage had been feeling flat for a long time and I didn't know what to do. She journeyed for me to look for a significant past life between me and my husband. When she returned she recounted her journey. She'd flown over a meandering river and forests. She saw a condor and realised it was a South American life, before descending to a mud hut with an old woman sitting outside rocking and humming to herself.

Patricia was then taken back into the woman's youth. She saw a vibrant young woman with her husband and many children. The woman was bathing her husband's feet. She appeared to be nursing him, but he died and she was left to bring up the children. It was a struggle alone, a hard life and she never found anyone else. Her dying thought was, "I will be with him again." There was a sense that this man was my husband now.

I journeyed into the same life with my raven to see whether I could learn anything more. The old woman was very lined, but proud looking. I embraced her and a wave of sadness and grief passed through me; she'd been lonely for so long.

I travelled back in time. The man's feet were infected; I felt he had died from blood poisoning. As I watched I found I was sending healing from my palms to his feet and then I saw myself chewing green herbs and packing his wounds with them. I realised I was rewriting the script, healing him so that he would live to an old age. The scene shrank and became encapsulated in a translucent golden heart shaped box.

I asked my guides what the learning was for me and was told that I didn't have to nurse my husband any longer. Now he could literally 'stand on his own two feet'. This was very pertinent as although I truthfully didn't want to be in my marriage I felt guilty about leaving him.

That night I told my husband about the past life journey. As I described the scene I watched the blood drain from his face. He stopped me before I could finish my story. "I have dreamed that life." He was irritated, "You are missing some of it. Yes you nursed me, but you were the one that injured me. You attacked me with a knife; you hobbled me, because you were jealous. You thought I was having an affair with another woman when I wasn't."

I sincerely hope that this lifetime we have balanced much of the karma that was created then and have freed each other in the process. The past life journey was a turning point. I stopped feeling that it was my duty to stay with my husband and I dared to imagine living my life outside of my marriage.

Sometimes when a situation isn't healthy, but isn't too uncomfortable, you need a catalyst for change and that catalyst came into my life within a year of moving to Llandrindod. In short I fell in love.

Twin Flames

*When your socks smell of angels
But your life smells of Brie
Don't marry her, have me*
The Beautiful South

I had been aware that I got on with a man I'd met in town uncommonly well. Nothing inappropriate was said or done, but I thoroughly enjoyed bumping into him. Whenever we chatted I felt myself come alive and the flow between us was animated and easy. I knew when he was likely to be around and I would time things to give me a good chance of meeting up with him.

Months after our first meeting, I realised that I'd fallen in love. I can still picture myself walking away from him with a huge grin on my face and my heart so ridiculously light that it felt like it had been filled with helium.

I knew these amazing feelings spelled the end of my marriage. I decided I would keep my feelings to myself and wait until I'd sorted things out with my husband. I rationalised that this was a small town and that my amour was unlikely to meet anyone else in the meantime, so we continued to chat and nothing was spoken.

As time passed I still hadn't broached the subject of separation with my husband. It was such a big step. Meanwhile my feelings for the other man were growing. One day recklessness overcame me and I felt compelled to meet up with him. I thought of a suitable pretext and obtained his phone number from someone who knew him. I rang and asked whether I could come over to his house. He said, "Sure," and so I quickly found myself standing on his doorstep with my heart pounding loudly in my chest.

Footsteps came to the door and a woman answered. I was taken aback and clung to a notion that he had a lodger. He had talked freely about his ex-wife and his daughter, but never mentioned anyone else. I was ushered through and I launched into my pre-planned excuse for dropping in. The woman brought us cups of tea and left us alone again.

Our conversation went on and then he dropped the biggest bombshell, "I'm getting married next month." I felt like someone had punched me in the solar plexus and I struggled to hide my emotions. I went away distraught. I'd fallen in love with a man who was not only spoken for, but engaged and about to be married very soon. How could fate be this cruel?

The next month was agonising. We continued to chat, now almost daily through email. Still the tone was light and frothy, nothing very flirtatious, but it gave me a lift every time I saw I had a message from him. We would send inane chatter back and forth and sometimes there would be five or six messages flying between us in a day.

I know I should have cut all communication as soon as I'd found out he was spoken for, but there was so much rapport between us and in my wildest fantasies I imagined him realising he really loved me and calling his wedding off. I would picture the life we could have together.

I meditated on what was happening and was told clearly, "You are twin flames." At the same time I saw a picture of us sitting face to face with all of our chakras aligned and connected by light. I'd heard of twin flames vaguely, but didn't really know about them. I found out that the belief was from Plato who said each of us has an equal and opposite half that we were split from at the beginning of time. We are always looking for each other to be reconnected and made whole again. The idea gives rise to terms we often use casually in our relationships like 'my other half'. Okay, this might explain the intensity of emotion and longing I was feeling, which was unlike anything I'd experienced before.

Over the next few weeks I had the phrase 'twin flame' pushed at me from unexpected sources. One day I went buying crystals, trying out a new supplier. Within minutes of my arrival the woman in charge launched into a very personal account of the hot affair she was having with her twin flame, from how they'd got together, to the intensity of their physical relationship and her frustration that he wouldn't leave his wife.

I'd never met this lady before; she had no reason to trust me with her story. It was all quite, quite bizarre! I remember thinking that I wouldn't be happy with the set up she had; being the long term mistress wasn't in my character and I didn't feel comfortable with the level of deception that was taking place.

A psychic friend recounted her own affair that had lasted for decades. The love of her life had never left his wife either. At his funeral she had to sit at the back of the church and listen to how devoted a husband he'd been and how much he'd loved his wife. It was a poignant tale and another warning that some men don't have the courage, or motivation, to leave their marriages for their loves.

Light behind the Angels

Our email chats continued. As his new best friend he even invited me and my family to his wedding reception, quelle horreur! I wriggled to find a way out of that one. I had dreams of running into the church shouting soap opera style, "You can't marry her, I love you!" Perhaps I should have spoken up, but I kept my mouth shut and my feelings hidden.

In the end I arranged a healing swap with another therapist on their wedding day. Stephanie had been trained in Cranial Sacral therapy. I turned up at her place a bag of nerves. As I opened my case the crystals tumbled out and rolled all over the floor. I somehow pulled myself back into healer mode and hope I gave her a passable treatment. When I got onto the couch I floated completely out of everyday awareness. I think I was just grateful to be taken away from my internal angst for an hour.

The happy couple had got hitched and I'd resisted the temptation to arrive like a bad faery at their wedding reception. They went off on honeymoon. I'd kept everything repressed and it was too late to do a thing about my feelings. And that should have been the end of it, twin flames or not.

Imagine my feelings when I received an email as soon as the groom returned from honeymoon. The messages started straight back up again and over the weeks we progressed to a regular routine of morning tea breaks taken with each other several times a week. It was so enjoyable to have someone on the same wavelength as me and I loved our chats. It was still entirely well behaved, although I didn't spell out how much time I was spending with him to my husband and I doubt he let his new wife know how often we met up.

We got on better than I had ever got on with anyone of either sex and it seemed our views on everything were matched. He was interested in the paranormal and psychic phenomena, and enjoyed regaling me with stories of things that had happened to him in his adventurous youth. I was someone he could tell his 'weird stuff' to, his wife being an ardent rationalist.

Some of his stories were entrancing. He had memories stretching back to babyhood when his mother would find him in the morning in his cot with muddy feet. He remembered being taken outside at night to dance with the faeries. He had an uncanny resonance with the faerie realm and I loved this otherworldly energy about him.

Instinctively I knew that Lancelot and my twin flame were one and the same. I'd already realised this wasn't the first lifetime I'd been so besotted with him. It felt too intense and too familiar for that. I knew this man better than his own wife.

I soon got my confirmation. I hadn't breathed a word of the Guinevere story to my twin flame. I was concerned he would think I was insane. One day we met for coffee and he recounted a strange dream he'd had. He'd been sitting in a boat on a large lake moving through mists. With him he could see me and a mutual friend. We were both dressed in long gowns. The mist parted and through it he could see Glastonbury Tor.

He laughed it off and put it down to eating too much cheese before bedtime, a curious bit of nonsense. I was tempted to enlighten him, but didn't dare. Was this a real past life memory I wondered? I couldn't believe that my feelings were entirely one sided, but he'd given me no sign of anything other than a close friendship.

Looking back I wish I'd kept things as they were, as he was a lovely friend for me, but my emotions were overpowering. I decided to email him a letter explaining how I felt, how uncomfortable I was that I had these feelings, and that I would leave him alone completely if he wanted me to. He invited me round to talk about it. I have rarely felt so intensely embarrassed, but I needn't have worried. He admitted he felt the same, but he also had a hatred of affairs and he couldn't be unfaithful to his wife. Could we be friends and just know that we had this special bond? We hugged and nothing more. At least it was out in the open between us and I could stop the pretence.

His marriage was already looking shaky and they were arguing a lot. We talked about having our time together in the future. Meanwhile he felt we could hold our heads up and know we'd done nothing to be ashamed of. I truly believed his marriage wouldn't last and that it wouldn't be anything to do with me. The pair seemed a real mismatch and a psychic reader summed them up as, "Square peg, round hole," and counselled me just to wait it out.

One fateful day I went round to my twin flame's house and we sat together chatting as usual, then we had a hug and that turned into a kiss. I simply melted inside. I'd never really understood the language of love in films and songs until that moment.

When I left his house I had a text from my husband, "What's wrong?" He'd had to leave a meeting to be suddenly and violently sick. Having a sensitive as a spouse didn't seem much of an advantage at that moment in time. Perhaps if everyone was so psychic the world would be a better place and no deception would be possible.

My twin flame had absolutely shocked himself and he pulled right back from me. For a while he didn't want to see me and when we

Light behind the Angels

next met we sat on the opposite sides of the room with the coffee table playing chaperone in the middle.

I really should have kept away at this point, but I didn't. These new feelings were so intense and so delicious. I would be sitting doing something quite ordinary and suddenly I would feel my heart chakra glowing with warmth and I would know he was thinking of me. It was beautiful, amazing and madly frustrating all at the same time.

The End of an Era

'Every so often the Heart says, 'Fill me' and this can cause great anguish if you don't know how. To me, the priority must be to listen. To listen to what the heart has to say.'
Maharaji, Reflections

My marriage was more strained than ever now and I knew I had to do something about it. My husband was a sensitive man and he guessed something was going on from the moment of that first kiss. He asked me outright, even naming the man and I had to tell him the truth. I must have been far too enthusiastic when I had spoken of him. As my husband put it, "You've got it bad!" We decided we should split up.

The hardest thing was to tell our children. Children rarely like the idea of their parents separating and mine were no exception. That was a painful time, especially for my husband who was, and continues to be, their devoted father. We agreed he would move out when he found somewhere suitable to live, which took some months.

We tried our best to treat each other with respect. We even went to a solicitor together for advice. She was most put out to be speaking to us as the divorcing couple. She told us that we wouldn't find a solicitor to represent us jointly and that because we had seen her together neither she, nor any other solicitors in her practice would represent either one of us. It still astounds me that the law cannot accommodate two people who mutually agree to part in a co-operative and amicable fashion. The law is set up to create combat. Simply terming a divorce Smith vs. Smith sets the parties up for a fight that need not be there.

When we returned from the appointment our cat Byron, the last surviving pet from our pre-married days, decided to die. He'd been ill for months with kidney failure, but the symbolism was clear. His death really marked the end of an era for us.

One of my students was staying in Llandrindod for her course and we decided to have a meal out together. This is unusual for me on a teaching weekend, I don't normally socialise on the Saturday night. During the meal she mentioned she was booked to go on a yoga retreat holiday in Turkey. That sounded like bliss. My husband had just moved out without too much drama, but I was feeling emotionally drained and needed to take some time out. She suggested I join her and by the end of our meal I had decided that I would go.

Light behind the Angels

She gave me a little gift of a tiny rose quartz Ganesha, said to be the deity to call upon if you want to clear obstacles. I popped him on my altar, little imagining how swiftly and efficiently he would set about his task.

I was running a holistic fair in town and was preoccupied with the organisation of that, so things were busy. My twin flame and I were having a mutually agreed break from each other. Neither of us could stand the emotional tension, he didn't want to leave his wife and I didn't want the role of mistress.

One of the stallholders at my fair was a friend, admittedly a male, devilishly bearded, good-looking friend. Selling crystals too he took much longer than everyone else to pack up. Crystals need careful handling and the job can't be rushed. Afterwards I asked if he'd like to pop back to mine for a brew before his long trip home. We had a chat and a laugh and then he left, first giving me a big hug on my doorstep.

Next day I had a nasty email from my twin flame making snide comments about me, "Going off with a crystal beardy man." As he hadn't attended the fair I could only assume he'd been spying on me! I found that a bit creepy and when I said so he went off at the deep end and ranted. I was torn to shreds by his accusations and had my eyes opened to a completely different and deeply unpleasant side to him. I can understand now that he was eaten up with jealousy and lashing out, but I felt shaken by the attack.

The holiday came soon after and I was relieved to be going away. We arrived late at night at the centre in Turkey after a long journey and I was told my husband had contacted the owners. My first thought was, "Can't he cope for five minutes on his own and give me a break?" but it was more serious than missing school uniform. My home had been burgled, ransacked actually, almost as soon as I'd left. He wanted to know whether I had left any credit cards there and told me he had been putting everything back and tidying up for me.

Both children were put on the phone in tears and from somewhere I had to find my rock-steady-cope-with-anything persona to console them. What a start to my first holiday as a free woman! The thought of my husband putting all my personal belongings away was quite sickening. He was being thoughtful and doing the best he could in a bad situation, but I felt like I'd only just found my own space and he was back there already. I dearly wished he'd kept quiet about the break-in until I got back as it tainted my holiday from the word go.

Generous quantities of red wine helped to revive some of the holiday spirit that night. However I quickly became aware that my travelling companion and roommate wasn't as jolly as I'd thought. She was getting over a much less amicable break up than mine and was still shocked by the horrific death of her mother. Although her break up had been years before, it had devastated her and she couldn't leave it behind. She talked about it in ever decreasing circles.

I was still stunned by the row with my twin flame. At least I got to take a turn to process this one, and my roommate referred to him as, "Voldemort: he who cannot be named," as I continued to protect his identity despite his angry outburst.

I hope and trust the holiday marked something of a turning point for my travelling companion, and I know she has been able to put some of the heartache behind her now, but at times I felt like a live-in therapist and the fact we were sharing our cabin meant there was less peace than I'd have liked to unwind. I'd gone on holiday needing to top up my batteries and looking for deep relaxation. I realise looking back that if I'd explained she probably would have honoured my wishes, so there was a lesson for me in setting boundaries.

The holiday had its highlights. The weather was just beautiful and so was the setting, a dramatic rocky shoreline overlooking crystal clear seas. I loved lazing on the kosk's outdoor cushions overlooking the sea and reading. The group atmosphere was friendly and the vegetarian cuisine scrumptious.

We had moments of great hilarity. One morning an elderly lady travelling alone came to breakfast looking shaken. In the night she'd been woken by a series of knockings in her cabin. I calmed her down, asking, "Have you lost someone dear to you?" I thought a loved one in spirit might be trying to contact her.

A day later we were chatting to another woman who was complaining about the rats at the centre. "I can't see them, but I can hear them running over my cabin roof at night." She'd got so fed up she'd taken a broom handle and started hitting the ceiling. My companion howled with laughter. This lady's cabin adjoined the elderly woman's. Sometimes phenomena have a rather more earthly and rational source!

As the centre was on an organic farm they didn't spray against mosquitoes. We hadn't expected so many and when we arrived in the dark that first night we couldn't see them so we'd settled to drink wine without putting any anti-mosi stuff on or covering up. I got seriously munched on and as bites become raised red blotches on me I soon looked less than glamorous. My roommate was so irresistible that her lower legs swelled and she had to take a day off to rest by mid week.

While she rested back at the cabin I had a fabulous day exploring the stunning Kabak Gorge. Surrounded by mountains and only accessible by foot, or from the sea, this is a very special place. It has a chilled out hippy feel, with camping available in tipis and tree

Light behind the Angels

houses. There was a choice of laid back veggie cafés. The beach was so hot it scorched the soles of your feet and we ran across the sand to cool our feet in the sea. I had plenty of time to talk to the others and found I got on really well with a girl from Manchester called Carmel.

At the end of the holiday Carmel and I swapped contact details and said we'd keep in touch, not something I've ever done. I like meeting new people, but don't feel a need to hold on to them when the experience is over.

I returned home to deal with the police. They'd caught the burglar, who'd been after money and electrical goods to support his drug habit. They were at pains to say how unlucky I'd been to be broken into in such a low crime rate area. I knew it wasn't about bad luck, it was about encouraging me to let go of the house.

Nothing of great sentimental value went. I suffered more from the invasion of privacy. One thing especially made me squirm with embarrassment. Before I'd gone to Turkey I'd made myself a manifestation box to attract a new romantic partner. Creating boxes to support big life goals is something I'd done before and I enjoy this creative way of setting an intent. This one was carefully decorated and contained symbolic items to represent a new loving relationship. It was the last thing I wanted my husband to see. To really rub salt into the wound the contents of the box had been tipped out by the burglar and the police had taken the lid away for fingerprinting! Perhaps the universe was telling me I wasn't ready for a new relationship yet.

I had dearly wanted to hold onto my dream house, but realistically selling up was the fairest thing to do and the burglary helped me detach from the property. It seemed every time I entertained a notion of retaining the house something unpleasant happened.

Previously my neighbours had tried to fix me up with a lodger and talked of grubbing up the hedge that separated our gardens to give us one large shared garden. They didn't want us to go. It was a tempting offer, but not fair play on my ex. Letting go of the house was the price of my freedom.

Whilst that discussion had been going on we'd had an unwanted visitor. I'd walked into town to pick up some printing for my students and left my daughter supervising my son at home. As I walked through my front gate I was confronted by a nervous looking youth coming up the side of the house from my back garden sporting a very obvious erection in his shell suit bottoms. I acted on instinct and stood in front of the gate barring his way. Looking back it could have been dangerous, but I drew on my school teacher's authority and demanded to know what he was doing on my property. He stuttered something about 'jumping gates with friends' which I knew was a lie and I warned him that if I saw him anywhere near my house again I'd be calling the police. He apologised like a school boy, "Sorry Miss," and I let him pass. Afterwards when the adrenaline had worn off I felt shaken and vulnerable. The burglary just a few short months later was probably unconnected with this intruder, but it was underlining my need to let go and move on. The house was put on the market.

Light behind the Angels

Angelic Encounters

'Angels transcend every religion, every philosophy, every creed. In fact, angels have no religion as we know it...their existence precedes every religious system that has ever existed on earth.'
St Thomas Aquinas

After the holiday in Turkey Carmel and I sporadically emailed each other. Although we made several plans to meet up we had to cancel them each time. Meanwhile I picked up the role of New Age Editor writing weekly articles for one of the world's largest women's magazine sites, Bellaonline. I felt blessed to have secured such a wide subject area for my writing and was thrilled to join a vibrant community of women writers from around the globe.

Towards the end of the year the sale on my house went through. We sold to a couple that viewed months before. I'd told the estate agent then that they'd buy it. She dismissed them as not ready to purchase and we heard nothing more for a long while. When they came back with an offer she looked at me askance and said, "Are you a witch?" It was tempting to nod, but I just smiled. I'd found another house in town. It was still very spacious, though not nearly so grand and because it was situated on the main road I could afford it by myself. At last I was in my own place and we'd divided the equity fairly so my conscience felt clearer.

I managed to create a good vibe in my new abode and people would come in and exclaim, "This feels just like your old house!" Space clearing is powerful and one visitor remarked on her second visit, "It feels so much lighter now you've decorated." At that point I hadn't lifted a paintbrush, merely cleansed the atmosphere.

I had various short and stunningly unsuccessful relationships. I'd left my marriage to look for true love and I couldn't be with the man I'd fallen for. I was determined to find love and tried dating other men. With my twin flame still in contact I found I couldn't get seriously involved with anyone else. Most of these men were capable of wielding an axe as in Clive's vision, so it wasn't easy to decide whom he'd pictured in that first reading. Amusingly one, an ex boxer and bodyguard, even turned up bearing his shiny new axe to chop firewood in my garden!

It had dawned on me by then that my poor husband had never been the man in Clive's vision of a man chopping wood. At the time my husband had even considered Forestry Commission jobs to try and fit his prediction. Take this as a warning to remember that no psychic reading is ever 100% accurate and predicting timing is always difficult. In this case Clive had assumed the man was my husband and that the cottage was imminent. At time of writing I'm still not in the cottage. I'm convinced it does lie in my future as Clive has seen it clearly several times, years apart, forgetting that he's already mentioned it, and always giving the same description of, "a stream no wider than a table."

Carmel and I continued to email each other. As two single women most of our emails were about men and the difficulties of finding a really compatible partner. It was entertaining to compare notes. Meanwhile life went on and in my case that meant there were a few strange happenings.

It was close to Christmas and I was standing in the back room wrapping presents ready for a family visit that I'd be making next day. Talk about leaving everything to the last minute! I was tired out, I'd been healing into the early evening, fitting people in so that I could take some time off, and the final client had some difficult energies with her. I was aware that my protection wasn't as strong as it should have been and something had sneaked through my guard and attached itself to my aura around my head. I wasn't scared, but it left me feeling headachy, like I had a weight sitting on my crown.

Normally I follow a set procedure to clear unhelpful energies like this, but I was busy with present wrapping. Standing there I called upon Archangel Michael to remove the entity from me. I continued wrapping until I became aware of a huge bright energy with me. It surrounded me and then went right through the core of my whole body. I got the impression that it was made of golden light. The feelings were so intense that I seriously wondered if my heart could take the strain. I thought my body might be found next day with not a mark on it.

I knew I just had to stand stock still, mid wrapping, and surrender completely to this force. Curiously although I wasn't sure I could survive it I wasn't at all scared and I felt privileged to be experiencing it. I knew this was the Archangel and he meant business. He dragged something from out of the top of my head. It was a sensation like pulling stretchy toffee away and then his work was done and his energy left me. I felt clear headed and simply continued quietly with the job of wrapping.

I was honoured to have felt some of the power of the Archangel and was given some insight that evening into the force of energy that exists in the Universe. I am under no illusion that there are energies that would burn out our circuits in an instant, not because

Light behind the Angels

they are bad, but because they are more intense than the human body can withstand. From then on I became more aware of angels in my healing and several clients sensed angelic energies whilst they were on the couch.

I knew many of my students would be interested in working with angelic energies and so invited a lady who did angel readings to lead a workshop. She pitched the content rather too low for my students and her experience of angels was on the sweet and fluffy side, but she did conduct a meditation to meet a guardian angel. I'd never bothered to ask who my guardian angel was, preferring to shout for an appropriate archangel if I needed one, so it was interesting to meet a very feminine angel. She was a tall figure of light and she held a seeing bowl in which the night sky was reflected. I asked her name and she replied Galadriel. I queried this, knowing the Lord of the Rings well I thought I'd supplied the name. She smiled, "Who do you think he got the name from?"

Later in the day we conducted angel readings for each other. An angel for Victory was drawn for me. It meant little to me at the time, but looking back it was the prelude to great changes that were to come. I made notes:

"Your prayers have been answered. Gold light, taking your light into the Universe. Aura expanding out. Spreading your wings. Phoenix rising from the ashes. Blowing your own trumpet. Energy lifting. Opening to new avenues."

Gone with the Wind

'Bliss has not to be found outside, against sorrow. Bliss has to be found deep, hidden behind the sorrow itself. You have to dig into your sorrowful states and you will find a wellspring of joy.'
OSHO, Tarot in the Spirit of Zen

I continued to see my twin flame, though not as often as I would have liked. Most of the time we were incredibly controlled and kept the lid on our feelings. We'd sit and chat and drink tea, just enjoying each other's company, but at times it all became too much to repress and we'd find ourselves rolling all over the floor like two teenagers.

Something very strange happened to both of our energy fields when we held each other. Kissing was enough to make us both light-headed and my legs would turn to marshmallow. Often I'd warn him to be careful crossing the road after we'd kissed goodbye as he seemed to be floating several inches above the ground. It was wildly intoxicating in a way I'd never experienced before. For a short time after he'd left I could feel myself glowing radiantly and then the yearning to be with him would kick back in and I would be counting the days until our next meeting.

I found I was living for a few stolen hours. From the time of his arrival I knew it was just a short while until his departure and then it might be another week or two before we could meet again. We never spent longer than a few hours together and never had a whole day in each other's company. He was terrified his wife would find out and I knew he was torn within himself, hating himself for seeing me.

Several times we argued and stayed away from each other for weeks or months. The tension was too much to bear. Any glamorous notion I might have had about mistresses went out of the window. Loving a man who despises affairs was hard work and rather than showering me with gifts he showered his wife with them. It was nauseating to see the cards and flowers on show on his mantelpiece and although I knew he was easing his conscience it upset me.

I would walk away and try to have a normal relationship with someone who was truly available, but no-one could even approach my heart. I met some interesting and very talented men; a gifted stained glass artist from Birmingham who lived on a narrow boat and played Spanish guitar beautifully stands out in my memory. He was prepared to trek across the country to see me bearing gifts. It wasn't fair on him

Light behind the Angels

or the others. My heart wasn't free to love elsewhere and these suitors were quickly doomed.

I looked for support in psychic readings. I still felt I was destined to be with my twin flame. Most readers would pick up on him and the intensity of the feelings; they were so strong I might as well have been wearing them written on a t-shirt, but seeing the love and resolving the impasse were two different things.

Occasionally a reader would predict a different future. I didn't want to hear it. I would bristle and cling to my belief I was destined to be with my love. A reader in South Wales told me outright, "It isn't him, you will be with someone you have heard of on a distant path." I was irritated. How could she dismiss my great love affair so lightly? I'm afraid she got a stony reception for the rest of her reading which I dismissed as 'total nonsense'.

I realise now that I'd been going to readers only to hear one message. Anything else was discarded. One Romany reader offered to fix things by magical means. He said my love and his wife were more like brother and sister than a couple and he sensed that it would be a relief for all concerned if they released each other. It was a temptation, but I couldn't let him work his spells. Although I wanted my twin flame in my life more strongly than I'd ever wanted anyone, I wouldn't take a magical route. I knew that I wouldn't be satisfied if he came to me in that way. I needed to know he wanted to be with me enough to change his life of his own free will. I wanted a man courageous enough to take action for himself.

He said many times that he'd made a promise to stay with his wife as every other man had walked out on her. It had been a foolish promise in my opinion, after all the others must have had reasons for walking, but he was determined to stick by it and instead talked about us being together when she left him. I think he was genuinely hoping fate would take a hand and save him from looking like the bad guy. One day Patricia saw his power animal, large as life in the corner of the room. She announced he had a chicken. For long afterwards she would ask, "How's the Big Chicken doing?"

Gradually the pain of loving someone who wouldn't be with me outweighed the pleasure and our breaks became longer and longer. We went for months at a time without talking. The feelings were always just as strong when we got back in touch. I decided to finish it one last time.

Our farewell scene was like something from a Hollywood film. Scarlett and Rhett never had so much charged emotion between them. He told me I was beautiful and that the man who got me would be lucky. I recognised he was defeated, that he never expected to be with me. He then pointed to my third eye and my heart centre and said, "We will always be connected, here and here." This was interesting as I had removed energetic cords between us in preparation for this, but couldn't bring myself to sever the two beautiful healthy ones at the third eye and at the heart centre. Our last kiss was one of those epic numbers and I almost didn't dare let it end. I knew that was it. Final. When he left I ran to my room and sobbed like I'd never sobbed before, my whole body was wracked in grief and I could truly term myself heartbroken.

Later when I'd calmed down I sat and channelled one of my guides. *"You are doing the right thing. We will help you. Believe in yourself. You are a remarkable woman. You attract followers. Your light is shining out across the world. We will help you to stay protected from those who would bring you down. Be yourself. When you are true to yourself miracles will happen. Be prepared to be elevated. You will be heard by many. This is a necessary time. We cannot stop the pain, it is helping you grow. You understand so much more about love now. This is his gift to you."*

Light behind the Angels

Past Lives and Future Selves

'There are no unnatural or supernatural phenomena, only very large gaps in our knowledge of what is natural...
We should strive to fill those gaps of ignorance.'
Edgar Mitchell, Apollo 14 Astronaut

I holidayed alone in Crete that year, trying out a retreat centre as a possible venue for teaching abroad. It had been a wonderful break and I'd been welcomed on my arrival by the sound of a raven's distinctive cawing and looked to see him flying low across the veranda. I assumed this was a regular spectacle, but the owner assured me that she had never seen him do this before.

I loved Crete and felt very at home there. The food was terrific and the views sublime. The centre was all I was looking for in a retreat space, with beautiful marble faced areas for groups to work and a tranquil meditation room. I loved having no particular timetable and I split my time between healing and massage swaps with the resident therapist, bathing in the sea and dozing in the shade to recharge my batteries.

When I returned I went to a Shamanic evening that Patricia was holding. We were going to do some past life journeys for each other. I was paired with an experienced shaman. We didn't know each other and didn't have any chatting time, we just went straight into the journeys. I was surprised to go to a past life for him as a Roman centurion in charge of a legion. He had been full of thoughts of honour then and was proud of his station in life.

The shaman journeyed for me and came back with a life as a Minoan temple priestess. He'd seen me healing with snakes. I was reminded of the Minoan goddess statues that show a snake held in each outstretched hand. He said I'd been in the temple from childhood and had died there. He had the impression I taught other healers as I got older and that when I died I was buried beneath the temple itself. I realised it was no wonder that I'd felt at home on Crete as the island was the centre of the Minoan empire and also saw that my liking for snakes could have stemmed from this past life of healing.

I began to receive strange messages about beings from other dimensions. It began with a student who was a devotee of the Indian guru Sai Baba and has made a lifelong study of mysticism. She told me about Golden Beings who wanted to come to help us raise the vibration on Earth.

Not long after, during a healing, Patricia realised she needed to do a soul retrieval for me, but for a part of me I had never had in this incarnation. She saw a piece of my soul standing in golden light at the top of a mountain with arms outstretched like the figure of Christ above Rio de Janeiro in Brazil. This part of me wasn't ready to come back yet but there was an assurance that I was being prepared to receive it.

I went to Glastonbury alone to seek answers. The Isle of Avalon always has revelations for me. On this occasion I had booked a reading with a psychic who promised to 'sing my soul'. I'd been a bit taken aback by the cost, more than I'd ever paid for a reading before, but I did feel drawn. When I met her it was like being greeted by a technicolor faery. She was very bright, from her vividly dyed red hair to her acid coloured clothing and she couldn't help but skip across the floor.

The reading was a mixture of song and channelled messages. Most unusual! She sang of connecting with a dove at my heart and of a being from the Pleiades, an aspect of my soul that was close and wanted to join with me now. Only at the time I heard it as 'Palladian' which put me in mind of Saturday Night at the London Palladium! She told me I had to invite her in.

Fortunately the reading was recorded onto a CD and I listened again travelling back to Wales. I realised that I'd misheard 'Pleiadian' for a start. I was already aware of the importance in which the Pleiades are held by some New Age thinkers. My own crystal healing teacher had supplied us with a symbol of the Shekinah Dove mapped over the constellation of the Pleiades for clearing unhelpful energies. I'd used the symbol with great effectiveness for years, but mostly focussed on the Shekinah Dove and not the star system behind the image.

Back home I decided I would take the reader's advice. I spoke aloud in bed that night, making a formal invitation to my Pleiadian self to join my energy if she wanted to do so. It felt right; I wouldn't ask just any being to connect with me! Next morning I woke feeling incredible. I felt strong and strangely upright. By synchronicity I was going to see the student who'd first mentioned the golden beings to me as we had arranged a therapy swap. In the car I felt my backbone was ramrod straight. I couldn't possibly slouch. It was as if I'd grown several inches in the night. I felt so good in fact that I didn't have a full treatment, I didn't need one.

The Elementals

'Life is in the flow and the change. Life is rhythm and movement. What you were once informs who you are now, but is not the same as who you are now. You are more, but each moment of growth contains a letting go.'
The Elementals of Water channelled by Lauren D'Silva

One of the bonuses of writing the New Age site at Bellaonline has been the opportunity to receive books for review. Some of them have been wonderful, some just okay and some downright dreadful. One of the more unusual books was 'Elementally Speaking' a series of nature spirit messages received by American psychic Cheri Barstow. She'd contacted me as she was travelling to the UK to take part in the Goddess Festival in Glastonbury and she wanted to visit Wales and meet up. Knowing how much she enjoys the company of elementals I took her to my favourite waterfall which is situated in a gorge and is vibrantly alive with faeries and elementals.

We both settled down to channel. I hadn't tried talking to the nature spirits before, but I held my notebook open and extended my consciousness out, asking for any light beings in that place that wanted to communicate to come through. I sensed a feminine white energy protecting the waterfall which felt quite angelic. The resulting channelling was very beautiful and some of the guidance applies to the whole human race.

'You are welcome to bring those that stand in the Light. Be discerning please and let no dark ones to this place. I am healing for you. Let me take away the worries and the heartache and replace them with lightness of being.

You are on the path of your destiny and must not allow any to sidetrack you. You are learning discernment. Stand aside from harshness and those who are critical. Embrace those who support your light and development. Learn that people are privileged to know you. Be aware of your own light and proud of it. They want to be close to you so they must earn the right.

You trod these hills in ancient times and have been brought back now with a purpose. Uncover the unwritten history of the place and awaken the seekers who gather here. Be not afraid of those you meet for they are all pointers on your path. You are close to the edge of things now and when you walk past that unseen border your life will unfold with new vistas and you will leave the old pain behind.

Walk forward and don't look back. We support you and bring you all the help you need, seen and unseen. Come here whenever you need support and refreshment. It is always here for you. You are loved and blessed.

Arthur will walk in these hills again and you will walk beside him. This time it will be different. You have learned about betrayal and right thought. Difficult decisions. You must choose. You have not identified the carrier of Arthur's energy yet. You have indeed met the Lady of the Lake and she wears the moon on her brow. You guide her and she guides you.

At this point my consciousness shifted and I found I was tuning in to a multitude of small voices chattering in unison:

Listen to us we are the stones of the stream bed. We are many yet one. The water caresses us and we lie in the sun and shade ever smoothed and chattering. We are happy to just be and do not chase dragons as you do. Be stiller like us stones and you will hear much to enlighten you.

Shifting again another gentle and poetic voice spoke to me:

Each drop of water allows itself a moment of sparkling sunshine before falling to meet the waters of the pool where the rest is brief before running into the stream. You don't see the water droplets trying to hold on do you?

Let your life flow like water. As you let go you move onwards leaving the past behind and growing ever larger, ever more connected with others. Resistance simply holds you back, prevents you from fulfilling your life purpose.

Life is in the flow and the change. Life is rhythm and movement. What you were once informs who you are now, but is not the same as who you are now. You are more, but each moment of growth contains a letting go.

Move freely, move with grace. You are learning. Never hold on. Those who call you back will have to run to catch up with you. Don't hold back for them.

See the light shining through the leaves, illuminating them within. They have nothing to hide. They are One. They work together yet stand alone. They are not lonely. They are connected always to the whole, yet each has their own identity.

Be like the leaves, clinging not to others, but allowing the connections. Do not mourn those who fall away. There is never really loss and separation is an illusion.

Show your beauty and radiance and allow others to bathe in this and raise their own spiritual light to meet yours. You point the way for so many and we are grateful for this.

Looking back at this channelling I am again struck by the beauty and grace of their messages. As my experiences unfolded further I could understand and accept their wisdom.

Light behind the Angels

A Suitable Suitor

'When one door closes another opens. Expect that new door to reveal even greater wonders and glories and surprises. Feel yourself grow with every experience.'
Eileen Caddy, Opening Doors Within

It was a full year on from our Turkish retreat when I received an email from Carmel written in hushed and scandalised tones. She had been out with a man from her yoga class and he turned out to be a *White Witch!* This was all too exotic for Carmel and she'd decided the relationship was a non starter, but they stayed friends. Lucky old Carmel I thought. A male witch might be lots of fun, what a shame he was in Manchester and I was in Wales.

At that time I was wringing my hands over the ex boxer and realising I couldn't really have picked anyone much less suitable for me. Opposites attract indeed! I'd known him from the school for several years as one of the dads and we'd been friends. He'd always been so sweet and helpful. When I'd split from my husband he'd taken me out for tea and cakes and at that time had been at pains to tell me he didn't drink. The first time he came over on a date he brought a bottle of wine with him. It didn't ring the alarm bells, it seemed normal behaviour, but when he started hiding vodka bottles in his wellies I knew the guy had a bit of a problem.

This was a relationship straight from the land of soap opera. His life lurched from drama to crisis. At least he took my mind off my twin flame for a while. Investigating this very strange attraction I saw that I'd been his mother in Victorian times. That made sense, I felt protective over this great hulk of a man and furious with his own mother who was an incredibly cruel and controlling woman.

It was autumn 2006 when I finally managed to make the trip up to Manchester to see Carmel. I knew the relationship with the boxer was going nowhere and I caught myself thinking en route, "I wonder if Carmel would introduce me to that White Witch guy?"

I had a great visit, lots of bemoaning the lack of decent men and plenty of wine. No introduction to the witch, but Carmel was due to see Steve AKA the White Witch that weekend at a Mind, Body, Spirit Exhibition in Manchester. I'd been flicking through the brochure and pointing out the people I'd met. I pointed at a picture of Lui Krieg from Glastonbury's Stone Age and she said, "Steve looks a bit like him." Not bad then, long curly hair and the air of an aging rock god, that would do me nicely! She said she'd mention me.

Light behind the Angels

She didn't think Steve was up for a serious relationship, although she suspected he might be the sort to drive to see someone special.

Back home weeks passed and there was no news. The boxer was finally dumped after yet another broken date. I'd had enough of his excuses. Apparently expecting to keep a lunchtime date he'd suggested himself was 'really heavy pressure' and getting too serious for him!

Exasperated I texted Semele to see if she could do lunch as I needed to vent my spleen to someone who'd understand. She's a great listener fortunately, although my text must have carried some angry energy as she thought she was in trouble for some reason.

Driving down the valley to hers I was crying, shouting and swearing about the useless men that had been sent my way. It's lucky I was in the car as I really let it all out! I was not best pleased with the Universe and demanded something better; no more wasting my time and energy on men that didn't deserve it! Sometimes it's good to rant; much healthier than keeping the frustration pent up inside.

We lunched in a quiet café and Semele patiently listened to my woes and frustration with men in general and this one in particular. "Why am I going through all of this hassle, why is it so tough?" I asked.

Semele looked into the middle distance and said, "I can see a sword, they say they are tempering you."

"Ha! Bad tempering me more like," I quipped. A ghost swept through the café, disappearing into the wall, oblivious to the current layout of the building, a memory of a moment in time I thought. "Did you see that one?" I asked.

"Yes," said Semele and carried on eating. Suddenly, her fork poised halfway to her mouth, she said, "There is someone coming who will be much better for you. They will only show me his knees!" The knees were inspected as closely as possible and pronounced, "Very nice knees, a bit hairy, quite tanned, slim."

No more information was forthcoming. I suppose my guides were wise enough to know I'd be scrutinising every face for a match if they gave me any more clues about what he looked like! Hmmm I thought, "I have a pair of knees coming my way. This had better be good!"

Feeling much better I drove back home, declaring aloud my intention to meet someone worthy of my time and attention. I was ready to extricate myself from energy sapping relationships. Thank goodness for good girl friends!

I am a big believer in the power of clear intention and manifestation. I'd had enough of half measures in men and decided to

47

send a cosmic order to the Universe for a really decent man. First I brainstormed the qualities I'd want in a man and then I wrote out my order in my journal:

"I ask the Universe to bring me a partner who is good looking, strong and tall, accepting of healing and psychic work, talkative, witty and a good storyteller, tactile and a good lover, vegetarian or accepting of vegetarianism, good with animals and children, exciting, sociable and not too materialistic. Someone I can fall in love with for a long, long time, plus he must be available or become available very quickly and I must have him close by so that I can see him often enough. I now ask that this amazing man is brought to me by the end of November 2006. May this or something better now manifest."

I wasn't asking for much was I? However I have learned with manifesting to set your sights high, state what you really want and be careful what you ask for!

To help the energy along I chanted a Sanskrit mantra for attracting a spiritual man making a beautiful string of glass mala beads to help me focus and count the repetitions. I chanted the mantra for one full mala a day over forty days. The chant was taken from Thomas Ashley Farrand's excellent book, 'Healing Mantras'.

Sat Patim Dehi Parameshwara
"Please give to me a man of truth who embodies the perfect masculine attributes"

Farrand recommends this chant for women who ask, *"Where can I find a man who will honour me and respect my power, who will use my energy honestly and unselfishly, without anger or resentment?"* I thought that this was perfect as the boxer had deep personal issues and was full of old anger. He had been manipulative and very draining. He was good at teaching me to set my boundaries, by trampling all over mine in hobnailed boots. My new man had to be a shining example of manhood.

The weeks went by and a relative calm set in. I started to enjoy more peace of mind and ironically for the first time ever I could see the potential in life with no romantic attachments at all. Then an email arrived in early December. Carmel was off to explore the Antipodes and had promised to fulfil one last duty before leaving, "Before I go, I have a little job to do. Monsieur white witch AKA the lovely Steve is interested in meeting/talking to you but being a gent he didn't want to be pushy and ask for your number so he suggested I give you his mobile phone number. You could text him?"

I had his number. There was no pressure on me and I could take it or leave it, so I left it, for a whole fortnight. Here I was single and quite content at last and suddenly there was a possible man on the horizon. I'd put out the cosmic order, but now I wasn't so sure I wanted a man in my life.

Just before Yule I suddenly decided nothing ventured, nothing gained. I texted the witch 'Solstice Greetings' and went out shopping. I got a response immediately while I was out. Encouraging *and* keen. There followed several quick exchanges, including the usual, "What do you do?" as Carmel had told me very little.

The reply came back, "A motor mechanic, wand maker and part time model."

I quipped back, "Life model I hope?" and found my gut instinct was quite right. Meanwhile I revealed my therapist's credentials and witchy leanings.

Back home Semele was round for a cuppa when more texts came in, including a photo of the guy, Steve, a bit unkempt looking, but he had been working under a car all afternoon. Semele and I had a giggle and she snapped several photos of me on my phone until I approved of one and sent it.

When we finally got to talking on the phone our first call lasted nearly three hours. Steve's a Gemini so he could win a gold medal in talking and I'm not often stuck for something to say. He sounded genuinely lively and interesting. It wasn't a romantic call in any way, but it was a lot of fun and we seemed to be operating on roughly the same wavelength. Our phone calls continued and so just after Christmas we met up.

Our first meeting was on neutral ground. We went to the small Welsh town of Montgomery which was sort of half way between Llandrindod and Manchester. I took my Springer Spaniel as my chaperone and our first walk together was marked by being dragged all over the little castle by my over-enthusiastic hound. Montgomery seemed to be asleep that day so we jumped in my car and headed off to find somewhere open for lunch. We found a very nice country house hotel by Offa's Dyke and had space to sit and talk over an excellent meal, then went off to visit Mitchell's Fold Stone Circle where it was blowing a gale. It was impressive, but not somewhere to hang about in that weather.

I didn't know what to think of Steve at first. He was very tall and skinny with long curly grey hair. I was wary. I'd been let down too often in recent years and I didn't fancy the heartache again, so I played things cool. We had a drink in a little hotel bar before going our separate ways. He sat smoking his cigar and announced, "I eat meat and I smoke cigars and I won't change that." I expect he felt he had to get his position in quickly with my vegetarian credentials. I wasn't too bothered, as long as he didn't want me to eat meat!

When we parted we left things open. Steve said, "Let me know if you'd like to see me again," kissed my cheek and we drove off in opposite directions. I wasn't sure. This felt like someone who would be a fantastic friend, but was it going to become a romance?

It is testament to Steve's patience that he made the long journey from Manchester for quiet walks and chats several times before he got so much as a first kiss. I needed to see such dedication after the offhand way I'd been treated by the boxer and as he proved himself worthy my barriers gradually came down.

Sometimes we can't see where a chain of events is leading us and even our perceived mistakes may be important steps on our journey. The Universe has a way of orchestrating key events and you have to trust and follow the signs that you are given. Now we have travelled more of our journey together we've realised that our guides must have had the whole thing set up from the moment I went out for that meal with my student and discussed the yoga holiday. Without her I wouldn't have gone to Turkey and would never have met Carmel. Staying in touch was key, but if I'd managed to visit Carmel earlier on as we'd planned she wouldn't have made friends with Steve and so wouldn't have mentioned him to me. We are both full of admiration and gratitude for what Steve calls 'the logistics team up there'.

I'm sure my guides thought my cosmic order was highly amusing, but having said that it was very accurate. I did get what I wanted almost to the letter. Steve is all the things I asked for and though he was 'delivered' a few weeks after the target date Carmel had spoken to him and procured his number to give to me by then. He wasn't close by, but he drove the 120 miles between Manchester and Mid Wales almost every week.

By now I'd been separated from my husband for close on two years and I felt the need to have my own identity. I didn't want to go by my married name any more, that belonged to him, nor did I want to revert to my maiden name, that would represent a step back into childhood for me. A year or so before I'd adopted a nom de plume, which I'd simply made up. I was Lauren Ravenstar when I wrote my New Age site on Bellaonline. It was a very twinkly name and fit for the purpose, but not a name to take down to the supermarket. I wanted a proper name, not a made up one, a name that I could use every day, yet would really reflect who I was. I'd been searching for some time but nothing felt right.

Light behind the Angels

On New Year's Day I was motivated to have a bit of a clear out in the spare room. There was a stack of books in there that didn't fit downstairs on the bookshelves. Sorting them out I found a baby naming book and started to flip through it. Something urged me to look up my middle name, Sylvia.

Silvia and its alternative spelling Sylvia mean 'of the wood'

I read on that Sylvia is derived from the Latin word *Silva* meaning 'a wood'. I knew I'd found my new surname straight away. I have a love of woodland and tree energies. I'd been using tree essences and attended the Tree Spirit Healing course. To find that my middle name actually meant 'of the wood' was moving to me. I simply turned my middle name into my surname. In truth I'd always been called 'Lauren of the Wood' and it felt completely right. Strangely my first boyfriend's surname was Woods, perhaps it was his name that subliminally attracted me?

I rang Steve, wished him a happy New Year and told him I had a new name to go with the New Year. I felt Lauren Silva needed something extra. Steve suggested, "Hi Ho." Very funny. I settled for D'Silva which I knew was a common surname in Portuguese and so wasn't in the least made up.

I won't go into all the details of our budding relationship, but it is worth returning to the vision of the knees. When I met Steve he was tanned. His knees were indeed hairy and nice. In January 2007 I hit the magical age of 40 and decided to throw a fancy dress party. Steve came with Carmel who was dressed as Medusa. He arrived in an Egyptian pharaoh's costume cut just at the knee. When Semele arrived I pulled her giggling into the back room ostensibly to introduce her to Steve, but most of all to check out the knees. A positive identification was made, these were indeed the right knees and for quite a while after that we referred to Steve as Mr Knees!

Pretty Stones

*"I am a spirit guiding stone.
In my rainbows you will discover whatever answers you wish."*
Labradorite, Stones Alive with Twintrees

At first Steve thought my crystal healing was just pretty stones. He recognised that I was a healer but didn't understand how the crystals worked with me. He admitted much later that walking into my healing room used to make him feel nauseous.

The energy in my room is beautiful. It is so clear and high that new clients and students often draw a breath in wonder as they walk through the door. I have only felt its like in special places in nature and occasionally in a church or temple. It is a sacred space and is only used for healing. My children respect it utterly. My daughter commented once that it is a 'magic room' that feels like it is in a different place from the rest of the house, so much so she often forgets it exists as it doesn't belong in the mundane world.

There are hundreds of crystals in my healing room and to someone sensitive who isn't used to crystal energies they can be a bit overpowering. I remember a client walking in to my room for the first time asking, "How can you sit here with so many crystals in the room?" Her husband was so sensitive that if she slipped a crystal under her pillow without saying anything he would complain until it was removed. She went on to become appreciative of the energy, and trained with me as a crystal healer.

Steve's awakening to the power of Crystal Healing came during that first spring of our relationship. I had a new student, who was starting late. I put on a special one-to-one session for her to bring her up to speed with the others. Steve was there that day, so I suggested he might like to be a body for her to practise on. He played along to be helpful.

My student was a natural and she chose the crystals intuitively to balance Steve's chakras as she'd been shown to. I was happy with what I was observing, however Steve looked uncomfortable and asked, "How big is the stone at my heart centre?" It was a little piece of golden labradorite, no bigger than my thumbnail. He said that it felt very heavy. I double checked the choice of stone and found it was precisely the energy he needed. He said he could cope and so the treatment proceeded.

Light behind the Angels

Fortunately this was the last exercise of the day. My student finished and left happy. As she went out of the front door Steve walked out of the back door into the courtyard. I waved her off from the doorstep listening to Steve hacking and coughing in the background. He'd proudly boasted several times that despite his heavy, long term smoking habit he'd never had a smoker's cough. Within half an hour of golden labradorite being placed on his chest he had a cough that any smoker would have been proud of.

Now my student was gone he described the sensation of the stone on his chest, "It was as if someone was putting all their weight on their thumb and pressing it right into me." He was astonished when he saw the little yellow stone. Steve felt there was still a big heavy lump stuck at his heart centre once the crystal had been removed. As it had been my student's first ever attempt at crystal healing he hadn't wanted to say just how uncomfortable the stone had made him because he didn't want to knock her confidence.

I put Steve back on the treatment couch and dowsed for something to make him more comfortable. A hand sized cluster of celestite, larger and heavier than I would normally place on anyone came up. I put it on somewhat apologetically. What amazed Steve was that despite its actual size and physical weight it felt much lighter than the little piece of labradorite had done. The sense of something stuck was lifted, but the cough remained. It was a productive cough that lasted for the next four months and he hacked up horrible amounts of gunk from his lungs in the process. It didn't stop him smoking but it did give him a new respect for crystal healing! The little golden labradorite was extremely proud of itself and developed a beautiful rainbow that hadn't been there before.

When I buy crystals I often go to a big wholesaler based in Huddersfield. It is like a crystal supermarket, you even get a trolley to wheel your crystal shopping around in. Steve took me along that spring to save me the driving as it's a five hour trip from Mid Wales each way. I noticed that when we arrived he veered off in the showroom and he kept wandering off as I shopped. He always seemed to have disappeared to the same corner.

An hour later he was brandishing a very nice labradorite massage wand. "Do you mind if I buy this?" He couldn't remember the proper name for the stone, or he pretended not to. He preferred to call it 'dog rock'. So the dog rock wand returned to Mid Wales with the other purchases. I don't think Steve had the first idea why he'd bought it, only that it pulled him over to it so many times that he had to have it. It was to prove its worth to us later on.

Back home we decided to visit my favourite waterfall. We took my son and chose some crystals to cleanse there. Steve took his dog rock. I felt my large smoky elestial quartz would appreciate the outing. When we arrived Steve held his wand in the waterfall, but I felt my crystal wanted to get right in and have a good soak. I placed it gently in the pool where the waters were churning white and left it for a while.

When it came to retrieving it I was sure I knew exactly where I'd put it, so imagine my concern when my fingers only touched slippery stones on the bed of the pool. I'd had my elestial for years and loved it. My son and Steve waded gamely into the pool to help, freezing cold water slopping over the tops of their wellies. I stood back and gazed at the pool. We'd need to leave soon, we were all wet through and getting chilly. I wondered if the crystal wanted to live in this beautiful place instead? In my mind I asked, "If you want to come home with us please show me where you are." I then stepped into the pool, some distance from the place where we'd been searching. I reached down and my hand fell straight upon the crystal. I picked it up and cradled it. My son was still plunging in enthusiastically yelling, "I think I can see it!" I took a fair bit of ribbing from the pair of them for pointing to the wrong spot, but secretly I was delighted. My crystal liked living with me and wanted to come back home.

Not long afterwards we went to a Mind Body Spirit show in Cardiff. My friends run an aura camera business and take their camera around to the shows. Steve had never had his aura photographed before. As soon as we got through the door I felt compelled to get our auras done and I dragged him off to meet them. I still have no idea how the technology can possibly work, but I've had my aura photographed on numerous occasions and you can clearly track changes as my life has unfolded.

Steve was sceptical that a camera could pick up something as fine as an aura, but he played along. I went first. I'm usually greens and blues with some purple but this time my photo came out bright yellow with a core of purple at the centre and some pinks, blues and greens.

Alan was interpreting my picture whilst Liz took the photo of Steve. Suddenly I heard Liz say, "Oh my word, you won't believe this!" She placed Steve's photo down beside mine. It was almost an exact mirror image. Alan was adamant that we should work together and were a perfect balance for each other. I felt elated that we had 'visual proof' of being well matched. Ever the sceptic Steve hung around for a while checking the camera wasn't just churning out big yellow auras for the day. It wasn't of course!

Light behind the Angels

A few years later we had our birth charts printed off for an Astrology and Crystals workshop we were on together. Then we realised that it wasn't just our auras that were mirror images of each other. Steve is a Gemini with Aquarius ascendant and I am Aquarian with Gemini ascendant. No wonder we talk so much and share the same off the wall sense of humour! The theme of twins, of being opposites and equals, was to become very important as our story unfolded.

The Caduceus

'And this tattooing had been the work of a departed prophet and seer of his island, who, by these hieroglyphic marks, had written out on his body a complete theory of the heavens and the earth, and a mystical treatise on the art of attaining truth.'
Herman Melville, Moby-Dick

I'd decided to get myself a tattoo shortly after meeting Steve. He'd had a flaming pentagram done just after we started texting each other. He'd sent me a picture of his fresh ink, still a little reddened, before I'd even met him. I'd wanted a tattoo for years, but the seedy image of tattoo parlours had put me off. The salon in Manchester where Steve had got his tattoo was apparently kept spotlessly clean and so I thought it was time to go for it.

Choosing what to have wasn't hard. As soon as I'd made the decision to go ahead the Caduceus was everywhere I looked. I'd open a book and the symbol would be there. This ancient symbol is familiar to us today as a medical logo. The central staff has two snakes entwined around it, rising from the base, one light, one dark, representing the polarities, the energies of yin and yang infusing everything on the planet. At the top a pair of angelic wings unfurl representing enlightenment. The staff and wings represent the union of Heaven and Earth.

The staff is also symbolic of the spine, the Sushumna or central channel through which energy flows and the snakes can be seen as the twin energy currents of Ida and Pingala, as they rise up the spine. I am reminded of the serpent energy of Kundalini, normally coiled and dormant at the base of the spine, awakened and rising to meet her consort Shiva.

I felt that my tattoo was about nailing my colours to the mast, stating "I am a Healer and that is my purpose." It was only later when I was researching the Goddess Hygeia that I found out the original symbol of healing was the staff of Asclepius, her healer father. It has just one snake wound around it. The staff with two snakes is the symbol of Hermes the winged messenger of the Gods. Interesting that I'd been shown the symbol of the messenger; perhaps my writing and teaching was as important as my healing?

Steve booked me an appointment at the tattoo parlour and I got drawing as I wanted my bit of ink to be a one-off and I couldn't find the exact image I wanted in books or the internet.

Light behind the Angels

A week before my appointment I made a visit to my parents. We took the kids to the playground. It was a warm day and people were wearing short sleeves. A woman walked by with a tattoo on her upper arm and suddenly Mum launched into a diatribe about how much she hated tattoos and what she thought of women who had them. She was sitting by my teenage daughter, and asked her to promise not to have one. I kept very quiet. The exchange took me right back to my teenage years. "Don't you do this, don't you do that, you do promise me don't you?" All those broken promises, some had been broken before they were even made. I had possessed a very guilty teenage conscience.

I wasn't about to change my mind on having my tattoo, but I wasn't going to argue either. At 40 I didn't need parental permission; however the whole episode made me squirm. I told my daughter in the car going home that she never had to promise anything and what she did with her life was her own business. To her credit she replied she didn't want a tattoo, but she hadn't made a promise either, she'd just grunted and shrugged. I felt rather proud of her!

Getting the tattoo was interesting. As promised the parlour was very clean and the tattooist seemed quite spiritual himself. There were statues of Buddha to welcome me, which gave me courage, as did holding Steve's hand tight. Being tattooed is not for the squeamish. Mine was being done on my lower back so I straddled the reclining chair and leant forward on my arms. The very first line was a shock. It felt like a slowly moving wasp sting. I nearly chickened out there and then, but the thought of living the rest of my life with a number one tattooed on my back as a permanent reminder of cowardice overcame the pain.

I determined to see it through. I went deep into myself, and found I could watch the pain from a distance, completely detached from it. Halfway through the tattoo artist commented, "You are one tough lady!" as I sat silent, still and unflinching. The results were well worth it; I loved the design. I felt a euphoric high walking out of the shop and could understand why some people get covered in tattoos, it could easily become addictive.

For the next few visits I hid my tattoo carefully from my parents. I didn't want a row. It did remind me of being a teenager again and I knew at some point I would have to show my mother, but I was putting that day off.

Egyptian Mysteries

'Read, children of the future, and learn the secrets of the best, which are so distant to you and yet in reality so near. Men do not live once, in order to vanish forever. They live several lives in different places but not always in this world, and between each life there is a veil of shadows.'
The Papyrus of Ani, the Egyptian Book of the Dead,
translated Dr Ramses Seleem

That summer we camped at the Quest Festival in Newton Abbot. There was an exciting mix of esoteric talks and workshops to attend, stalls to look at and entertainment for the evenings. I'd booked for the workshops David Wells was running as I admire his powerful clairvoyance and spiritual integrity.

When I arrived for his Tarot card workshop the room was almost full. I walked in at the back and a woman waved at me enthusiastically from the front row gesturing to the empty chair beside her as if she'd been keeping it for me. I'd never met her before. It turned out to be an auspicious seat as not only was I right at the front of a crowded room but David passed the Major Arcana cards around the audience as he spoke about each one, handing them to me first. He was using the Crowley Thoth tarot deck, which was the first I'd owned, buying my own at 18 years old, so I was very familiar and comfortable with the images.

We were all assigned a tarot card to work with using the numerology of our birth dates. Mine is a master number, 11, the number of the Spiritual Messenger. Looking further into the significance of 11 I found many messages that resonated powerfully with me, including this one from Magellan Numerology on the internet: *'In the ideal, the master number 11 is on a journey to find its own truth (illumination), using spiritual inspirations as a guiding light, and then bringing these illuminations to others to help raise spiritual awareness on the planet.'*

We were reducing the numbers that day and so I became a 2 and worked with the High Priestess' group. David led a meditation whereby we entered the card. The High Priestess told me to study the Mystery Schools. When I asked for help developing my clairvoyance she took her athame, plunged it into my skull splitting it in two and placed a crystal in my head at the level of my third eye. She did heal the split afterwards, but it was a good reminder to be careful of what you ask for!

Light behind the Angels

One session at Quest was purposefully avoided: a talk on crystal skulls. I've always found them a bit repulsive and when a reader once told me I 'literally had a rose quartz crystal skull in my heart' and that I should connect with it in meditation, I'd shuddered inwardly and resolved to do no such thing.

A friend was also camping and she came over to our tent enthused about the great reading she'd had. I hadn't had a reading for a while and booked to see the same lady. When I sat down with her she asked me to choose whichever crystal skull was drawing me. Ah, she was the crystal skull lady, oh dear! To be polite I picked out a labradorite skull, mainly because I like the stone. I kept my hand on it over the course of the reading and by the end had quite bonded with it to my own surprise.

My reading with Beryl turned out to be truly prophetic, though I had no idea at the time. She sensed that I had been through a lot of sorting out in my heart chakra and had much more to come, "We have to burn away the past in order to start again." She saw transformational energies coming into my life taking away the things that were still holding me back. I was informed that I'd picked 'the Egyptian skull, Ptah' and I needed to look at the Egyptian Mystery Schools and that these initiations would be important for me. I was impressed; I had just come from the Tarot workshop where I'd received the same advice.

"Before you can undergo initiation you have to be taken to the Temple and cleansed. I'm feeling quite emotional now. Fire cleanses, it burns away. You are training for the final initiation on Earth, you then become self-realised. You will be taken out of your crown chakra, taken back to Source and given your mission. You offer your life to service and have your part revealed to you. When you work for Spirit nothing must compromise it. You are on the Emerald Ray; look at the Emerald Tablets of Thoth. The Egyptian initiation culminates in the Gold Ray of healing."

I returned from my reading quite intrigued. Beryl was certainly 'out there' and good at what she was doing. I persuaded Steve to book a reading with her, which he did for the next day.

Steve came back from his reading highly amused. Halfway through Beryl stopped herself and said, "Oh my goodness, I told a lady almost exactly the same yesterday." That lady was me. Steve explained he was my partner. "There is a connection between you on a soul level." When I listened to the recording of Steve's reading they were certainly similar. As it was she picked up my work with crystals, my teaching and several other facets that were different to the love of ritual she sensed around Steve. Again she'd spoken of the Egyptian

Mysteries, the Emerald Tablets and the Gold Ray of healing. She urged Steve, "Do explore the Egyptian Mysteries; there is a powerful connection with your soul."

Egypt had been coming up sporadically for me over several years. Shortly before meeting Steve I had reviewed Judy Hall's past life novel 'Torn Clouds' for Bellaonline. In it the heroine moves between her present day self and her remembered past life in Egypt. She mentions the statue of Sekhmet at the British Museum in London. When I went there not long after I determined to seek Sekhmet out and when I found her I greeted her and took her photograph. It was only when I got home that I saw what appears to be light emanating from the Goddess' mouth. I'm pretty certain that it isn't a reflection from the window or from my camera flash and it remains one of my favourite images to the present day.

Light behind the Angels

The Twin Flame

When I fail, may I know forgiveness for myself.
May I dance naked, unafraid to face my own reflection.
Rae Beth, Hedgewitch

Steve became aware of the twin flame from only a few months into our relationship. One of Steve's friends in Manchester was having a passionate, but difficult and clandestine affair with a man she referred to as her 'twin flame'. My reaction was less than romantic; I advised she should get out of it as fast as possible and save herself a whole lot of heartache. Out came my own painful experience of twin flame romance. I didn't mention that my heart was still aching. I was keeping my distance and 'being good'. Steve had been faring much better than any of the other suitors in that respect.

We visited Glastonbury during that first summer together. Glastonbury gives you answers if you go with a question; underneath it is still the magical 'Isle of Avalon' and the energy of the place is very special. I get struck by a longing to return a few times a year.

Steve hadn't been before and he was wowed by the esoteric shopping experience. Whereas any normal town would be lucky to have a magical shop, a crystal shop, or an esoteric book store, Glastonbury is packed with them and much more besides. How many other places can boast a shop dedicated to incense and candles, or to colour healing?

A strange and rather lovely piece of synchronicity happened on this visit. I'd seen a pack of tarot cards I liked at Quest but they were priced at over £30 so I didn't buy them. In Glastonbury we did the rounds of the bookshops and went into a store which sells second hand esoteric books. I picked up a few crystal healing books that I thought might be interesting and paid for them. Steve found a book and went to the counter to pay with a £20 note. While I was waiting I continued to browse and spotted the tarot deck I'd liked, unused and still wrapped on the shelf in front of me. I went to Steve to show him. It was half price at £16, which just happened to be the exact change he was holding in his hand. He bought it for me there and then. This was lovely as traditionally you should be given your tarot cards and not purchase them yourself.

It was the end of the day and we were feeling peckish and weighed down with books. We went back to the car to drop off our bags, but I couldn't wait to examine my new deck of cards, so I kept them with me. We went to Galatea for our tea, a relaxed art café I've eaten in many times.

Settling down we made our order. There was a woman at a table over by the counter offering tarot readings. She had a sign propped in front of her, Rae Beth. We'd only mentioned her name earlier in the day. There had been a copy of Rae Beth's famous book 'Hedgewitch' for sale in one of the shops and Steve had stopped me from buying it as he already had a copy to lend me. Steve said, "Do you think that's THE Rae Beth?" I felt it was unlikely to be anyone else! I encouraged him to have a reading with her. As we'd already ordered food he said, "Let's wait 'til we've eaten and if she's still available then I will do."

I unpacked my cards and started to lay them out and get to know them. The Sacred Circle Tarot is a beautiful photographic deck with a British Isles Celtic feel to them. Our food arrived and we ate. Rae Beth was still there when we were done.

Steve got up to ask for a reading, but she said she was about to pack up and go for her bus. He came back to me looking a little crestfallen. For some reason I felt it was important that he should get his reading and I said I'd have a reading too if she'd hang on for us. Rae decided to catch a later bus and asked Steve to take a seat whilst she went to the Ladies room. I wandered over to keep him company. There in front of us on the table were the Sacred Circle Tarot cards she was using too. I felt it was a good omen.

I can't remember all of the details Steve told me about his reading, but he liked Rae Beth very much. He respected her writing and was pleased to have met her in person. She'd said she was equally honoured to have met him, which he was touched by. She saw in him the ability to 'work in dangerous places' which is certainly part of his spiritual calling. He is prepared to clear out the difficult energies others have unwisely summoned or inadvertently let through.

I went over for my reading. Rae Beth looked at me with understanding eyes and said, "I'm seeing a lake." It was Avalon and Lancelot again I knew. She saw the two men vying for my attention and warned me that the other man would want to keep me as his muse whereas Steve would support me to walk my own path. She could see the turmoil still churning within me and treated me with great empathy.

Neither of us wanted to drive straight home after our readings as we'd planned. We needed to talk things over. We went to the pub and sat down over a beer. Steve went off to the loo and came back highly entertained; he'd been mistaken for Lui, the flamboyant proprietor from Stone Age. That was the same guy I had pointed out in

Light behind the Angels

the Mind, Body, Spirit Festival programme and Carmel had commented that Steve looked rather like him. I conceded that they are rather alike to look at.

We had a long and serious discussion about my feelings of a past life connection with Avalon. I hadn't told him the Guinevere and Lancelot part of my story before. It seemed too outlandish. Steve was sympathetic about my heartache. He'd had his own painful soul mate experience which had ended in disaster, driving him to a suicide attempt that should have cost him his life. Somehow Spirit had intervened and saved him.

With the twin flame back out in the open I made the mistake of trying to resume contact with my old love just as friends. Looking back I can see it was foolish of me, but I'd missed him terribly and I didn't want to lose him out of my life. He'd been my closest friend for several years. At this point I hadn't seen him at all for six months. I decided it would be okay to visit and keep to safe topics of conversation.

I was wrong; I couldn't cope with the resurgence of emotion that welled up as soon as I saw him. I left his house with my hands shaking like leaves and feeling sick. Despite being in Manchester, Steve picked up the vibes straight away. I'd parked in a lay-by to have a good cry about my lost dreams and immediately received a text from him, "What's wrong?" Trying to keep secrets from Steve would be as impossible as keeping them from my ex-husband.

I'd reopened communication channels and we would see each other occasionally for a coffee, though not with the frequency of the past. I was restrained and we kept the physical attraction at bay, but it was clear that we both had strong feelings for each other and he didn't seem any happier in his marriage. In a moment of madness I asked that he would either do something about our relationship by the end of the year or get right out of my life. To me it made sense. I needed closure and if nothing was going to come of this I wanted to know for certain so that I could put it all behind me.

I was still hooked into the twin flame's energy. I couldn't erase all the psychic readings that had indicated I'd be with this man, all the hopes and dreams I'd invested in him. Steve would pick up any contact we made, whether it was face to face or by email. It was rather unnerving.

There were other possible predicted futures and I remembered the reader who'd said, "There is a second marriage ahead of you. That person will come in over the next 3 years and it isn't someone you technically know. What I mean is you might have heard of the person on a distant path. It'll be someone you meet interlinked with the spiritual side." I realised now that I'd heard of Steve almost six months before I met him and the distant path was Manchester and Wicca.

Now the Twin Flame was back in touch it was costing Steve his peace of mind and he began to receive strange guidance about the man in the autumn. One evening I was socialising with my old neighbours, drinking wine in their garden, celebrating their granddaughter's birthday. I had a quick mobile phone chat with Steve in Manchester, as he was sorting out some shopping for me. Manchester has a lot more shops than Mid Wales! He said, "Remind me to tell you later about a bizarre dream I had. I think it will mean more to you than it does to me."

When I got home we had our usual late night chat. I reminded him about the dream. He seemed more reluctant to tell me by then and later confessed he'd felt he shouldn't share it with me. He'd dreamt he'd been following the skeletal figure of Death seated upon a pale horse. He walked behind wearing a long black cloak. They were travelling on a cobbled road and Steve was leaving fiery footprints in his wake.

In the dream he came up with the exact name of the village the twin flame lives in, which I'd never disclosed, and he was walking up and down looking for a place which sounded very similar to the estate he lives on. I let Steve know that he had the name of the village right and gave him the real name of the estate, and then I doubted whether I'd done the right thing.

The dream scared me and I rang Semele, distraught. She calmed me down and pointed out that knowing about this old love was playing on Steve's mind and being so psychic he'd been given the information he sought. Still I felt uneasy. Images of Death weren't cosy! Who was this man that I was sharing my life with?

Our relationship was turned upside down. I didn't want to lose Steve but I was unsettled by the way the information was coming through and I didn't want my twin flame to come to any harm either.

That week we went into town. Steve popped into the ironmongers to pick up a few things and I went into the bank where he joined me shortly. As we left and started to cross the street my legs suddenly felt like they were going to give way. By the time we got to the other side of the road Steve had received a text on his mobile phone. I said we had to go straight into a café as my legs felt like jelly. I sat down and Steve bought us a coffee each.

In the café Steve looked at his text. The sunshine had been too bright in the street to read it. His expression froze. His last girlfriend Ashley had sent him a nude picture of herself fresh from the shower

Light behind the Angels

saying how she missed her High Priest and how much she wanted him back.

I'd known they'd been in touch, supposedly just as friends. It hadn't bothered me and he'd often read her messages aloud to me. He'd told her when he started seeing me and she would send me her regards. It didn't feel like he'd been hiding anything. Despite his protestations that he hadn't done anything to invite this more intimate contact I was unnerved, especially by the immediate physical reaction I'd had as the message arrived.

That night we went and sat on a hilltop together in the light of the full moon. We weren't angry with each other, but we were both badly shaken. We decided to call it a day. I couldn't cope with the feeling that he might have been unfaithful back in Manchester and Steve had been more and more provoked by the continued contact with my old love as time had gone on.

Steve told me he'd asked for balance that morning; he certainly got that. Now I'd had a very physical taste of how he'd been feeling. Next morning we still felt the same. We went to the nearest earthworks and sat on the embankment. I cried, he cried. We talked for an hour. Neither of us wanted to split, but we just knew we had to part company. It was the most bizarre of break-ups, both of us shaking, crying and neither wanting to let the other one go. Then he drove off back to Manchester, perhaps for good as far as I knew.

I went to Semele's that evening. I was surprised by how upset I was. I had been so bound up in my old feelings that I hadn't realised how deeply I cared about Steve. Semele did tea and sympathy and was as ever the most soothing shoulder to cry on.

Our relationship didn't end there. Steve stayed in contact by text. We'd agreed to give it a clear fortnight to see how things stood, but just over a week later we were back together to discuss our future. Our problems weren't just about ex lovers, there were other things about Steve's behaviour that had annoyed me and this seemed like the right time to sort everything out.

During our time apart I had composed a long list of positives and negatives about Steve and I suggested he do the same for me. It was time to be absolutely open and honest with each other if we were to continue together. To Steve's credit he listened to the list of his faults and accepted them as fair comment. He'd made his own list for me, but it only contained positives. I don't imagine for one minute I am faultless, but he wanted to stay with me and he wasn't about to jeopardise that.

Steve was back, more serious about our relationship than before. Splitting up had made us realise that our bond went deeper than we'd given it credit for and we'd really missed each other. Steve told me he'd composed a text while we were apart to express what he'd been feeling. Sitting in an old fashioned tea shop on the Welsh Borders he sent it across to my phone.

"This is a record of my willingness to commit to our relationship, for over a month now I have felt a deep yearning to tell you how I actually feel about you and the level of commitment I am happy to make but with the cloud [meaning the twin flame] *it was not appropriate as there needs to be balance and that has not been there. I will protect myself when threatened and not be vulnerable. I see us spending our lives together, I would like us to be handfasted and if you wanted even do the civil wedding thing. I am willing to find regular work to bring in money although that scares the hell out of me but for you I will do it. There is of course the but, but for this level of commitment there can only be two in the relationship, no Lancelot, no Ashley. These are my innermost thoughts, scary huh!"*

What girl could resist? I had to clean up my act. I couldn't even pretend that a friendship with my twin flame would be okay any more. I cut all communication. He made a few attempts to start chatting again, but his emails went unanswered. It was tough to do, but necessary if Steve and I were to stand a chance. I couldn't erase the old feelings so easily, but I could avoid fanning the flames.

Light behind the Angels

Initiation

> *'And thou who thinkest to seek for me, know thy seeking and yearning shall avail thee not unless thou knowest the mystery; that if that which thou seekest thou findest not within thee, thou wilt never find it without thee.'*
> Doreen Valiente, The Charge of the Goddess

Steve's role as High Priest of a Wiccan coven was fine by me; although I'm not Wiccan it was good to have a partner with a strong sense of spirituality. Our beliefs didn't completely match up, but there was respect for each other's viewpoints. I had worked in a gently magical way for quite a while, intuitively using sympathetic magic and I was happy to be shown more sophisticated techniques, which quickly became essential knowledge. It was as though Steve was guided to teach me whatever I'd be needing next.

I became concerned about a middle aged local man who'd been taken suddenly and seriously ill with breathing difficulties. The hospital had been unable to make a diagnosis. His plight had been brought to my attention by several different people and although I'd never met him I knew his wife. I was aware that they'd recently bought the same shop with living accommodation above that I had first noticed on the internet all those years ago. Since living in Llandrindod I had found out more about that place. A couple had bought it shortly before we came house hunting. They'd intended to open a Victorian costume business together, but within weeks of moving in and starting renovations the husband had a sudden heart attack and died. Their business had never opened and his widow had now sold up and moved to be closer to her family.

Now the new owner had been taken suddenly and dangerously ill. I felt the building was the connection. I knew something wasn't right and happened to mention it at Semele's when I visited her. Grabbing her tarot cards she discerned that the attack had come from an astral being that had lain dormant under the ground. It had been disturbed and had attacked the man. He appeared to have a dark entity which was very black and heavy sitting on his chest. It looked a bit like a large stingray. She saw that he had little time left and if we were to help him we had to act quickly. This accorded with a rapid deterioration in his condition. He'd been sent away to the Midlands to a specialist intensive care unit where he was unconscious and on a respirator.

Knowing that no amount of drug treatment would pull him back whilst this creature was attacking him I spoke to his wife and asked permission to organise some absent healing. She was grateful for any help, though I doubt she believed it would change anything. Semele could see it needed the power of three to shift this creature. I contacted Steve who was in Manchester at the time. Only the previous week I'd been taught by Steve to draw magical sigils. I showed Semele how it worked. Before we could start we had to create much stronger protection around ourselves than normal. Semele was guided that we should use the 'full armour of God'. She lifted down her Biblical Concordance, referenced the phrase and found the passage in her Bible.

"Put on the whole armour of God, that ye may be able to stand against the wiles of the Devil. For we wrestle not against flesh and blood, but against principalities, against powers, against the rulers of the darkness of this world, against spiritual wickedness in high place...Stand therefore, having your loins girt about with truth and having on the breastplate of righteousness; And your feet shod with the preparation of the gospel of peace; Above all, taking the shield of faith, wherewith ye shall be able to quench all the fiery darts of the wicked. And take the helmet of salvation, and the sword of the Spirit, which is the word of God." Ephesians 6, verses 11-17

Thoroughly prepared and protected we wrote out a clear intention to remove the entity from the man's chest and have it taken to a place where it could harm no-one else. Together we drew our sigil. Back in Manchester Steve was drawing his own sigil and we co-ordinated our efforts with his. Synchronising our timing we stared at the sigil to empower it. Semele and I were amazed and heartened to see that the seemingly random design we had created of letters coalesced as we gazed into a glowing stingray shape. We three then released our intent upon the astral plane at the same moment.

Fortunately distance doesn't matter in magic. I contacted the man's wife the next day to ask how he was. After spending a week in intensive care with no change he had suddenly shown some improvement overnight and looked like he would pull through. She was delighted to inform me that the hospital said they had worked out what was wrong now and thanked us for sending some healing. I was pleased we'd achieved our result and knew we'd saved a man's life, but I didn't spell out what we'd done.

Later, when I bumped into her I did tell her that the energy that had attacked him had been dormant in the ground under the building until it had been disturbed. She went pale; her husband had indeed been taken ill after working on the drainage in the cellar.

Light behind the Angels

I've always called myself spiritual, not religious. I know there is a Divine Source and that there are many truths in the religions of the world, but there is much falsehood and hypocrisy too. When I find a spiritual truth it 'clicks' somewhere inside of me and I just know that it is right, I find I can sift out the manmade dross that has been added to religions throughout history. No-one dictates what I may or may not believe. Standing outside of organised religion I can appreciate the connections between the faiths more than the differences that cause so much hatred and bloodshed.

Early on in our relationship I had to scotch Steve's notion that I might want to come to his coven meetings. Covens and organised religious groups in general are not for me. At first Steve interpreted my refusal as shyness, but soon he realised this was a real personal choice and respected my decision. He was bothered that I was working magically but hadn't been initiated as a Priestess and offered to conduct my initiation himself.

I thought long and hard about this. I couldn't and wouldn't nail my colours to a religion. I work with diverse energies. How would a Wiccan work with Jesus Christ? How would a Christian call on Ganesha and power animals? I wasn't about to shut out any of my helpers and guides because a religion didn't recognise them.

Steve felt I should have the same status as himself. I already felt equal but I could see where he was coming from and although initiation was not high on my personal agenda I eventually agreed to go through with it. Steve was pleased, but I insisted on examining every vow minutely beforehand with him and he rewrote until they met with my approval. I believe very much in the sacredness of vows and I was not about to promise anything I couldn't wholeheartedly embrace as my truth.

Steve chose to initiate me through all three degrees on one evening. This was a strange decision as normally initiations are spaced out and elevation from a Novice to High Priestess may come after years of training, or not at all, but Steve felt I was already working at the level of a High Priestess. I had some conflict about that. I have long felt that Reiki for example is being damaged by those who fast track their attunements and do not take on board the full spiritual commitment that originally went with the title of Master. I didn't want to take on the mantle of High Priestess without earning it. We agreed that we would stop after each initiation and check whether it felt appropriate to continue to the next level.

Our biggest stumbling block was over me being bound to be led into the sacred circle for the rite. In Wicca each candidate is introduced naked and bound. Even though I knew it was only going to be me and Steve I wouldn't allow myself to be bound. He assured me it was symbolic and that he wouldn't tie the cords tightly so it wouldn't hurt, but that wasn't the point. Steve got frustrated with me. He'd already written new sections into the rites and left other phrases out that I didn't agree to. He wouldn't allow any member of his coven to personalise their initiations and state their terms like this. I pointed out that I wasn't in his coven and neither did I want to be. I would not allow myself to be led bound into that circle and I knew it was important to dig my heels in. I was absolutely prepared to ditch the whole thing and so, reluctantly, Steve backed down and agreed that I could walk in freely.

On the evening everything ran smoothly and flowed naturally and so I was made a High Priestess. Steve presented me with a beautiful copper athame that he'd hand carved from a solid bar of copper. It is one of my most cherished possessions. He also gave me a wand of crystal and elder wood and a pretty silver pentagram pendant that I wore until a more personalised protection replaced it.

I felt that my initiations simply put a more formal wrapper on work I was already doing, but also allowed us to work together as magical partners of equal ranking. We found later that our equal status as High Priest and High Priestess was essential for unravelling our soul journey together.

Light behind the Angels

Pyramids of Gold and Ice

*'Your vision will become clear only when you can look into your own heart.
Who looks outside, dreams; who looks inside, awakens.'*
Carl Jung

As the partner of a teacher of Crystal Healing Steve got used to being a 'demonstration body'. I think he mostly quite enjoyed it and he has probably had more crystal healing than most crystal healers have themselves in a lifetime.

I was demonstrating a more advanced way to clear the chakras to a second year group. The method I use is to relax the client, take a large quartz point in my left hand which receives the energy from the Universe and channel it through me to my right hand which massages each chakra in turn. At the same time I guide my client through their chakras and we see what they pick up. Often it is just colours, sometimes there are visions of objects or symbols. It has the potential to get to the root of any chakra related issues.

We started at Steve's base chakra. All seemed quite normal and healthy down there and a burst of fresh red energy was all it needed. At the sacral chakra Steve saw a pond choked up with green pondweed. A man went in wearing waders and pulled them out, putting them on the bank. The Sun came out and frazzled them and the pool was left lovely and clear. The imagery made a lot of sense as the sacral is linked to the element of water.

At the solar plexus the images became more complex. Steve saw a golden pyramid covered in sand. The wind blew the sand away and uncovered a doorway. He walked in and found the place was choked with sand. It needed sweeping out. As he did so he uncovered flagstones and steps. He climbed the steps and cleared the floor. It was stained glass coloured in blues and golds. The background was blue and the symbols on it were gold. The only symbol he could remember clearly afterwards was a seven pointed star.

At his heart Steve saw another pyramid. My hand felt very chilled over this chakra. At first Steve thought it was a pyramid made of silver, but when he looked closer it was made of solid ice. His heart chakra was frozen over. He drilled the ice and dynamited it away. When it was broken into chunks we brought in the power of the Sun to melt the ice and the ground beneath began to show as a brown patch of earth. Once the Sun warmed it grass started to grow and a beautiful meadow emerged. I was pleased with his progress, green being a great balancing colour for the heart chakra.

At the throat Steve felt there wasn't much work to be done. Some clouds covered a blue sky. They just needed to be blown away for a beautiful blue to be revealed. We moved swiftly on to the brow chakra. At this point Steve physically flinched. He felt my hand was burning hot (it was several inches above his forehead). He saw a bonfire in a woodland clearing and figures in black dancing around it widdershins. Steve was greeted with warmth. He felt that he had returned to lead this coven and he was invited to join their circle. He knew they were performing a dark rite.

Steve went in, sword drawn, as his magical persona and was joined by his white robed Gemini twin self. Together they ousted the coveners and then he put out the fire. Steve seemed quite shaken by this and aware that my students were watching he kept the description of events to a minimum. Once it had been cleared out the brow chakra looked like a dark cave. He seemed to want to move on at this point and so knowing that the brow can seem to have unfathomable depths we did so.

Later, in private, he told me that when the coveners' hoods were drawn back and he saw their faces they all looked like him and the cave appeared to be a gateway to the Underworld, like an open fanged snake's mouth. In the cave a pale horse was awaiting him. He recognised it from his dream of walking in the wake of Death. Wisely he'd felt the full description might have rattled my students a bit and kept quiet. To our mutual relief the crown chakra was full of the Sun, the Moon and the Stars and it needed no work at all.

Even spared the full details this had been a heavy duty demonstration and my students had eyes like saucers by the end. I had to reassure them that this had been a really unusual healing and that they were very unlikely to get anything quite so challenging to deal with.

Just before Christmas I was giving a lesson to a psychic student of considerable clairvoyance. She had a lot of raw ability and had worked hard over the year to hone her skills. I didn't have any guinea pigs lined up for her so I let her read for me. She became quite troubled. She claimed that I wasn't seeing dark energies growing around me because the perpetrator was so close he'd got in under my defences. She had a vision of black roots creeping from under me sending up shoots that would trap me and had the image of me as a dove in a cage. She was apologetic but felt it was Steve doing this, that he hadn't told me everything and was keeping a dark secret.

Light behind the Angels

I had been really looking forward to the arrival of Steve later in the day to spend our first proper Christmas together. Now I was on my guard. I thought he'd been really open about his life, the highs and the lows, and I couldn't think what this dark secret could be.

I did know that Steve's soul mate relationship had driven him to the depths of despair and I knew from the way he still talked about her several years on that he must still be corded to her energy. I asked him if he would like the cords cutting and he agreed that it would be a good idea. Cords can hold us to people from our past and are commonly found in relationships where the couple have played power games and manipulated each other. Cords are an 'easy access' into another person's energy field and I advise that whenever a relationship ends, or is in difficulty, it is worth scanning the condition of the cords. In this case Steve was still chatting to his ex girlfriend's mother and would be cheerfully and regularly told, "She still hates you."

Steve confessed that he'd especially like to have the energetic return of 'a piece of his heart'. When he was truly, madly, deeply in love, he'd made her a stamp for her card crafting hobby. The handle was based on an old fashioned post office stamp and he'd hand carved it from a piece of apple wood from his garden. The silver heart-shaped stamp had been cut from an oval of solid silver which had his name engraved upon it. One sliver of the heart was cut away and presented to her separately with the sentiment, "You'll always have a piece of my heart." He'd reinforced his message by carving it in runes upon the wooden handle of the stamp. Very romantic, but 'always' is a long time. This little sliver of metal had been playing on his mind in recent months.

I took him to the healing room and laid him on the couch. The cord cutting technique I use most often is adapted from Phyllis Krystal's book 'Cutting the Ties that Bind'. All went smoothly with a multitude of twisted and angry cords removed from each of the chakras. When we asked for the piece of Steve's heart however she was unwilling to return it and had to be persuaded by his guides to finally give it up. Once it was all over Steve felt a lot lighter and this healing seemed to open the floodgates on his clairvoyance.

The Fix Her

*'If you're breaking down, don't give up hope
If I can't fix it, baby, it ain't broke'*
George Thorogood

I'd been having trouble with my back for a good while. I would wake with backache every morning and the problem was getting steadily worse. I'd tried a range of remedies, including yoga and regular massage, but nothing worked for long. I'd bought a new bed as my old mattress was worn out, but there was still no real improvement, although a fresh new mattress felt like a good investment on the energy front. Heat gave some relief, but it was all a temporary fix. I felt more intensive healing energy was needed to get to the root of the problem.

A few months previously my back had gone into spasm and I was unable to get up or even change position without help. Steve tried hands on healing then and within a few hours I was much better, but he had wiped himself out transferring so much energy. It was then I decided he needed some tutoring. Healers readily transfer life force energy to another. Untrained and unwitting healers often wear themselves out by giving their own energy away instead of channelling the boundless energy that comes from Mother Earth and Divine Source. Once the problem is identified it is simple enough to sort out.

Having taught Steve to channel healing energy safely he was keen to work on my back in an intensive way, as small parcels of healing were not giving more than temporary relief. At Christmas he was staying longer than usual, so he made fixing my back his holiday project. I use the word 'fix' deliberately- as a motor mechanic, Steve didn't consider himself a healer and preferred to call himself a 'fixer' spelt F-I-X H-E-R, as in his hero George Thorogood's lyrics.

His decision to start healing seemed to trigger an influx of clairvoyance. Although Steve had natural abilities he didn't regard himself as exceptionally psychic. Suddenly guidance flooded in. Special hand positions were shown for healing that I hadn't seen before. One position was given for drawing stale energy out, another for putting good energy in and yet another for injecting etheric anaesthetic, which I felt numbing my back. He found that by creating a viewing 'window' between his hands he could see inside my body and describe the state of the energy there.

Light behind the Angels

At first the energy of my lower back looked muddy and dark brown. Elsewhere it was much brighter and there was a lot of gold light. He decided that I needed to become 'all gold', not really knowing why, but trusting the guidance he was receiving.

There was so much dark stagnant energy in my back that a few sessions of hands-on healing wouldn't shift it. Steve found that he could draw the energy up though his hands into his forearms, using energetic tourniquets below his elbows to prevent it rising higher. He was given two handmaiden helper guides who would stand either side of him and clear away the sticky energy from his forearms. He would hold his arms out in a special sequence of movements for the cleanup. It looked very like a surgeon scrubbing up for an operation.

Steve sensed that the dark energy pooled at my back was largely emotional rubbish I had stored there over a long period of time. This part of the lower back is also related to the rear aspect of the sacral chakra and the emotions, so I felt he was correct. I remembered a shamanic healing I'd had a year before. Patricia had dragged all sorts of old junk from my lower back. Temporary but welcome relief had been gained. Clearly my lower back was my favourite dumping ground.

Daily and sometimes twice daily sessions of healing were scheduled now. There was too much debris to take it all out in one go. Gradually, the colour was getting lighter and clearer. More and more gold was shining through and we were reminded of the 5 of Disks in the Thoth tarot deck, entitled Worry. This card depicts dark, leaden disks, resting upon a sea of gold light just waiting to be uncovered.

Next Steve was guided to extract more stubborn, stagnant energy by sucking it out, something new to him, but I recognised this as a traditional shamanic technique. I've never tried it as this is an unappealing method and it wasn't the pleasantest by all accounts. It left Steve retching, coughing and dry vomiting. He also had some fiendishly smelly bowel movements afterwards, so I guess a label of 'don't try this at home' applies, or at least 'don't say I didn't warn you!' Steve described the taste of the energy as stale and old; I had freshly bathed, so I'm quite confident that I didn't smell stale on the physical level. Steve was reassured months later when he read 'The Last Confessions of a Sin Eater' by Ross Heaven and found that the sin eater, a traditional Celtic healer, would eat the bad energy from the body of the newly deceased to leave them cleansed and ready for the afterlife. He would then dry vomit it into the ground. Steve was just rediscovering an old technique.

My back was getting much easier day by day and I was really pleased with the results. Steve kept working on me until my energy was golden all over. There wasn't much to shift elsewhere in comparison. We didn't recognise how important the colour gold was for me until later.

When you have daily pain you don't notice how much it affects you until it lifts. Waking without backache felt amazing. However Steve felt that to get to a place of permanent improvement I would have to process the old emotions that went with it. The 'dogrock' wand had formed an important part of the healing. It was good to see it in use and it became Steve's choice of stone. As he used it we saw it begin to change. It became more translucent in places and started to show gold highlights. The blue seemed to get more brilliant too.

After Christmas we had a brief lull in proceedings. My ex had the kids so we decided to go to Hereford and do some shopping in the sales. We chatted as we went along about all sorts of things. The road to Hereford from Mid Wales is long and winding. It takes you through several of the Herefordshire black and white villages, old places that I'd never stopped to explore with a couple of kids in the car anxious to get on with their shopping. In one of these I'd noticed a café come second-hand bookshop and we took the opportunity to stop and check it out. We wandered around the bookshelves. My eye was caught by a coffee table tome on Ancient Egypt. We'd looked into going to Egypt to take initiations into the Egyptian Mysteries as Beryl had suggested, but finances weren't quite up to the expedition. We still felt a draw towards Egypt and hoped to go at some stage.

We ordered coffee and buttered tea cakes and wandered through to the quaint tea rooms, all lacy tablecloths and china knickknacks. It was very quiet, we were the only customers. Our discussion drifted back onto the programme of healing. Steve started talking about his last girlfriend, Ashley of the text message, whom he'd only seen for a few weeks. She'd had a major psychic awakening in that time. By the end she was seeing her room as full of angels. He felt that this was his 'job done'. They weren't compatible and it was a relationship for a purpose.

Steve admitted that he had a nagging worry that once he'd completed the healing on my back the relationship between us would be over. Perhaps he'd only been brought into my life to fulfil a purpose? Frankly it seemed improbable to me, but he was serious. Even so it felt like there was no going back. The healing took priority. My system had to get cleaned up for me to move on and he was the one to do it. When it was complete we would see whether we still wanted to be together.

Light behind the Angels

The end of year deadline that I'd foolishly set in the summer when I'd last seen my twin flame would soon be up. I'd told Steve about it at the time of our temporary break up, thinking it was good to be totally open and honest. It wasn't quite so thoughtful from his point of view and now it makes me squirm with embarrassment.

Unbeknownst to me Steve had confided in his best friend. We were due to go out for dinner when a voicemail came through. Steve put his phone on loudspeaker and I listened horrified as his friend joked about the Sword of Damocles hanging over Steve's head. A furious row ensued as I felt my privacy had been invaded. No-one but myself, the twin flame and Steve had known of the deadline. Here was a virtual stranger making jokes about my personal life. I knew in my heart that the twin flame wasn't coming for me and I wasn't even sure what my reaction would be if he did turn up, but it had been playing on Steve's mind.

Dinner was a strained affair and all I can remember was the laver bread arriving. I'd expected an actual bread dish. It turned out to be a traditional dish of seaweed in a cheese sauce. I'm still learning about the Welsh culture!

Happy New Year

*'If we only ever reveal what we believe to be acceptable,
we can only ever feel unacceptable.'*
Joanne L. Hall

I had been feeling increasingly upset over the past year by my relationship with my father. Several times when we'd spoken he'd got dictatorial with me and I'd automatically gone on the defensive. Sometimes I'd even put the phone down. I couldn't cope with his energy and I didn't know how to sort things out.

My childhood had been happy enough, but my father was very much the disciplinarian. As soon as I got to university I went wild, but I tried to keep that wildness hidden from my parents. I knew my mother worried when I didn't phone home or visit nearly as much as she'd have liked. I split my identity for them. Once I dyed my hair a gorgeous shade of pink, which I just loved. Whenever I looked in the mirror it made me smile and I felt so fantastically confident sporting this candyfloss confection. Long before I was tired of it I dyed it black to visit my parents and that was the last of my glorious colour.

I tried to present myself as the daughter they wanted me to be, but I wasn't and they weren't fooled. The inner conflict between the real me and the acceptable me took me nose diving into bulimia nervosa. I couldn't cope with my sadness and guilt, so I tried to blot it out with enormous quantities of food. This cycle of binging and purging went on for several years, gradually getting worse until it dominated my life, only resolving itself when I found some emotional security with my husband.

From that time on my relationship with my parents had never fully healed. They assumed that my eating disorder was due to my lifestyle choices and I just distanced myself from them. I never sat down and fully discussed my issues; I kept most of my life a secret. In my adult years we would have some peaceful times and make pleasant visits, then the flare ups would come and we'd stop talking for months. I'd get my husband to screen phone calls in case it was them. I know he got much of the blame as he'd make excuses for me, or say I was out, but it wasn't his fault. I couldn't be myself in their presence, I only showed them the little bit of me I felt they would be proud of and we would fall into the old destructive patterns all too easily. I aimed to make just enough visits and calls to keep them from getting annoyed with me and I got it wrong frequently.

Light behind the Angels

Since meeting Steve and turning forty the issues had been brought right up to the surface and I couldn't dodge them anymore. My sister and her young family had recently moved away from the Midlands to the Lake District. She'd always lived within a short drive of my parents and within months they announced they were moving to Cumbria to be near her. Although my logical mind could see that this was a sensible move for them, my inner child felt unbelievably hurt and abandoned. I was shocked by the strength of my feelings. Inside me a little Lauren was crying, "That's not fair, they love her more than me!"

I couldn't hide my emotions when they told me and instead of understanding why I was upset my parents were angry, feeling I was being unreasonable. The whole issue ballooned into another big row. My sister, then in her mid thirties, took care of me and my feelings, and I realised for the first time that she wasn't just my little sister, she was a capable woman. The row made a real change to the dynamics between us and brought a more balanced harmonic to our sisterly relationship.

That summer I'd had a reading with a clairvoyant who was adamant that my issues with my father were holding me back. She told me to cut my cords with him and move on. I must admit I'd buried my feelings so deep inside of myself for so long that I was shocked she'd picked this up.

At the end of November my father's Aunt had her 90th birthday party down in Essex. The family all hail from Essex and Steve is always highly amused that I'm an Essex girl. My parents had decided not to go, but I felt drawn to make the journey. I hadn't seen most of these relatives for years, but the warmth with which I was received was very touching. Seeing how close knit other members of the family were made me regret the gulf that had grown between myself and my parents. I cried myself to sleep that night wishing things had been different.

On New Year's Eve Steve decided to drive over to the crystal shop in Llanidloes and buy his own copy of the Arthurian Tarot. It was a strange decision as he doesn't consider himself a tarot reader and he knew he was welcome to use my deck. We had the house to ourselves that night and Steve was planning to do more work on me. Steve pulled cards on the healing to come:

Grail King, Grail Queen, Two of Cups, The Tower, the Fool.

He saw the King and Queen as representing us and the two of cups as working on each other out of love, a process we were engaged in together. The Tower represented the need to break down the old structures to bring in the new. The Fool card in this deck is depicted as the seeker stepping out on the rainbow bridge and starting a new journey with Spirit. He surmised that the healing was a way to clear out the old stuff and help me along my spiritual path. Steve felt the process would be completed by my birthday in January and that the results would be significant. At that point we had no idea how significant and accurate his prediction was.

I decided I didn't want to spend another year carrying the baggage of my past. Events had served to draw my attention to the issues and stop burying them. We decided the time to clear out the rest of my psychic junk was long overdue.

We started by looking at the relationship with my father. We could see a little of this baggage stemmed from childhood, but most of it seemed to have been accumulated in my teens. I'd been carrying unhealthy connections for far too long. I don't think my Dad was a bad father, but the energies between us had got twisted. There was a personality clash between a dominant Leo male and a strong minded Aquarian female. When I was a child he'd held the position of power and things were fine, but I'd kicked against him as I'd grown up and wanted my independence.

Steve worked from a script to guide me through the cord cutting process and to prompt me as and when I needed it. We set up a golden circle for me to stand in as a place of safety and in my mind's eye I saw golden flames whizzing around me, quickly resolving themselves into a golden ouroboros, a snake biting its own tail.

The first cord I could see was repulsive. Pallid, fleshy, grotesque, connecting me to my father like an obscene umbilical. It had to be torn away and I found it so hard to look at this repugnant thing that I turned my back and allowed my guides to do the work. It actually scared me and I cried hysterically, my body wracked with sobs as I lay on the couch. Once it was removed I felt a huge sense of release which is hard to express in words. It was like nothing I'd experienced before. Imagine you are in the middle of your worst nightmare and you are suddenly and unexpectedly rescued and taken from the scene. That's the level of relief I felt. There was still plenty to do, but from here on nothing could be as scary.

The next cord led into my solar plexus and was as big and firm as a tree trunk. No wonder our relationship was so rigid and inflexible. When that was gone it left splinters that had to be removed with tweezers. I flinched physically each time one was dug out.

Next I found I was wearing iron shackles on both wrists. I could physically feel them there and they needed to be unlocked. My father carried an iron key, big and heavy, which he passed over without fuss. It unlocked the shackle on my right wrist, but it didn't

Light behind the Angels

unlock the one on my left. Dad said, "It's with your mother." I had to ask my guides to visit my mother and ask her for the other key. When they arrived back it made a striking contrast, being dainty and golden.

Reflecting later I felt the energetic shackles had been placed on me for slightly different reasons. My father was very focussed on controlling my behaviour when I was a teenager, stopping me getting into trouble, whereas my mum always worried too much and wanted to protect me, therefore the shackle on my left wrist was more about keeping me out of harm's way. Their motives may have differed subtly, but the end result was just the same and they'd unconsciously been holding me back on an energetic level decades later as these controls had never been removed.

My cord cutting script prompts the therapist to encourage the client to forgive the other person. I truly believe that forgiveness is the only route to complete freedom, however sometimes the client isn't quite ready for this step. In my case when Steve prompted me I screamed and shouted all the things I wished I'd said to my father over the years and had held back from expressing. I was stunned by how much old anger I had been holding onto. In my mind's eye Dad took it meekly without defending himself. When I was finished I sent him away and he left without argument.

I was left with a huge pile of old cords heaped in my circle. My emotions were in full flow and I went into peals of hysterical laughter looking at the outrageous size of it. I lit a big bonfire and threw them all on. The horrible meaty tie sizzled and cooked. A big black dog appeared, looking like a black wolfhound and I got the words 'hell hound' in my head. Whatever it was, it was glad of the meat, scoffed it and ran off again.

I was left with the iron manacles to destroy. They were melted down in a furnace. I decided not to get rid of the metal, instead I fashioned a doorstop with them. Until that moment the manacles had held me back, but now the doorstop would hold the door to my future open wide. There was a feeling of rightness and a huge sense of personal satisfaction in doing this.

The next stage in the cord cutting process is to look at what you are wearing, as your clothing is often symbolic of the nature of the relationship. I looked down. There was a scaly reptilian armour over my back; not very attractive. I think I'd donned the armour myself and the fact it was reptilian suggested I'd dealt with my issues in a cold blooded way. I strained to see what was underneath the armour and got the words 'sackcloth and ashes'.

I saw a hessian tunic-style dress, textured like old potato sacking, very drab and very rough. Underneath that were dirty looking linen pants and a matching vest. Altogether very poor, uncomfortable clothing that I certainly didn't want to hang onto.

I took everything off, made a pile of the clothes and threw petrol from a can all over them. I tossed a match onto the heap and watched them go up in flames with an almighty whoomph. Then I turned and in an act of supreme naughtiness warmed my bum on the flames. It gave me a tremendous feeling of freedom and I knew no-one could tell me off any more!

Next I found a body of water to bathe in. My pool was just beautiful, a tropical lagoon. I floated lazily on my back like Baloo the bear from Disney's Jungle Book, squirting little fountains of water from my mouth. When I got out I turned cartwheels on the shore. I found an ash tree and climbed up it to find a protective garment, a soft grey woollen robe like a monk's habit with a nice big hood, done up with cord. It felt very comforting and I could snuggle myself into it and hide completely.

When I got off the treatment couch I looked at the time; we'd been working solidly for almost two hours. I'd been through the most intense healing I'd ever experienced and it was almost the New Year. We just had time to go downstairs and see in 2008 with a glass of champagne. I felt a bit washed out, but I was relieved it was done.

Later I went on the internet to look up the meaning of 'sackcloth and ashes'. Although I'd heard the phrase used I wasn't fully clear about the meaning: *Penitent dress, shame, repentance.* It was a curious thing to be wearing. The clothing in cord cutting represents how you feel you are seen by the other person. Although I knew I carried a burden of guilt for not being the dutiful daughter it seemed a bit extreme.

Next morning, New Year's Day, my father called to wish me a Happy New Year. We had a short but pleasant chat with none of the underlying tension that normally characterised my conversations with him. At last I had removed the old, habitual defences and patterns which I'd kept in place for decades and I could be more relaxed with him.

Whether cord cutting is real on the astral level as I believe, or just a very clever psychological technique, it can transform relationships. I've seen this plenty of times with others. Either tensions dissolve, or it becomes easier to walk away from old entanglements. In this case the relationship with my father became much less angst ridden and it stayed that way for several years despite some of the past life revelations that emerged later.

Light behind the Angels

The Altar

> 'Freedom is a heavy load, a great and strange burden for the spirit to understand. It is not easy. It is not a gift given, but a choice made, and the choice may be a hard one. The road goes upward towards the light; but the laden traveller may never reach the end of it.'
> Ursula Le Guin, The Tombs of Atuan

For weeks I'd been talking about setting up an abundance altar. I felt I needed some help on a financial level, especially as I wanted to move house. The house I live in is great, but the main road we are on is busy and I found the noise intrusive.

On Wednesday 2nd of January 2008 Steve woke and said, "Today is the day you set up your altar." That sounded great! However, events that day brought strong feelings out. I went to the estate agents to speak to their financial advisor about a mortgage. He gave me a kindly but firm reality check on how much I could afford to borrow as a lone buyer. It wasn't much.

When Steve had left his wife for his soul mate relationship six years before he walked away with just his personal belongings. The family home was sold and his wife kept all the proceeds. I expect this was very soothing for his guilty conscience, but it infuriated and frustrated me, as there had been no thought for the future. When Steve met me he had no property, apart from a battered old Mondeo, no savings and he worked barely enough hours to keep him in cigars, clothe and feed himself. The situation wound me up incredibly, especially as I'd been conscientious in making sure my ex had enough equity from our marital home to put a decent deposit on a place of his own when we split up.

Now I would be trying to buy a new property and I couldn't afford anything I wanted. I felt Steve would expect to move in, having contributed nothing to the purchase. Whereas he described his lifestyle as 'living light' and 'going with the flow', I saw it as lazy, irresponsible, self-indulgent and sponging. What made my frustration more acute was that my twin flame was a hard worker, right at the other extreme, a workaholic if anything, and he had a pleasant home of his own. When I'd been seeing him I'd dreamt of us being able to put our two properties into the pot and buying something beautiful together. That wasn't going to happen now and I was just going to have to manage it alone.

I know this wasn't a spiritually enlightened viewpoint to take, but I am human! I returned from my meeting with the financial adviser in a particularly foul mood. No excuses, I just felt annoyed about the hand I'd been dealt.

Steve gauged my mood in an instant and suggested I take the dog out and have a good shout about it on the hilltops, which I did. It's great up there, there is absolutely no-one around and the wind takes your voice away. You can scream your lungs out and clear the anger from your system. It is incredibly therapeutic and much less harmful than shouting at the other person. I returned feeling a fair bit better.

Having helped me to separate all worldly links with my twin flame, Steve had received more guidance that morning. Enough was enough. We were just over one year into our relationship together and although the twin flame thing had started to fade after I'd guillotined our contact, energetically and emotionally there was still a big pull on me. In my mind I was comparing the two men although I didn't mean to and sometimes, as on this day, these comparisons were spoken aloud.

Later Steve described his behaviour as an inner knowing that this was the day decisive action had to be taken. The children were going to their dad's at tea time and we would have the evening to ourselves. When they were gone Steve told me to sit down at the kitchen table. He had an air of stern formality I'd never seen in him before and his whole demeanour was cold. It was quite unnerving and he was not like his normal self at all.

"Tonight is the night you make your choice. You have three choices and whichever one you choose will happen. Your choices are Enlightenment, Abundance, or your Twin Flame. Whatever you choose it has to be your heart's true desire."

I was stunned, shocked. Tears sprang to my eyes and I started to plead with him, but his tone was dispassionate and detached. Steve was in an authoritative High Priest mode as I'd never seen him before and I had no doubt at all in my mind that he could and would bring about whichever one of the three choices I made. Crying did not move him at all.

Now normally if someone was this high handed and authoritarian with me they'd be informed of some unimaginative, but painful places to stick their demands; I don't take kindly to being ordered around. In this case I knew I had to comply and give him an answer, however painful the process and so I stayed seated at the table.

Light behind the Angels

This had to be the craziest situation I'd ever been in. Steve stopped being my boyfriend that night, he became a High Priest just doing his job and if his job involved setting me up with another man he would do it.

"You have three hours to make your decision, now choose." Steve stalked off upstairs and left me alone in the kitchen crying. The contrast between us couldn't have been wider. I was all emotion, a melting sea of misery; he was the picture of cold, pitiless, heartless efficiency.

I had never been in such a dilemma before. It was surreal, something out of a play. For three years I had begged Spirit to bring me my twin flame. My chance had arrived and now it was here did I want to take it?

In the past I had turned down magical means as unethical, but my twin flame had told me that summer that he wished I would do something to make it all happen for us. I had his express permission. That was when I'd set the unwise deadline for him to act. It wasn't for me to do. I'd sorted my life out and left my husband, he couldn't expect me to sort his life out for him too. I needed him to show courage and choose to be with me instead of his wife.

My twin flame hadn't rowed with me, I'd simply cut him out of my life so that I didn't destroy my relationship with Steve. I knew that he was still only an email away and he would want to see me if I made the contact. If I chose this route Steve would be gone from my life as soon as the altar was set up. I couldn't expect anything more from him and yet he'd been such a big part of my life for the last year. Did I really want to lose him?

I got out my cards. Deck followed deck until the kitchen table became a patchwork quilt of different packs and layouts. The cards couldn't make my choice, I had to do that for myself, but I valued their guidance and their company. I couldn't talk to anyone and I felt too emotional to meditate, so I talked to Spirit through my cards.

I had a brainwave and I tried a fourth option. What if I could make the altar for me and Steve, something to draw us closer? That would help wean me off my twin flame wouldn't it? That would show I was committed to our relationship despite our difficulties. The cards told me, "No!" in no uncertain terms. The choices had to be examined just as they'd been offered, no further options were allowed.

Suddenly an Abundance altar was easy to dismiss. Although I'd been thinking about money and living in a quieter setting against the other two choices it seemed a trivial matter. I was left with a choice of Enlightenment or Twin Flame. At a higher level I knew which one I was *meant* to choose. I believe enlightenment is every soul's eventual goal, but the worldly love I'd had with this man who had consumed my energies for so long couldn't be turned down easily.

The Twin Flame option was tempting certainly, but I knew it was wrong. All along he had sat back and waited for fate to step in and make something happen. This was something I despised about him. Choosing this option might give me some short term happiness, but I was sure it would lead to disaster because he wouldn't have taken the initiative, he wouldn't have wanted to be with me badly enough to act. I felt angry with him. I am worth more than that! I am worth making the effort for!

To choose my twin flame was to hand myself to him on a plate. I remembered the warning given to me by Rae Beth in Glastonbury that this man wanted me to be his muse and as flattering as that would be I couldn't let it stop me on my spiritual path. Yet the love I still had for him paralysed me and left me unable to choose. To close the door once and for all on this man, to deny myself what I'd longed for, that action felt like more than I could cope with.

Three hours passed and I still hadn't made my decision. Steve gave me a short extension to my time limit. He had been told that it all had to be completed and the altar set up and activated by midnight. I knew I had to obey.

I can't capture the full gamut of emotions I went through that night. This was the final giving up on a dream, a folly in the eyes of others perhaps, but a much cherished dream nonetheless.

A little calmer now I moved away from the table to meditate. My guides wouldn't choose for me. It was to be my decision alone, but in the peace and stillness I could make a choice that truly came from my heart.

I decided on the Enlightenment path. I'd known it was the right choice from the start, but I'd struggled so hard to make it. The last card I pulled confirmed my decision: 'Creator: Awareness, Co-creation, Change' from a deck of Native American cards. The accompanying message moved me to shed more tears, but tears of gratitude this time.

"There is a strong desire for change and redirection in your life. Here you are given the gift of awareness. A hidden truth may be revealed to you, or a new understanding unveiled to you in the near future. This newfound information will bring about necessary changes."
Linda Ewashina, Spirit of the Wheel Meditation Deck.

This message proved to be accurate beyond my wildest imaginings. If Steve was relieved in any way by my decision he didn't show it. He was still locked into cold, detached High Priest mode. While he'd

Light behind the Angels

waited for me he had been sewing a golden altar cloth and had changed into his ceremonial robes. I dressed myself in my 'goddess dress' and a beautiful silk frock coat a client had given me. Together we set up a golden altar in my bedroom. Steve had intuited that the altar had to remain in place for three weeks. On reflection it had all been threes: three choices, three hours, three weeks. When we checked on the calendar three weeks took us to the date of the next full moon and the very eve of my 41st birthday.

I added the Native American guidance card to the altar and wrote out the affirmation that went with it:
"With the greatest of honour I open myself to the complete truth of who I am. I trust, Great Spirit, that you will assist me on my path. Help me to build my dreams and develop my potential for the higher good."

I drew a Goddess card to accompany it, Parvati, Mother of Ganesha, depicted with the wheel of fortune. Her message seemed most appropriate given the choice I'd just made:
"Be assertive in saying no to anything that diverts you from your path."

Next I placed a feather to represent my winged helpers and the element of air. My crystal ball was added to symbolise seeing more clearly and a carved tiger's eye owl joined it for wisdom. We blessed and consecrated the salt, water and mead and then lit a golden candle for the fire element and to symbolise enlightenment. Finally, I lit incense to take my prayers to the heavens.

As a sop Steve let me place my Christmas present from him, a little fat bellied iron cauldron, at the foot of my altar with golden pound coins surrounding a tea light to draw abundance. By the time the altar was fully activated it was just on midnight.

I took a photo as a record. Months later when I downloaded it from my camera I noticed a clear orb hovering in front of the cloth on the left.

We went to bed that night leaving the tea light still burning in the cauldron. A cold stream of spirit energy swept past our faces like a cool breeze. This sensation lasted for ages moving across our faces from right to left. We both had the impression that a long procession of spirits were passing through congratulating me on making the right choice.

Much later Steve let me see the notes he'd made in his journal that night. The cold detachment he'd shown was absolutely genuine, he was not putting on a brave face or acting:
"I tell Lauren I need to talk to her, give her three choices for the altar: Abundance, Enlightenment or the Twin Flame. Total surprise, shock and tears

from Lauren. I don't care, I'm just doing my job. I will not influence her in any way, but I do know that whatever her choice I will make it happen by 23rd. Leave Lauren to it. I am so removed from all this. Drink coffee and smoke. Can't see what all the fuss is about. Oh yes, the decision has to be Lauren's 'true heart's desire'. Those boys really know how to twist the knife. Tonight is her best chance to get the Twin Flame for good.

Lauren has several tarot decks out on the table. She's spreading them in three columns, Abundance, Enlightenment and Twin Flame. She tries a fourth pile. Can the altar be for Lauren and Steve? The cards say, "No you're joking, bugger off." That column is swiftly removed, followed by Abundance. Good girl, now we are left with Enlightenment or Twin Flame. The former would probably strengthen our relationship and the latter kill it stone dead. WHATEVER.

Lauren is still in floods of tears working thorough the cards. I put a time limit on the decision making. The altar is tonight or not at all. Lauren goes upstairs to meditate and think. I sew an altar cloth, drink more coffee, smoke again. Lauren has made her choice. Enlightenment. To make it she has been through so much heart searching. I think she has been unlocking boxes that have been closed for years. The Twin Flame situation was looked at from every angle, past, present and future. I still don't care, the swingometer is going towards Enlightenment and staying there. Cool, that's what my deck said in the afternoon, but I don't read the cards, so I take no notice. Once again I ask, "Are you sure you've made the right choice?"

Time to set up the altar. I Hoover bedroom, move table, place cloth on (nice job on the cloth) place chalice, salt and water dishes I had polished up that morning in the shed. We both dress for the occasion. High Priest robe for me, dress and lovely frock coat for Lauren. I ask for a few minutes alone at the altar, do my stuff and say my words. I just know she is going to get enlightened. Lauren does her stuff.

Went to bed still feeling nothing. Don't often have to do the proper job, but when I do I'm bloody good at it. Night Babe."

I activated the altar every night for the next three weeks as instructed and we grew used to going to sleep with the light from the cauldron shining on the ceiling. The shadow created by the corner of the table cloth and the zigzag beading on my lampshade thrown onto the ceiling made the outline of a large bird wearing a crown flying over us each night. I grew very fond of my royal bird and rather missed the image when the altar was dismantled. The mead had a strange reaction with the metal of the chalice and turned an intense emerald green over just a few days. We didn't risk drinking it!

Light behind the Angels

I have noticed since that time that if I gaze out of the window for a little while and then look away I see that same vivid green wherever I look. It is so bright and solid that it obscures my vision. The sky becomes a strangely fluorescent pinkish mauve too. This same lurid shade of green is being seen increasingly by my clients whilst I'm healing and many of my students have mentioned seeing it spontaneously too. It is always the same otherworldly shade, almost fluorescent in intensity and not a green found in nature. Is it linked to the Emerald ray, to the Emerald Tablets of Thoth, or am I glimpsing another dimension?

Looking back at that night I still find the whole sequence of events hard to believe. It seems so unreal, so out of step with 'normal life'. To choose to be with someone who was behaving so dispassionately, so lacking in any empathy, is alien to my being. Faced with Steve's almost callous and robotic coldness I can imagine readers asking, "Why didn't she choose her twin flame?"

I can only answer that my love of my spiritual path is beyond measure of any romantic relationship. I would sacrifice, and did sacrifice, big love for it. Neither of us knew that night that my Enlightenment would come so swiftly or take the form it did. Had I known the pain enlightenment would entail I wonder whether I'd have had the courage to make the choice I did.

The Light behind the Angels

*'Religion is a candle inside a multicoloured lantern.
Everyone looks through a particular colour, but the candle is always there.'*
Mohammed Neguib

When we woke the next day the energy felt tense. Everything seemed so unreal, dreamlike, and yet there was the evidence, the altar had been set. It had happened.

We decided that we deserved to take things easy, and so we went off to the health spa together, I swam a little, we sat in the steam room and the Jacuzzi, not really wanting to discuss events of the night before, trying to be a 'normal couple' whatever that might be.

We followed with lunch out at a cafe. Things were quite calm and civilised until Steve trotted out a really crude sexual remark. I saw red. I bit my tongue, but when we got home I ripped into him. All the pressure had been piled on my shoulders to choose and I had duly chosen; I felt I deserved some respect in return. A furious tirade was launched. I'd turned down a man gifted with the silver tongue of the Irish to be treated to this filth from a foul mouthed mechanic! I wasn't going to put up with that!

I flounced off feeling utterly self-righteous and went to sit at the computer. Our roles were reversed; this time it was Steve looking stunned and nonplussed at the kitchen table. Good! A few minutes later he followed me into the room and looked at me with teary eyes, shaking a little.

Looking at him trembling before me, seeing his soul appear vulnerable and meek from under the thick layers of bravado, my anger towards him evaporated. Something made me say, "Sit down, your guide wants to come through you." Obediently he sat opposite me and within moments he started to channel.

I grabbed pen and paper. This was true trance channelling. I felt Steve was still somewhere in the background, but I was face to face with someone or something else and whoever or whatever it was, it was powerful. I didn't know if I wanted to communicate with this guide, especially as the first comment it made directly to me was,

"You have to use your dark side."

I replied emphatically, "I won't do that!" and was ready to banish the being and bring Steve straight back to the fore when he replied, *"You answer well, but you need to know what is there."*

Light behind the Angels

He invited me to ask questions. I was totally unprepared for this, neither of us could have predicted it was about to happen. I asked why he was speaking to me.

"*You are one of us. Before Egypt you were of the Holy Order. Go back to the Bright Light. You were there. He is one of us too. He listens better than you. We are beings of gold and blue light. Not as humans see and paint angels, we are the Light behind the angels. We are the Chosen Ones.*"

Again I toyed with sending the being away. The phrase 'the chosen ones' made me uncomfortable. It has been used by man as an excuse to dominate others. It smacked of white supremacists and fascism. I let the being continue but decided I would be the judge of what had come through for myself.

"*You will do new healing, but it is old healing already in you, although it will feel like a revelation. You must go back and remember.*"

This mention of healing caught my interest. I asked about my psychic development. The reply was stern, "*What do you want? Party tricks?*"

At the time I'd been developing my mediumship skills by sitting in Circle once a week. I found I was consistently getting impressive results with psychometry. Several weeks running I'd been given a mystery object in an envelope and described the contents with an accuracy that astonished me. I confess it had given me a buzz to be spot on, although I knew of course it was only a parlour game and of no real importance.

I felt this being was both powerful and humourless. It was reminiscent of the way Steve had behaved the night before and I wondered if he had been channelling this same presence then. I replied that I didn't want tricks, I wanted genuinely to help and heal.

"*2008 will be your golden year. Use the opportunities. You must discern. You will need to look after your power wisely as you will have much power.*"

My audience was at an end. Steve came back to the fore completely unaware of what had passed. He was tired and needed to lie down and rest. He also had a case of the shakes, trembling all over. Later when Steve had recovered I asked him to go back into trance. I wanted to know more about this guide. Who was he, what was his role? We hadn't been prepared before, but now I had my questions ready. Steve sat down, took off his glasses and quickly slipped into a trance state.

"*I have never incarnated. It is my work to look after the Chosen Ones, to help. It can be frustrating as it is the nature of humankind to listen to only what they hear. They do not listen to what they know.*

It is through your human emotions of sorrow, hurt and suffering that we may most easily make contact. To those of us who have stayed behind human emotions are not understood. We feel only what you call love.

Some of us chose to incarnate with humans, while some stayed behind. It was thought to be radical. The purity would be lost once in human form. We are not subject to karma and at the end of each human life we have the choice to return to the Light. The emotion of happiness stops you from hearing. Once we have your attention you can remember and we can communicate. We of old can help you of new remember.

You will help those humans that have the wisdom to seek you out. In each life you are born with knowledge but the older you become in human terms the less you know. You have forgotten, but there comes a time in your human life when you are awakened. I cannot make you listen, but I can help and that is what I am here for."

Steve came back to the fore, again with no recollection of what was said. It was almost as if he wasn't there at all. I was impressed by how readily he trance channelled. I've never let go of my sense of self enough to channel like this. I can channel guidance by sitting with a notebook and pen and allowing the words to flow through me, but I'm still aware that I'm me, just taking a 'back seat' in my mind. I decided to sit down and I invited the guide to speak through my pen:

"I am speaking now, you have to trust my voice in your head. I have been speaking for a long time. I am still of the old ways, the ways of the Light and you are of the new, but you will remember and the bridge will be formed between the two worlds. I am always there for you.

We are all aspects of the One. You do not need names, for names are limitations and we are unlimited beings. We are the power of the splitting of the atoms and we can create or destroy, it is a choice."

This felt odd, although it touched a memory in me, something I'd read, or something I'd heard. I had come across a story of creator beings that incarnated and became human, rather too human. Had that really been our path? The gap between 'little me' and this idea seemed much too wide to assimilate.

Next morning, Steve casually wandered into the kitchen rubbing his hair dry with a towel. "What's El-o-heem?" The word had come to him while he'd been in the shower; this being was 'El-o-heem'. It meant nothing to him, but I knew the word from somewhere. I knew it was something from the Old Testament, something to do with Judaism and that these were very high and powerful beings indeed. So high it scared me.

This was all too much to take in. The El-o-heem claimed we were of the same order but incarnated? If that was the truth it would take some getting used to and it really needed questioning. Could this be some elaborate ruse to inflate our egos and mislead us?

Light behind the Angels

Researching El-o-heem on the internet we found references to the Elohim as creator gods. Just as the guide had claimed they were placed somewhere between the angels and the Divine Source.

Later that day I encouraged Steve to channel again. I felt we had to get to the truth:

"After Atlantis fell the keys to healing were split up and sent around the world. To work fully they need to be together again. They are held by the leaders of the religions of the world. They won't give up their keys and join them with the others. They are none of them wrong, but none of them right.

When man has the wisdom to join the keys together the Earth will be at last as it was intended to be at its Creation. Humankind has been set many tasks and has failed each one miserably. Each religion thinks it has the answer, but none will relinquish their key and so humankind must stay as it is."

I still find this an intriguing message. It feels absolutely right and is aligned with my own beliefs about the major world religions, that each is holding a part of the truth, but that no single religion holds the whole truth, even though they each claim that their way is the only way to reach salvation.

As a writer and healer of the New Age I pray that the barriers between religions will eventually come down. Many people are starting to simultaneously work with different faces of the Divine, linking to Jesus, Buddha and Kuan Yin without fear of contradiction, because they are all aspects of Divine Source. There is a sense of spiritual liberation and a realisation that you don't have to sign up to a specific religion, or worship through a priesthood.

It was time to do a home visit. I had offered the bereaved husband of a client who'd recently passed from cancer a free healing when he felt ready and he had called me. I was very fond of his wife and had spent a lot of time with her over the years. It was her frock coat I'd worn when setting up my altar. I felt the offer of a healing was a fitting gesture. He had loved her very much and was now coming to terms with life on his own. As I left Steve made a strange gesture with his hand over my head and said, "You'll get a taste of the healing that is to come today."

Arriving at the client's house I set up my treatment couch and started a normal crystal healing. He told me that he'd locked up his wife's room. At first he'd thought it would help him to sit in her room and sort out paperwork, but soon he found that spending time in the space made him feel depressed. I wondered whether something was wrong in the room and I was just about to ask whether their cats spent much time in there when he said, "Even our cats won't stay in the room." I knew this meant there was some unpleasant energy trapped there as it used to be a friendly and welcoming space where the cats would drape themselves over chairs and laze around whilst I gave his wife healing.

When my client was nice and relaxed on the couch I was guided to stand back and simply allow the energy through. This felt right and so I held the healing space open. My client exclaimed, "How extraordinary!" He felt as if a stream of energy had passed right through him taking away all the heaviness. Afterwards he described it as, "Dispassionate and impersonal, like being in the path of a river, it did its job and left."

He then showed me into his wife's bedroom. The heaviness in the atmosphere was tangible, the air felt thick and suffocating and it was as cold as the crypt. I could see why he'd locked the room up. It had none of the feeling of his lovely spiritual wife, more of the ugly, consuming cancer that had carried her away.

I hadn't come prepared for space clearing. I rooted around in my kit box and found a sage smudge stick. We located a brass bowl and lit it, leaving it to burn safely. Then we closed the door on the room, locked it up, and walked away. I made arrangements to return with a proper space clearing kit in a few days time.

When I returned home I found Steve lying in bed with a bad case of the shakes. He'd been lying with his face under the covers whilst I'd been healing, as he put it, "Hiding from all the weirdness for a bit." He'd seen a bright blue light and sent it over to me to pass on. I felt this was the cleansing energy that had passed through my client.

The Three Wishes

> 'A sound head, an honest heart, and an humble spirit are
> the three best guides through time and to eternity.'
> Sir Walter Scott

A few days after the first channelling Steve received instructions for a ritual that we were to carry out together. He was given a word of power to use, which neither of us had heard of before, but he found it through the internet later. It has a profound energy which could easily be misused. I believe that if you are meant to know certain esoteric information it will be revealed to you at the right time, therefore I'm not about to share it here.

Steve would need my co-operation for this ritual, so I was offered a bit of a carrot, "*As your reward for this you may choose three gifts. Be wise with your choices.*"

I laughed out loud, how crazy could my life get? Had I landed in a fairy story? I'd seen and heard too many 'impossible things' lately to discount the message. I have a background in storytelling and I love the patterns of myths, legends and traditional tales. Stories connect us to our ancestors, they are the way humanity has passed on wisdom through millennia. I know some funny stories where the traditional three wishes get wasted by foolish people, so being wary of the pitfalls I asked myself, "If I really had three wishes what would I choose?" Truth or not, it would be an interesting creative exercise, the sort of activity I used to set a class in my old incarnation as an English teacher.

I ran through some possibilities. Perhaps I was unusually focussed on my spiritual development, as travelling the world, or living in the lap of luxury didn't cross my mind. To the forefront came the abilities I'd been working on. I jotted ideas in my journal:

- To be able to see energy clearly, particularly within the human aura and to see the energies within and around the body.
- To be a clear channel for my guides and to be able to channel guides for others.
- To be able to communicate with the crystal kingdom.
- To be the best healer I could be.

That was four wishes, greedy girl! I needed to hone them down.

Next I asked my tarot cards about the coming ritual. I used the Thoth deck. What was it all about? I pulled the Tower, symbolising the breaking down of old flawed structures, often suddenly and violently, to make way for the new. It is a card that worries people, but I see it as necessary change, even when it is uncomfortable or challenging. In the Thoth deck it bears an all seeing eye radiating gold light. I looked up the Tower in Gerd Ziegler's 'Tarot: Mirror of the Soul'.

'You are in the midst of an extremely intensive transformatory process. Whatever is destroyed or shaken within you serves to purify you and make room for something new. Allow it!'

That was spot on. Steve was even having physical shakes to purify him. I asked what the outcome of the ritual would be and pulled the Ace of Disks which is about internal and external riches, wholeness and unification of body and soul. Next came The Star, normally a card of hope, especially after a difficult passage. Ziegler also spoke of Cosmic inspiration, self recognition and clear vision. The cards were very encouraging. It felt like the results of the ritual would be positive, though not necessarily comfortable to deal with.

The following day dawned pleasant though chilly. We needed to get away from the house for a bit. It had been too intense and the kids deserved an outing as they were still on holiday. Living in Wales it delights me to be able to take day trips to the beach, so very different from the landlocked Midlands in which I'd lived so long. I drove through the Welsh landscape artistically lit by the winter sun. On the journey Steve was preoccupied and spoke little. I headed for Ynys Las, the Blue Isle, my favourite beach. It's never crowded, but that day in January it was deserted and we had the place to ourselves.

Steve kept his counsel and didn't tell me what was happening until we were walking alone by the edge of the sea, leaving the kids playing together in huge sand dunes. Steve had been given more of the coming ritual during the journey. It seemed straightforward enough, although I hadn't anything to compare it with.

The ritual was scheduled for the next day whilst the children were at their dad's. Clive happened to ring for a chat, so I asked him whether he could pick anything up for us. His guide said we were being given something big and we were to wear white and purify ourselves by water. We had already planned to visit the waterfall together first.

Light behind the Angels

First I had to fulfil my promise to cleanse the room at my client's house. Steve came along with me as the energy was so unpleasant I felt I might need help to shift it. How surprising when we got there to find the door to the room unlocked and the cats wandering in and out. My client had been in after the smudge stick had burnt down and found the energy transformed. It was astonishing to find that sage alone had made such a difference. The temperature was now just the same as the rest of the house and it felt quite pleasant to walk into. We did a little more to clean up any lingering residues of the illness, mainly using my Tibetan singing bowl to raise the vibration in the room. Steve was surprised to find he could see the energy of the bowl as it circled the room, vibrating outwards.

After we'd finished we were offered tea and my client went through his healing experience again. He'd had time to think about it and said a fairer description would be a warm sirocco wind passing through him. I saw him a few weeks later in town. He looked great, so much lighter and brighter. If this was a taste of things to come it was very promising indeed.

Back home we dutifully bathed and dressed in white, travelling on to the waterfall to prepare for the evening's ritual. On the journey Steve turned to me and asked, "If you had to choose just one of the wishes which would it be?" Something in the tone of his voice told me this wasn't an idle question. I ran through the 'glamorous' options in my mind, the crystal communicator, the superb clairvoyant, the amazing channel. I realised these were all well and good, but first and foremost I'm a healer and what I really had to ask for was to be the best healer I could possibly be. Clearly I had given the right answer. The Elohim answered through Steve's mouth, "She is ready."

Back home we set up our sacred space and enacted the ritual we'd been given. It involved combining and balancing our male and female energies, so I'll leave you to imagine how that might happen. At the end of the ritual Steve chanted the word of power he'd been given three times and I watched fascinated as his whole ribcage was inflated with huge yoga-style breaths. It looked as if he was 'being breathed' rather than breathing for himself, an incredible thing to see.

Next the shakes came in, much more violently than before. Steve's whole head and torso were lifted and shaken. I've never seen anything stranger outside of horror films, but although it was forceful it didn't feel threatening to either of us. We trusted the process was necessary and knew it was a purification. Although he was picked up bodily and shaken like a rag doll it was done in such a way that he hit nothing and was unharmed, although it made him ache to the bone afterwards.

Over the coming weeks Steve would have more bouts of shaking. It is difficult to explain how severe this was or how surreal it was to watch. Clive tuned in for us again and his guide described the shaking to Steve as 'spiritual Jeyes Fluid' clearing his channel. I felt this was right, he was being cleared to take a higher vibration through his system and although it felt unpleasant and was tiring, it wasn't harmful or a psychic attack. The Tower had been the most apt card to describe the process: a forceful clearing.

Steve found that putting his glasses on slowed things down. I felt they short circuited his energy meridians and this disrupted the flow. I would see him trying to talk normally to people, hands clenched tightly around a coffee cup and all muscles tensed, the shaking reduced to an almost imperceptible tremble. As soon as we were alone again he'd relax and the shaking would resume.

I encouraged Steve to just let it all flow, as I knew it was happening for a reason and it would be better not to prolong the process. I had seen nothing quite like it, but a book I have read since on the awakening of the Kundalini energy through the spine describes bodily shaking and spontaneous yoga kriyas. Looking back I wonder if this was what was happening.

Light behind the Angels

An Execution in Egypt

'The doors will finally open and we shall see all the places where our feet have trodden since the dawn of time.'
The Papyrus of Ani, the Egyptian Book of the Dead,
translation Dr Ramses Seleem

A week or so after our ritual Steve rang me from Manchester whilst I was still in bed. He cheerfully told me about the faeries that had been whizzing around his bedroom the night before, mostly bright green lights, but some red ones too. They'd been zipping about like little meteors, but some had got so close he'd been able to see their wings and then they'd realised he was watching them. One would approach him then zoom away, then another would come in close, taking turns. He could almost hear their excited whispers, "He can see us!" I was really pleased for him; his clairvoyance had opened up beautifully.

Steve changed the topic of conversation and casually asked, "Can you choose which past life you visit?" Although I love doing regression therapy for people it was something I'd never done for Steve.

"Why?" I asked, sensing something was being left unsaid.

"Oh I was just shown an execution in Egypt this morning."

"And?" I knew there was more.

"It was you being executed."

I'd known it as soon as he mentioned Egypt. I'd seen this one before in my mind's eye. "Did you do it?" the accusation escaped my lips before I could stop it.

"No I was just watching the scene." He sounded awkward and evasive. The liar!

We said our goodbyes. It felt like Steve couldn't wait to get off the phone. I went about my morning, but I knew he'd been more involved in my execution than he was letting on. I could picture the scene all too clearly.

Steve rang again a few hours later, speaking in a confessional tone. "I've been shown a bit more. It was me that gave the signal for your death."

I was filled with rage, "You bastard!" A torrent of abuse spilled from my lips and Steve abruptly ended our call.

I went off to the health club to sit in the steam room and stew. I must have given off 'leave me alone' vibes as I was mercifully left to it.

When I teach past lives I always say we have all been the good guys and the bad guys trying out different roles over different lifetimes, learning the lessons we need. I teach that we reincarnate with other members of our soul group and I do believe we agree to test each other in various ways before we incarnate, therefore your biggest challenger can be your truest soul mate.

That's all very well as a theory. Now I had to find forgiveness for my partner for putting me to death. Would I look at my boyfriend and only see my executioner? Thousands of years is as nothing to the eternal soul, and the sorrow and fear I felt at my execution was as tangible to me as any memory from this life.

When I next spoke to Steve I was still simmering with rage, so I wasn't very receptive when he said, "It was your fault, you broke your vows." For that one comment I could have finished my relationship with him on the spot. Something stopped me slamming down the telephone and I let him speak. More of the story had been shown to him.

It was Ancient Egypt. I'd been the High Priestess and he'd been my High Priest. As such we had both taken vows of chastity. I'd been seduced and fallen in love. When my sins were discovered he had, in his words, "No other option but to have you executed."

Perhaps you can imagine the vitriolic diatribe that I launched into, spoken from the perspective of a liberated Western twentieth century woman? In the midst of my furious rant he slipped in, "I've also been told that you need to seek forgiveness."

"Excuse me! Am I missing the point somewhere? Who executed whom? If anyone needs forgiveness it's you!" Again we rang off barely speaking.

I felt this was the end of our relationship, ironically only days after I'd turned down the opportunity to be with the big love of my life. I was certainly being 'enlightened' and I didn't like it at all. At this point if I could have gone back to the night of choices I would have chosen anything but enlightenment.

Steve stayed at a safe distance in Manchester. I didn't want to see him anyway. More details came through and it only got worse. Steve had been the High Priest who had ordered my execution, but it wasn't that simple. One morning he rang me, "I think I may have put an eternal curse on your soul. Oops!" He tried to make light of it. Not a good tactic! Grovelling for forgiveness may have helped, but Steve isn't the grovelling type.

He'd uncovered the nature of the curse. It ensured I would always fall deeply in love with my seducer, but that I would never be able to stay with my love.

Light behind the Angels

As eternity is a very long time that curse was still fully functioning. I knew for certain it had already caused me utter heartbreak this time around.

The man I'd fallen for in Egyptian times had been a Roman. We'd had a brief and clandestine affair, meeting secretly, so we'd thought, and he had encouraged me to leave the country with him. We were found out and when I arrived at our agreed meeting place he'd deserted me and fled to Rome.

The curse had been constructed to ensure that we would meet again and again, lifetime after lifetime, that I would always fall in love with him and always be left alone and heartbroken. There was no doubt in my mind that my twin flame, Lancelot and the Roman were all one and the same soul.

No-one had ever captured my heart as my twin flame had, nor had anyone been so capable of inflicting such sorrow and pain. Our relationship had been so convoluted, so unsatisfying and yet so irresistible. I'd always known there must be a past life connection with him and I'd already been shown that I had loved him and lost him time and again. Semele had said a year before when I was trying to break free from him, "I can see a stack of tombstones on your heart."

It had taken all of my strength and determination to cut the ties between us and choose a different path this time. Even on the night of choices the curse was at work tempting me to take the unwise option. Had I done so this revelation would never have emerged and the eternal cycle of heartbreak would have continued unabated.

Discovering that my partner was the author of a curse that had caused me more pain and grief than I can begin to describe was simply devastating to me, worse even than the news he'd had me executed. Hysterically I begged, "Get it off me, take it off me now!" I knew exactly where it was lodged, right over my heart, which had always felt like it had a cold hard lump in it. My ex husband had accused me of having a heart of stone. It seems he was at least partially right. Steve pointed out reasonably, "You've had it for millennia, you are going to have to wait while I find out how to remove it." I didn't have much choice.

I let Steve return to Wales just to remove the curse. I don't think he relished seeing me, but to his credit he was determined to find out how to lift it, whether the relationship between us ended afterwards or not. He couldn't just wave his hand to magic it away and he made that much clear. This was not a simple matter, it had been an expertly crafted piece of Egyptian magic that had lasted through the ages and the solution would need some fathoming out. We called a truce whilst he went to work.

Steve received a message sitting at the kitchen table and scribbled it down on the back of an old envelope, "*I was weak. We were duped. You need the key. I loved her as a sister. She was my sister. They will try and stop you. The key.*"

The message didn't feel that helpful. More talk of keys. How do you get hold of an Ancient Egyptian key when you live in Mid-Wales?

My anger abated a little when I saw how much Steve genuinely wanted to lift the curse and was working to solve the problem. There was no sense in antagonising him. If I got too annoying he could always run back to Manchester and leave me carrying the curse forever.

More information came through to him, "The other night was a test and for once you didn't choose the love option. You put others before yourself. That was the first key." Steve also smelled burning paper several times over the day and realised that the curse had been written on papyrus and then burned.

Our lives took on the air of an ancient mystery play over the next week. We spent a lot of time meditating on the problem. Many more details came through. It was interesting to find that if I meditated on the Egyptian lifetime I could see what had happened.

Steve would test me by asking specific questions about aspects of our lives and writing down what he'd seen on a piece of paper to show me once I'd given my own account. All of our visions tallied. Steve asked me whether there were any children at the temple complex we lived in. I closed my eyes. Yes, I saw lots of children, but no parents, as if they had been given to the temple. Then he asked how I behaved with them. I imagined a High Priestess would be haughty and standoffish, she'd carry herself regally. I closed my eyes. There I was as the High Priestess, a beautiful young woman, full of playfulness. When I'd walk into the courtyard the children would rush over joyfully calling out my name. I watched as my Egyptian self disappeared giggling under the swarming heap of children who climbed all over her. I saw the disapproval on the faces of some of the older priestesses; such undignified behaviour from their High Priestess!

Steve asked, "What was the mood of the crowd at your execution?" I imagined a stereotypical public execution scene, shouted insults, booing, rotten vegetables and stone throwing. When I closed my eyes I was touched. The scene pulled on my heartstrings and made me cry. The crowd was almost silent and their mood was sombre. There were many sad faces and some were weeping. The public didn't want this to happen. I was a 'Priestess of the People'. They really loved me and were grieved to see me humiliated and taken from them. Their

Light behind the Angels

mood reminded me of the public displays of grief on the day Princess Diana died. Shock, sadness and loss permeated the atmosphere and it was incredibly moving.

The Shining Ones

> *'Not in entire forgetfulness,*
> *And not in utter nakedness,*
> *But trailing clouds of glory do we come*
> *From God, who is our home.'*
> William Wordsworth

Further information about our Egyptian selves was uncovered and our story grew to sound more like a Hollywood blockbuster daily. It was hard at times to accept the information and to recognise how important we'd been, but the evidence kept coming in, not just from us, from others too, and we knew we weren't taking off on flights of fancy.

The evidence filtered through as fragments in no particular order, so here I've rearranged the pieces to make sense of the story. Semele picked up on our origins. Discussing our Egyptian story so far I mentioned that we didn't know where we'd come from, seeing ourselves on arrival in Egypt as small children. She had 'Sumeria' straight away and I immediately thought of a picture of winged, angel like beings carved in relief which I'd seen in an angel book demonstrating that the belief in angels existed in ancient cultures.

Her next revelation was even more extraordinary. She had a picture of our Sumerian mother, a beautiful virginal peasant girl, and sensed that she had been 'visited' by one of these winged beings and conceived us as twins in much the same way as the Virgin Mary conceived Jesus.

She was told that the Egyptians were guided by their knowledge of astrology and their priests saw our arrival heralded in the stars. That startled me a little as I had just that morning read the chapter of Ursula Le Guin's 'The Tombs of Atuan' in which the girl who is chosen as Arha, High Priestess of the Tombs, is told of how she was located in the very same way.

Semele called us the 'chosen ones' confirming Steve's earlier channelling of the Elohim. The Egyptians sent their ambassadors to Sumeria to search for us and we were taken from our mother to be brought back to Egypt as small children of only five or six years old. That was the last we were to see of our birth mother.

Steve saw that we travelled by boat from over the seas and our arrival in Egypt had been eagerly anticipated. We arrived as children in the Light, literally surrounded by swirls of blue and gold light.

Light behind the Angels

We were the essence of purity and were called the Shining Ones. As children we had a job to do, we knew we were special and different. We were met on the shore by a welcoming party of the most powerful people in the land, it was a great occasion and from then on we were treated like royalty.

We were taken to a beautiful palace which was faced in white marble and had luxurious suites of rooms and many servants. This was to be our home for the rest of our lives and I loved the coolness of the marble contrasted with the heat of the sun. For a while I questioned the white marble as all of the excavations of Egyptian palaces and temples I've seen on television have been made of sandstone, however the buildings stubbornly remained white marble in my mind's eye however hard I tried to rationalise the marble away. Perhaps the marble was stolen and reused when the buildings eventually fell into disrepair? We both saw the same building when we meditated and I could guide Steve through the corridors to our rooms.

As twins our strongest bond from infancy to adulthood was always with each other and we needed no other friends, no others would ever be able to communicate as we did together, and much of what we shared was telepathic. We would often join foreheads to read each other's minds. We were One and whole, "I am her and she is me."

Despite our high status we saw that we played together like normal children, long raucous games of hide and seek and chase. Our guardians did not always approve of our lively behaviour as they felt we lacked the appropriate decorum, but they didn't manage to quell our spirits.

Everywhere we went we were accompanied by huge black eunuchs armed with scimitars. This included our own chambers and they guarded us around the clock so that they were almost a part of the furniture in our eyes, not to be spoken to, just there. It was interesting to see the eunuchs as a psychic artist had told me I had a huge black eunuch holding a curved sword protecting me. At the time it had seemed strange, but who better to stand guard?

As children we would lay on the bed whispering to each other or connecting our foreheads so the guards couldn't hear us. We would giggle, sharing jokes together. Often we just lay on our sides facing each other, relaxed, happy and complete in each other's company. Although we were very alike as twins our chambers contrasted in their décor. My rooms were decorated with swathes of ornate gold drapes. It was very opulent and in the centre stood an enormous and luxurious bed. My brother's suite was adorned with lapis lazuli blue, just edged in gold, darker and more sombre than mine. We went freely into each other's chambers all through our lives. We had nothing to hide from each other, but we were always watched by our eunuch guards.

When I was in my bedchamber alone I could enjoy a semblance of privacy as my guard would politely turn his back, but when my brother joined me we were watched constantly. This was annoying! Even as adults we kept up our habit of lying face to face, whispering and usually giggling, trying to stifle it.

We received strict training throughout our childhood. Although we lived in a palace it was part of a temple complex and we knew it would be our destiny to lead the Priesthood. The nature of our training was different. Mine was Priestess training in the healing arts; my brother was trained as a Priest in the magical arts. Although we were shown what to do we both had innate knowledge and power that we had brought into this incarnation and from childhood our techniques and abilities were often beyond those of our teachers.

As young adults we became the High Priestess and High Priest over Egypt. I know that some resented our fast elevation and were angry and jealous. I'm sure some did not believe in our Divine parentage and felt we didn't deserve our status over them. We certainly had our enemies, although everyone was careful to be humble and courteous to us on the surface.

As High Priestess it was my duty to train the other priestesses in the healing arts. I saw that my healing rooms in the temple were very light and airy and there was a round space in the ceiling open to the rays of the Sun. We used large quartz crystals to channel healing light from the Sun into our patients. I remember showing the other priestesses how to channel and work with the energies of light. Several priestesses at a time would channel energy through the crystals into the patient who lay on a white marble slab.

I have come across other accounts of similar healing carried out in Atlantis and I believe we were in Egypt long before the pyramids. Perhaps it was the time after the surviving Atlantians had dispersed and taken knowledge of their arts with them?

My brother's temple chambers were carved out of the rock. They were sandstone, subterranean, much darker, being windowless and lit by flickering torches. These were secret places that the public never saw, unlike my Temple rooms where healing could be sought. My brother was teaching magical formulae and ritual to the priests. There was writing on papyrus and a more scholarly, academic feel to his work compared to mine.

It seems that the sexes were separated in their esoteric work. The Priestesses were the healers and the Priests were mages.

Light behind the Angels

One evening whilst we were meditating Steve glimpsed a scene where we were preparing to go out hunting. I had a hawk on my wrist and was mounting a two wheeled chariot. He commented that I wouldn't like doing that now! I had a surprise for him. Despite being a long term vegetarian and detesting most blood sports I simply adore birds of prey and I am strongly drawn to hawking. I am always right at the front if there is a birds of prey demonstration and I'd love to have birds to fly of my own. He didn't know I had already seen myself as Guinevere out hunting with a hawk at my wrist and I knew how much I'd loved it then too.

Steve described me as being 'gutsy' back in Egypt, glad to be out hunting and free of the temple confines. When we went out we took the dogs with us. They looked rather like afghan hounds in build, but were short haired and sandy coloured with thin whip like tails. My favourite hawk was a large bird with dark feathers and she wore a jewelled cover over her face topped with plumes.

The Sky Turned Black and the Earth Shook

To deny the past is to deny the future.
A man does not make his destiny, he accepts it, or denies it.'
Ursula Le Guin, The Farthest Shore

We moved forward in time to see that tremendous preparations were being made in the main temple. A major event was to take place and it was a source of great national pride for Egypt. Steve was the carrier of the Blue Ray on Earth and I carried the Gold Ray. At the auspicious time we were to combine our rays to produce the Emerald Ray and this action was predicted to empower the whole of Egypt.

Foreign envoys were invited to witness this world changing event and we were at the centre of it. Flaming torches were lit and the temple was dressed with decorations of blue and gold. People were busy. Everything was being cleaned and purified. Steve watched the preparations through the eyes of the High Priest, 'Before you can enter the temple you have to be washed so that you bring nothing unclean in. Even to sweep the floor you have to be purified. They are excited and proud to be doing this, to have helped. I am just passing through, I don't need to wash, I am already pure.'

He described the altar as very plain, of white marble, with a circular hole in the ceiling above, similar to the one in my healing temple. It made a contrast with the rest of the interior which was highly ornate.

Thinking about this later it occurred to me how much Egyptian artistry draws on blue and gold. Lapis and gold are amongst the most precious of Ancient Egyptian treasures.

Of course not everyone would have wanted Egypt to become even more powerful and this is where our story takes on a quality of political intrigue. Remember Steve's note jotted on the envelope?
"I was weak. We were duped. You need the key. I loved her as a sister. She was my sister. They will try and stop you. The key."

One of the envoys from Rome was sent with a mission to disrupt the drawing down of the rays. He was a very handsome man and I fell completely in love with him. This was to be my downfall. I was naïve, never having had a romantic relationship and I thought he really loved me too and that I could get away with seeing him. I would sneak away from the temple to meet him in secret, with just my handmaiden knowing where I was, or so I thought.

Light behind the Angels

Steve viewed a scene where he was watching me mount my chariot to go out hunting one day. My Assistant High Priestess was trying to get his attention. We were aware that she was jealous of my position and wanted my power. I'd known she was talking about me as her eyes kept sliding over to me. It was clear she was trying to get me into trouble by tale-telling. My brother brushed her off angrily.

When Steve recounted the scene, I asked, "Do you know the Assistant High Priestess in this lifetime?" He looked sheepish and said she did remind him of someone. I knew exactly who it was too. Here was Steve's friend from Manchester, an artist, healer and owner of a whole food café. From that profile you might expect me to want to meet her, but I had detested her from the first time Steve mentioned her. I'd voiced my hatred of this apparent stranger with such a poisonous intensity that I think Steve thought I was crazy. The merest mention of her name used to provoke a long, vitriolic diatribe from me, yet according to him she was harmless and they'd had a platonic friendship for years.

It's not in my nature to detest someone I've never met and I had wondered why she raised such venom in me. Here was my answer at last. I named his friend outright and he had to admit it was definitely her; she even looked similar back then.

Next we were shown the Assistant High Priestess bursting into the High Priest's bedchambers. This was outrageous behaviour and he was angered. She was telling him that I had gone off with the Roman. He marched her to my chambers and was delayed by my loyal handmaiden who told him I was bathing. Unfortunately he swept her aside and went into the bathroom, which was empty. He demanded to know where I was and she refused to answer. He was impressed by her loyalty, despite his threats of death to her and her family if she didn't reveal the truth.

I recognised my handmaiden as Lin, a former client, turned student, who had remained part of my life, now doing my bookkeeping and taking in my ironing, still serving me well.

I had been found out. I was meant to remain pure. On my return he challenged me, "Had I lain with the Roman?" I could not lie but fell upon my knees weeping and begging him to understand that I loved this man. He was furious; the wellbeing of Egypt depended upon the success of our ceremony. In his eyes I would no longer be able to draw down the Gold Ray because I was impure. He cast me out, ordering me to leave Egypt and never to return. In a last gesture of brotherly love the High Priest kept my disappearance quiet from the guards for some hours.

I left with my handmaiden and went to my secret assignation place, but my Roman had fled Egypt without me. Whether he loved me, but was too cowardly to take me with him and risk pursuit, or whether he had simply coldheartedly completed his mission I do not know.

I saw myself sinking to my knees in the meadow weeping and my handmaiden begging me to get up and run into exile with her. Next morning the High Priest and the guards found me still there weeping with my handmaiden standing dutifully by me. She was dispatched from life with no ceremony on a command from my brother, run through with a sword. I was led back to the temple under guard.

I had let down my country at the highest level and for that the only punishment was execution. First I must be humiliated. I had been the highest of the high and for my crimes I must become the lowest of the low. My beautiful long hair was shaven from my head and all of my body hair was carefully removed.

Utterly naked with nothing to hide my shame, my hands were tied, my feet hobbled together and a rope placed around my neck. I was led by the neck like an animal, head bowed, through the subdued crowds by a novice priestess of the lowest rank. As I was taken to my death the sky turned black above our heads and the very Earth shook beneath our feet. This was the displeasure of the Gods.

Weeping and throwing myself onto my knees I begged my beloved twin, my brother, the High Priest for mercy, but he turned his back on me with a face full of scorn. He raised his arm in the air and simply gave the command to execute me by dropping his arm. I was run through the chest with a sword.

My body was dead, but my punishment was not yet complete. There was to be no Afterlife for me. My body was cut into quarters and each quarter was burnt in a separate pyre. Steve saw that the quartering was done above my knees so that I couldn't kneel to the Gods and ask them for mercy and at my neck so that I couldn't speak with them. My trunk was cut in half to divide my heart in two.

An eternal curse was created by the High Priest as a final punishment. It was written on papyrus and then burned. The ash from the curse was mixed into each of the four separate funeral pyres. My ashes were taken and scattered to the four winds.

Everything happened so quickly and my brother had acted in hot rage. Now he had to live with the fact that he'd executed and cursed his own twin sister.

Light behind the Angels

The ceremonial blending of the rays was still attempted, this time with the Assistant High Priestess taking my role, which had been her desire and motivation all along. It was disastrous. She'd expected my power to be transferred along with the title of High Priestess. Driven by ambition and ego she had thought that she'd be able to access the Gold Ray once she'd taken my place. She didn't understand it had been my birthright and had nothing to do with my status. Without the Ray the ceremony couldn't be completed.

It had needed our perfectly balanced energies as the Shining Ones to succeed and my role in the proceedings couldn't be usurped. We had been born to bring our rays, blend them and anchor the Emerald Ray onto the Earth. Now we had failed. Executing me had guaranteed failure. I suspect I would have retained the Gold Ray despite my transgression, but my swift punishment ensured that the opportunity was lost. It was this immense failure I realised I had to ask forgiveness for. I'd known what had been expected of me and however cruel my punishment looks from a modern perspective I had let everyone down and left my life purpose unfulfilled.

When the ceremony failed Egypt was humiliated and the High Priest was punished. He was distressed and deeply repentant for ordering my execution and laying the curse on me. We had been brother, sister, twins, magical partners and best friends; now the anger had died down he was left full of sadness and remorse.

He told me, "I was going to reverse the curse for you. The other priests realised this. Because I was high ranking they couldn't touch me and they blinded me with a red hot blade held in front of my eyes. I remember seeing that on a film once, it was happening to an Arab and it made my blood run cold." Now the High Priest couldn't see to revoke the curse. Steve admitted he has always felt very sensitive about his eyes. He had been relieved when he'd needed glasses as he felt they were offered some protection.

Humiliated and now blinded, the High Priest had taken a dagger and plunged it into his ribs. At this point we didn't know if his suicide was due to remorse and dishonour, or to follow the High Priestess into death to revoke the curse, but it was not a forced suicide, it was his own doing.

Steve's next view of the scene was floating above the body. He saw the other priests come in and kick his body, shouting insults, gleeful and full of spite. It was dragged away. His body was awarded the same fate as mine. To be quartered and burned. No Afterlife for either of us.

"I should have had the funeral of a pharaoh and been sent into the Afterlife, but because it was unbecoming of me to have taken my own life I was worth nothing. All gone. All the power and the glory."

I remembered I had already been told that I'd been a High Priestess in Egypt by a psychic and that I had disobeyed the rulers of Egypt and been severely punished. She'd warned me that to return to Egypt would make me feel very uncomfortable. Now I felt grateful that we didn't go to Egypt as we'd planned that autumn.

Throughout the Egyptian revelations Steve's 'dogrock' wand had been right by us. Steve had used it for some healing, but it was there more for protection and it stayed between us in our bed. We noticed it changing day by day. The colours became brighter and the stone became more translucent, more gold and sparkly. The most obvious transformation was at the tip which became quite colourless and clear. We started to examine it most mornings to see what it was up to. I wish I'd photographed it when Steve first bought it as I've never seen a piece of stone change so much.

As more of the story emerged, my anger subsided. I still felt the punishment far outstripped the crime and the pictures that came through upset me, but I could see why it had happened and knew my brother had truly suffered for what he had done to me.

Light behind the Angels

The High Priest

*'O You who change earth into gold,
And out of other earth made the father of mankind,
Change my mistakes and forgetfulness to knowledge.'*
Rumi

We needed more information. I was still carrying an eternal curse that had messed up my life this time and many other lifetimes. I needed the curse lifting if our modern relationship was to stand any hope of continuing. I sat Steve down in my healing room and set up a tape recorder. I wanted him to channel again and I was determined to capture every word. We started by chatting through the issue.

Steve: I have given this a lot of thought and it has come through, maybe as a conscience clearing, but he committed suicide because he couldn't resolve this in life. It was a written spell, written and burnt and put onto the astral, he had to put himself out onto the astral plane to sort it out. I'm proud to be a High Priest, but part of me can't just say 'Oh yes I'm a High Priest'. I always thought it was to do with keeping the ego in check, but I don't think so now. Now I know I've been a High Priest before and was not true to myself in that role. I think I was weak and I did what was expected of me and not what was in my heart.
Lauren: Maybe that is the message, about being true to your heart?
Steve: Maybe, because I do feel there was strong love between us. At the execution I had to turn my back. I thought it was contempt, but really I couldn't watch, turning my back was the easy option.
Lauren: Why did you have me killed?
Steve: It was expected, that's what I did.
Lauren: There is such a strong remembering of that humiliation. When you gave me my initiations last year I knew I'd been paraded naked and bound, that's why I wouldn't let you use the cords to tie me or lead me.
(At this point Steve started to sense the High Priest's persona. Within a few sentences he was fully channelling this distinctive personality and I found myself talking directly to my Egyptian brother.)
High Priest: There *(he points to the side of his ribs)* it was there. It wasn't the heart, because it would have been over too quickly. I didn't want it to be quick. I wanted to feel something of your suffering.
It was there, I can feel the pain.

Lauren: If you had me executed why add the curse?
High Priest: Because I was weak, because if I hadn't added the curse I would suffer the same fate as you. I wanted to save my own skin. I wrote it. It was on a scroll.
Lauren: What exactly is the curse?
High Priest: Let the punishment fit the crime.
Lauren: *(getting angry)* So you felt I deserved to be blocked from living with my love for eternity?
High Priest: I was humiliated. I wanted to save my soul. It was what was expected of me. Such mixed emotions. It was love right through to hate. It was heavier. If Egypt was going to suffer the High Priestess was going to suffer.
Lauren: *(Indignant)* She has!
High Priest: The scroll, the scroll, fury, hatred. I missed off the last two lines.
Lauren: Did you finish it?
High Priest: I was weak, I listened to others. I finished it. I burnt it. It was mixed with your ashes and spread by the four cardinal winds.
(The High Priest was getting distressed now) I'm against a pillar. I can't move back, hot, blinded as a lesson to others, worthless because I was weak. I could have revoked it, I had the knowledge, but I can't see to write. I can't do it. I can't do it. Such pain, my eyes. I'm still High Priest. Pain. I can't do anything about this. I can't see to write, I can't make the marks. I was weak, I can't stand the pain. I have to follow you. I have to right this wrong, find you on the other side. I don't want it quick. I want to feel your pain, suffering. I want to follow you, I want to find you. I want to set you free.
Lauren: Do you forgive me from the bottom of your heart?
High Priest: I truly forgive you. I can't forgive myself for being weak.
Lauren: What do you see now?
High Priest: Just black. They are standing over me, they show contempt for me.
Lauren: While you are still with that body tell me the words of the curse. If you really forgive me you would want to set me free.
High Priest: We need the key. Anuiset Sekhetae.
(It is hard to know how to spell this, but it sounded like An yoo set Sek er tay)
Lauren: *(It didn't sound like enough to me)* Are there more words? Will that set me free? What else do we need to know? What would you have done if you'd had your sight and you could have revoked the curse? What did you plan to do before they blinded you? Speak!

Light behind the Angels

High Priest: *(He's smirking now)* Just so easy. To reverse the curse write it backwards! I can forgive your actions, but I cannot forgive you forgetting your training!

Lauren: *(I resist the urge to hit him, he's so arrogant)* I don't know what was written. It wasn't just two words. Lifetime after lifetime your curse has worked on me. I have suffered over and over again. Please help me now, if you really care please help me now! Tell me what we were meant to have done in the rite. I can't remember that far back. Tell me what's happening, what are you seeing?

High Priest: *(I don't think he's been listening to me, he's drifted back to his death scene)* I'm shown no respect. "Is he dead?" They kick me, stab me, Ugh! *(he grunts)* A blade there *(he points to his heart)*.

Lauren: What do they do with your body?

High Priest: I am wrapped in white cloth and dragged.

Lauren: Where do they drag you? Where are they taking your body?

High Priest: It's too painful. I am being cut into four. Four separate fires. They have stopped me from going into the Otherworld. It is blackness.

Lauren: Is there anything in the blackness?

High Priest: Searching.

Lauren: Tell me what is under foot?

High Priest: Sometimes sand, sometimes grass. Searching strange lands, strange journeys.

Lauren: You have no body.

High Priest: Such pain.

Lauren: Ask for healing now.

High Priest: I want to feel the pain, want to feel the pain.

Lauren: Do you sense anyone else is there? Can you see anyone, are there other souls around?

High Priest: Many souls. They clear a path. They do not stop, they just go past. Fear.

Lauren: Are they afraid of you?

High Priest: Yes.

Lauren: Can you see the stars, the Moon?

High Priest: No. I must not rest, journey.

Lauren: Do you have any help? Any guidance?

High Priest: Alone, totally alone. Talk, talk to the faces, they pass, scared, fear, afraid. Looking for a ray of light. I must find it no matter how long it takes.

Lauren: What colour is the light? Did you have your own light?

High Priest: Blue, bluer than the bluest of skies, brighter than the brightest sun. *(This is most definitely the High Priest talking. Steve isn't given to poetic language, beyond 'The boy stood on the burning deck'!)*
Lauren: Did you give up your search?
High Priest: Never!
Lauren: How long have you looked for me?
High Priest: Forever. *(Steve wipes his face roughly by his mouth as though something was stuck there)*
Lauren: What was that? What did you rub off?
High Priest: Shame.
Lauren: Have you cleansed your body of the shame, your soul of the shame?
High Priest: I want to feel the shame.
Lauren: Where does it live in you?
High Priest: *(He beats his hand hard to his heart)* It's here. She was me and I was her.
Lauren: What is your intention when you find me?
High Priest: To lift the curse, to beg forgiveness, to explain.
Lauren: Can you set me free? If I can forgive you can you set me free?
High Priest: Searching and searching to set you free and you ask this of me?
Lauren: I need you to do it. You know you have found me now. We have found each other again. Do you recognise me?
High Priest: I see your Gold. So many times I thought I saw you, it was a mirage.
Lauren: I'm not a mirage. You have found me.
High Priest: Can't see, just blackness.
Lauren: Tell me what you need to lift the curse. You cannot fail me now.
High Priest: The search.
Lauren: *(Getting frustrated)* But you have found me now, which was the point of your journey.
High Priest: No strength.
Lauren: Give me your name, give me your name. I am still the same soul that you loved.
High Priest: No.
Lauren: Please! You have looked for me.
High Priest: All looks the same. I have journeyed far but I An-A-Huh must complete this task to set us both free. *(His name sounded like Ann-a-Hoo but later Steve saw how it should be spelt.)*
Lauren: Do you have your Blue Ray? Is there something I must do to be set free? I know I did wrong, do you say you have forgiven me?

Light behind the Angels

High Priest: I see your Gold but not my Blue.
Lauren: Ask and it is given. Ask.
High Priest: I am not worthy to receive the Ray.
Lauren: You must receive the Blue Ray to help me.
High Priest: I dare not look.
Lauren: You must, you must look. Please ask. You need to be in your power as I am in mine. *(He laughs)* Why do you laugh?
High Priest: The Ray. Seemingly once a High Priest always a High Priest. We have to blend the rays.
Lauren: Will that lift the curse or is the curse separate?
High Priest: It is not difficult.
Lauren: Do you feel the power returning to you? Does it feel familiar? *(A blissful look spreads across Steve's face as the High Priest basks in the Blue Ray. I can see him enjoying it as you might enjoy the Sun on your face. I let him have his moment.)*
High Priest: I have revoked the curse every day but it cannot be completed. I cannot revoke it without the tools. *(This was a real 'oh shit' moment. It isn't easy to get your hands on Ancient Egyptian magical tools in mid Wales! I tried to stay calm.)*
Lauren: What preparations do you need?
High Priest: I have done it so many times. Body and Mind and with the two rays the Spirit. Two shall become One. The Oneness shall be free. Two palms together, right hand to left hand, your right my left, my right your left.
Lauren: It can be done. Please describe what we are going to do together and the purpose behind the rite.
High Priest: Not yet.
Lauren: How many days before we can enact the rite? When can this come to pass?
High Priest: When the Moon is at its fattest. We shall purify. Stand hand to hand and the rays shall be One.
Lauren: Can I trust you?
High Priest: *(He makes a sign of honour beating one fist to his chest and holding the other arm at right angles to the side, hand held up, palm open. It looked like a sign someone might make if swearing an oath in a ceremony and it reminded me of a Roman gesture of honour I've seen in films.)*
Lauren: Please tell me my name as High Priestess in your time. I will follow your instructions, but will you tell me my name as High Priestess?
High Priest: I have called it so many times. Ankh-Ka-Dna.
(This sounded like Ankh Ka Deena)
Lauren: Thank you. Please step back now. I will talk to you again.

Almost before the words were out of my mouth Steve was back to the fore with me. He could remember very little of what had been said, his mind blank from the first few sentences until the end. This seems to be how he channels, he is 'kicked out' of his body and you feel you are talking directly to someone else. He finds it tiring and was relieved to read JZ Knight who channels the being Ramtha experiences it the same way.

Light behind the Angels

For Ancient Anger and Grief

'...for ancient anger and grief...reaching back into past lives to dissolve the roots of emotional dis-ease pervading the present life.
Gives off a spiral ray of golden energy.'
Judy Hall, Lithium Quartz, The Encyclopaedia of Crystals

Steve spent the next day transcribing the channelling from the tape we made. When I got in from running a training day in Cardiff I found him in very low spirits. He didn't feel he could even look at me; he was too full of shame. The shaking was very violent for him that night and I felt guided to place a small lithium quartz point on his chest. Looking up Judy Hall's commentary later it seems I couldn't have chosen a more appropriate stone and I'm sure it would have been effective had it not been stronger than Steve could bear. It caused him intense pain and I had to remove it quickly.

All that evening Steve was full of thoughts of self harm. He thought of taking a kitchen knife to himself, or even using a crystal point to injure himself. It was very frightening. The line between his past life persona and who he is now was getting blurred. He felt the guilt for his past actions so acutely he wanted to punish himself again.

Steve flipped back into watching the High Priest's suicide in graphic detail. Again he felt the pain in his ribs where the dagger had penetrated. He saw he was in a big room with white and gold drapes. My room, not his own chambers. Blood was running down his side and pooling on the floor. His chest was already bruised where he'd been beating it, punching himself as his way of expressing his sorrow. Steve felt his chest was now painfully bruised to the touch. Next he reported feeling cold and then feeling calm and peaceful. "I see myself on the floor. I must have been left handed. The knife is still stuck in me. It has a gold handle with lapis blue stones. Two pieces of lapis in the shape of an eye. Looking at myself now there is no pain."

The dagger he'd chosen was one that I'd presented him with in happier times. It was only intended as a ceremonial piece and I'd never imagined it would be turned on himself.

That night when I lit the candle at my enlightenment altar it wouldn't burn properly. All it mustered was a tiny blue flame, a little blue orb. Next morning I woke with strong guidance to hide Steve's car keys. I have never done such a thing to him or anyone else before or since, but the guidance was so insistent I hid them.

I went out to check on my chickens as I'd been out all of the previous day and had got back in after dark. Steve had fed them for the first time in my absence. I laughed out loud when I saw what he'd done. Their feeder was full of shell and grit. He'd picked up the wrong bag and fed them stones! Back indoors I took a coffee up to Steve, gently pulling his leg, "You fed those poor birds stones yesterday!" Wrong move! He was angry, "What do you expect? I eat the bloody things!"

Instantly Steve was all for driving straight back to Manchester and he stormed off downstairs to grab his keys and leave. When he got there his keys were gone of course. I wouldn't let Steve have them back despite his raging. I knew that if he left now he wouldn't be back again. That simply wasn't an option.

Steve went out to the workshop to smoke and sulk. Later when he'd calmed down he told me that he'd wakened in a bad mood. He'd had a dream in which I'd taken crystals away from a protective layout I'd designed for him and given them to the twin flame's wife who he dreamt was pregnant.

On his way outside he'd gone into my crystal cabinet and picked up a lapis lazuli palmstone that I'd just bought from a wholesaler. Now calm he turned it round to show me saying, "Look, we are on it." Sure enough on the back outlined in white is the shape of a taller figure with his head bowed over a shorter figure, or as a pregnant student commented, an ultrasound picture of twins in the womb. He insisted on purchasing this particular stone from me, rather than having it as a gift which I would have willingly given.

Whilst calming himself Steve had played with the crystals in his pocket. Some time before I'd bought a bag of natural citrine tumbles and pulled one out that was shaped like a crescent moon. I'd given this to Steve. Now as he'd been looking at it he'd noticed a rainbow the shape of a winged faery. He showed me the faery. He'd made contact with her and she'd told him she could lead him to where he needed to go.

Next day we discussed the situation as, although we'd made progress, we still didn't know how we were to lift the curse. I put the tape recorder on again as I had a feeling Steve might start to channel.
Steve: I need to get into the head of this High Priest who was me. Okay what would I do now to a woman who had really brassed me off?
Lauren: You were humiliated too.
Steve: That's the one! I was reading in Judy Hall's 'Hands Across Time' that there is a scroll on Egyptian sacred marriage, not just joining bodies, but minds and souls for eternity. Would I do that?
Lauren: You would have actually had to marry me to the other man.

Light behind the Angels

Steve: The High Priest would have the means to do it in their absence. This is magic.
Lauren: Before or after the death as a punishment?
Steve: Oh after death as a punishment, because the High Priestess went to meet him and he didn't show. I'd lock them into that forever. You let me down and you didn't just let me down, you let your country down. It wasn't just me you humiliated, it was Egypt. Egypt suffered because of this. It is something to do with the rays of the Elohim.
Lauren: And I would be locked into the same pattern, because in the Arthurian lifetime I did it all again, I let the land down again for a figure who looked very similar to the Roman.

We were getting a clearer idea of how the curse was intended to work, but we weren't much wiser as to how to lift it. I remembered that as we'd discussed the Twin Flame months before Steve had commented bitterly, "You're already married to him." I'd taken that as part of his frustration with our situation, but perhaps he knew more at a soul level. I picked up 'Hands Across Time'. Judy Hall states that the Egyptian mystic marriage was one of the strongest soul bonds which could be made and was prepared for over years by the couple so that they were connected on every level of their being, developing telepathy together.

I thought Steve had missed the point. I felt that the ceremony in the temple, the combining of the Rays, had been intended as the culmination of our mystic marriage as High Priest and High Priestess. Marrying twins was not seen as incest in Egypt, it was a way of keeping the bloodline pure and there are other records of twin marriages. All that time spent with our heads together reading each other's thoughts was not just play, it was preparation.

"Both parties had to be ready: one could not advance without the other. Once the souls were joined on all these levels, they were intended to stay together for eternity. They had spiritual work to do. Work that would not stop with death."
Judy Hall 'Hands Across Time'

No wonder my brother had been so beside himself with fury. I had been intended for him and him alone. I'd let him down personally. I realised that the curse he had constructed was a parody of the mystic marriage written in spite by a man that had loved me. Without any of the spiritual preparation I would be drawn back to the Roman for eternity. No wonder my brother had wanted to lift it when his anger had cooled. This had been our intended destiny. I realised the Roman was not truly my 'twin flame' as I'd believed, my own brother the High

Priest was, but the curse had been constructed to make me seek out the Roman as my twin flame. In cursing me, my brother had effectively cursed himself.

Steve channelled, "We weren't just brother and sister. We were twins. 'I am her and she is me.' We were twin flames as we were identical. We were brother and sister. We were so high. Our magic and healing was as easy as waving a hand. We were the Light. There was no Light brighter than us. We were Egypt's Light."

I dreamed that night I was looking into Steve's eyes and I knew I was looking back into my own eyes; our eyes were a golden brown. I knew we were not separate, we were the same. On waking I realised I'd been gazing into my twin brother's eyes in Egypt. In this life my eyes are hazel and Steve's are blue.

Light behind the Angels

The Novice

> *'It is here, my daughters, that love is to be found
> Not hidden away in corners but in the midst of occasions of sin.'*
> St Teresa of Avila

A cord cutting with my mother felt secondary to and less urgent than the cord cutting I'd needed with my father, however it seemed important that this was completed before the final ritual to remove the eternal curse. I found the compulsion to do this strange. My mother is a spiritual lady and a natural healer. If it hadn't been for her I might never have found crystal healing, as it was through my mother's yoga teacher that I had my first crystal treatment. We mostly got on well, although she had a tendency to fret about me.

We had enough on our plates really, but we followed our guidance and went ahead with the cord cutting. I set up the two golden circles again in my mind's eye. I stood in my circle and called my mother to come into hers.

At first she presented as a little old lady, hunched and shuffling. She was upset to be called; anxious and tearful. I felt there was a, 'Please don't be mean to me!' air about her. I have avoided broaching many a subject with my parents for fear of upsetting her in the past, so this made some sense. I told her to straighten up and present herself as she really was and she did so.

At first it was difficult to get an image of any ties between us at all. Scanning our bodies up and down more closely I spotted ribbon-like ties around my knees and heard 'Don't run too fast!' I felt these were ties she'd placed when I was little in an attempt to stop me falling over and hurting myself. I saw them as bright gingham hair ribbons like she used to tie bows when she plaited my hair as a child. They stretched from her fingers and it was easy to remove them at both ends using a pair of golden scissors.

Next I found a mass of gossamer threads between us. There was nothing substantial and these were whisked away with a feather. There were so many that the feather was covered in sticky cobwebs and had to be sacrificed and destroyed along with the ties. Steve suggested I look under my hair at the back of my neck, but I couldn't see anything there. However I could feel pulling under my left shoulder blade and when I looked I saw a very fine, almost invisible string. I then realised there were more, another one under my right shoulder blade, one at each elbow, one at each wrist, one at each knee, on each foot and at the crown of my head. Looking at them I realised that I was strung like a marionette! I felt that these strings were not much pulled on now and had been put in place in childhood to keep me from straying. My mother was holding the puppeteer's wooden cross piece in her hands and gave it back to me without a fuss. The golden scissors cut the strings away. My mum has suffered badly with arthritis in her hands and I wondered if there was a connection between the physical stiffness and an unconscious reluctance to let go.

Steve suggested I turn and raise my top to give mum a good look at my tattoo as at that stage I was still keeping it secret and hidden to save the fuss I felt it would create. In my inner scene Mum didn't like the tattoo, but I told her it wasn't her choice, it was mine. She was a little more accepting when she realised that it was symbolic of healing. Her attitude reminded me of when I'd told her about my new name, she hadn't approved then, expecting me to keep my married name or return to my maiden name. When I'd explained it was the Latin for my middle name, which she'd given me, she accepted it.

I sent mum away, forgiving her easily for being over-protective of me. The pile of cords were all burnt and turned quickly to ashes. Now it was time to bathe, Steve guided me to find a pleasant place and I found myself in my parent's bathroom. That was a strange choice as I'd rather bathe in my own home and it was even stranger to be in my mother's bath if I was truly free of ties from her. I got into the water but I couldn't relax and enjoy it as I normally would at this stage.

Suddenly I realised Steve had been right, there were more ties at the back of my head. I jumped out, wrapped myself in a fluffy white towel and redrew the two golden circles. Mum came back in, but this time she wasn't my Mum, I got a momentary glimpse of a young Egyptian woman in white robes with black hair piled up on her head. At this point my insides went cold as ice and I was gripped with visceral fear. I felt sheer terror and I found I was physically shaking and trembling on the couch. Steve had me draw a third circle touching the other two and stood himself in it to give me some of his strength and protection. I calmed a little and dared to look.

I realised the ties were silken white cords that went around my neck and around both wrists. They looked not unlike modern dressing gown cords. This was the Egyptian cable tow used to bind me and take me to my death. My own mother had been the young priestess who had been selected to lead me to my execution. I couldn't see the woman's face again, I don't know if I was too scared or if she was hiding it, but I was aware of a pair of female hands holding the other ends of the cords.

Light behind the Angels

As with the other ties she relinquished her hold on the cable tow immediately, simply letting it slip from her fingers as I pulled it. I cut away the ties from me using my pair of golden scissors. I had to cut my knees and ankles free too, it seems they had also been bound so that I could only hobble to my execution. They had made sure my final moments were as undignified as possible.

It was easy to forgive my mother for her part in my execution. It felt as if she'd been the unlucky priestess who'd been selected to do this, it wasn't something she had volunteered for; she wouldn't have had much choice. Steve confirmed later she'd been picked out because she was an absolute novice. They had chosen her from lowly ranks to humiliate me further. The ties were burnt and she was forgiven and dismissed a second time.

This time my body of water was a lovely tropical beach and I had a wonderful time exploring under the waves. As I went beneath the surface I transformed into a mermaid and found I could breathe easily. The waters were crystal clear and full of broken white pillars; the ruins of Atlantis. When I'd played enough I returned to the sandy beach. I was asked to express my new freedom and I lay and made a sand angel, then I let the rays of the Sun soak right into my body. It felt beautifully nourishing.

My tree this time was an old gnarly olive with a hollow trunk and there, inside, I found my grey monk's habit again. I felt this cord cutting explained much of my mother's over-protective attitude towards me this time round. She hadn't wanted to lead me to harm before and she would do her utmost to protect me now.

Having shown my mother the tattoo on the astral plane I decided I should show her on the physical level the next time we visited. When I did so her reaction surprised me, "It's your body. I don't like them, but that's me." I felt a big weight off my shoulders, another layer of pretence could fall away and I realised that I'd inflicted the angst upon myself unnecessarily.

The Land of Forgotten Souls

'It seemed to Arren that in this timeless dusk there was, in truth, neither forward nor back, no east nor west, no way to go.'
Ursula Le Guin, The Farthest Shore

Steve had followed the advice of the faery he'd met in his citrine moon and followed her into the Dark Lands to find An-A-Huh and ask how to lift the curse. He began by holding the citrine and meditating on a doorway he could see in it. He recorded his journey, careful to speak his findings aloud so that we didn't lose any clues:

A bronze door. I plunge my athame into it to hold it open for my return. Walking in it is almost total blackness. Silver dots, some come close, sad faces. No sunlight, no moonlight, just black. It feels as though I am walking on broken seashells.

I look behind me, there is a faint trail of silver dust, like leaving a trail of salt. I should be able to find my way back out. I feel we are going around a hillock, as if walking up a winding staircase.

We have just come to a stop. I can see nothing but blackness. The faery is just hovering there. She has put her hands to her face in the sign of a megaphone. I should try calling out his name.

"An-A-Huh! An-A-Huh! An-A-Huh!"
In my head I hear, *"Who dares look for me in the Land of Forgotten Souls, the land of no hope?"*
I reply, *"An-A-Huh I seek for you to make amends."* I can see a small blue glow, like the tiny blue light of the candle flame on the altar the other night. As I watch I'm not sure if it is moving towards me or growing bigger, towards me I think, very slowly. Now the blue sphere is close to me, just a sphere, no features. I ask three times for An-A-Huh to return to his human form.
"Who calleth my name?"
"I wish you no harm. If it is you, An-A-Huh, standing before me, please make yourself visible to me in the shape of a human." As I look at the sphere I can make out a vague shape, the shape of a man surrounded by blue light. He asks, *"Who are you?"*
I reply, aware this is completely surreal, *"I am you."* Understandably this is not the answer he is expecting. He speaks with the air of a man used to great power and respect, *"How can this be? What gives you the right to address a High Priest directly without introduction?"*
I decide to use my own rank as High Priest, I'm concerned that he takes me seriously.

Light behind the Angels

"I too am a High Priest. It is many, many years after your time on Earth. I work healing and magic, though not as powerful as yours. You met your sister a few days ago and spoke with her. I am you in another incarnation, we are of the same soul, you are of my soul. Help me become whole. You told her your story of great sadness, of how you had your sister Ankh-Ka-Dna executed. You cursed her for eternity."

He covers his face with his hands and then begins beating his breast in anguish.

"Stop! There is no need. We can right this wrong." An-A-Huh asks, "How do I know I can trust you?" I give him a password I was told whilst showering that morning. He isn't impressed.

"That does not prove to me anything. I have been duped before, you could have been given that password." Of course I was given the password, but not as trickery. I try using a ritual greeting from Freemasonry which feels right to me.

"I greet you as a brother, hand to hand, foot to foot, knee to knee, breast to breast, hand over back." This seems to have helped.

"What is your purpose?"

"An-A-Huh, you wish to revoke the curse upon your sister, Ankh-Ka-Dna. Your magic is very strong, it is still in effect. She has lived many lifetimes suffering the original pain, although you saw to it that her end was swift when you were last together on Earth. You have given me the word of power, I also need to know the ritual. Tell me what I need to do to lift this curse." An-A-Huh nods.

"Do you want to lift the curse?"

"Yes, yes, oh yes!" His reply is fervent.

"You have told me that the rite must be done on the night of the full moon and run through midnight into the beginning of the next day which is Ankh-Ka-Dna's birthday in this lifetime."

"You have the words."

"When do we use the words?"

"You place the symbol of the All Seeing Eye on the palms of your hands. On your left pointing to the Heavens, on your right pointing to the Earth and the opposite for Ankh-Ka-Dna. The same symbols on your foreheads; yours must point up, hers must also point up. You will stand erect, facing each other, the symbols on the palms are together. You will rotate slowly against the Sun three times. With each rotation you must say the words of power.

If you are truly who you say you are I need not give you the words again, for if you do not have the words, the lifting will not take place."

I'm checking the details, "Three revolutions, palm to palm. Three revolutions with the word of power and that will lift it?"

"That is only the first part. If you are who you say you are you will know the remainder. We will meet again and I will give you one chance to explain the last part of the rite correctly. If it is wrong then you are not who you say you are and the curse will stay."

I watch him going back into blue light and the blue sphere retreats getting smaller so that I can barely see it against the black. Then it is gone. The faery is flying again, back down the hill. I can see the silver trail, it has a sparkle, a shimmer. I'm running, having to run to keep up with her. I can see the doorway now. I go through the door and pull my athame out. Thank you kind faery.

Listening to Steve's recording of his journey I was both impressed and nervous. What if Steve couldn't find the rest of the ritual out? How would he know that the words and actions were correct? I thought it was interesting that he'd stuck his athame into the door to keep it open, as I'd been taught that portals to Faery could be held open with a knife, but I hadn't discussed that with Steve.

I could understand An-A-Huh being wary. Imagine wandering despairingly in a dark land for millennia and then someone comes visiting and says they are you and they want powerful information? I also remembered that early on Steve channelled, "We were duped." Of course he'd find it hard to trust us.

Researching on the internet Steve found that the arm position he had been shown, arms level with the shoulders bent at the elbow at right angles upwards was known as the position of 'Huh' shown in hieroglyphics and that Huh was a deity. The closest translations of his name that he could find were A Ne Huh meaning God of Eternity and A'a Ne Huh: Great of Eternity. Was he named after the deity or was *he* the deity? There had certainly been something of the 'Gods made man' in the way we had been born, found and venerated before our fall from grace.

The Egyptian curse had been well crafted and we knew it had been enduring. Our preparations for the lifting of the curse had to be exact and correct. Most of the work was done by Steve. He had laid the curse, so it was only fitting that he should lift it. He was told the magic was too strong to be destroyed completely, but it could be removed and contained. He'd been shown that he had to suck it out of me and blow it into a box which would then be sealed with the sign of the ankh.

Steve had been given guidance on purchasing the wooden box for the ceremony. That sounded easy enough, but as we trailed around town looking for a small plain wooden box with a tight fitting lid we found they aren't quite so simple to find, most are over embellished and not at all appropriate.

Light behind the Angels

Finally we ended up in a smart gift shop where I buy most of my greetings cards. It isn't the cheapest of places, but the owner has an eye for quality. There on the shelf was a lovely little triangular burr walnut wooden box. It was beautiful quality with a really snug fitting lid. This was the one. With trepidation I lifted it to look at the price sticker underneath. It was under ten pounds. Oddly it was a third of the price of a slightly larger rectangular box in the same range. I wasn't about to query this piece of providence, it was perfect.

Next we made an expedition to the chemists. We needed eye makeup in bright blue and bright gold for the All Seeing Eye design Steve had been shown in our earlier ritual. We were to paint this on ourselves again and we had found that the symbols hadn't shown up all that well before. Luckily fashion colours were gaudy and the eye pencils were cheap and cheerful, though my son was curious to know why Steve was trying the colours on his own hand!

Into the Darkness

Come you lost Atoms to your Centre draw,
And be the Eternal Mirror that you saw:
Rays that have wander'd into Darkness wide
Return and back into your Sun subside.
Farid ud-Din Attar, The Conference of the Birds

Steve felt he needed to return to the Land of Forgotten Souls with me. An-A-Huh was more likely to trust him if he saw I was there. I felt a fair bit of trepidation about this journey into the darkness. It sounded scary as this was a place with no landmarks. What if I got lost? Steve reassured me that the faery was a good and trustworthy guide. He showed me the bronze door clearly marked in the crystal through which we would pass and told me that the faery would lay a trail of faery dust again so we wouldn't get lost.

We lay side by side on the bed holding hands with the citrine firmly grasped in between our two palms, Steve holding his athame in his other hand to wedge the bronze door open. I was nervous and asked Steve to narrate the journey aloud as we went along to give me points of reference. We recorded everything so that we could retrieve information later.

Here is our journey:

Lauren: I can see the door, I see the faery. Tell me what you are seeing.

Steve: Blue and deep pink, purplish faery about six inches tall with silver wings. She is flying in front of us about three feet ahead at a slow, walking pace. The door is in front of us, we are walking steadily to the door. Glance to your left and you'll see I'm stood there.

Lauren: Yes.

Steve: I can see you. It is a single door and it is open. I've started to pass through and you are following. I've pierced it with my athame. I'm leaving the athame behind. Now on the other side of the door it is black, just black. It is just black going up into the sky. It makes me think of scenery in a play where it is painted on a black backdrop, but it is all black.

There is a faint silver trail that we left last time. I can see dull silver dots in the distance. We are following the same trail as before and veering to the left. Keep looking around. Amongst the silver dots we are looking for a little sphere of blue.

Light behind the Angels

Lauren: I think we may have to call him again.
Steve: We are now going around to the right. I feel that we are at the base of a little hill and we are taking a spiral path round it. Ascending. Nearing the top now. We've come to a halt. The faery is just hovering. She's put her hands to her mouth in a sign of making a call.
Lauren: Call out to him.
Steve: An-A-Huh! An-A-Huh! An-A-Huh!
Lauren: I can't see him yet.
Steve: We'll try calling again. An-A-Huh! An-A-Huh! An-A-Huh!
Lauren: Shall I call out for him?
Steve: I'll try once more. An-A-Huh! An-A-Huh! An-A-Huh!
Lauren: I think I need to call.
Steve: Don't be scared.
Lauren: I'm not scared. Brother! Brother! I have come for you, please come now! I am Ankh-Ka-Dna. I am your High Priestess. See me now. I have come for you. Brother, see my Gold light. You know you can trust me. Please come now. I think he's coming. Speak.
An-A-Huh: I am here. As ever you have been looking the wrong way! I am behind you.
Lauren: *(I found that I slipped easily and naturally back into role as his sister.)* Brother I am pleased to see you.
An-a-Huh: You look not like Ankh-Ka-Dna.
Lauren: I am she, but many lifetimes on from when we parted. I am the same soul. Can you see my light? Look at me.
An-A-Huh: Can it be true? My eyes have deceived me so many times.
Lauren: It is true. I want you to come out of this place with me. You do not belong here.
An-A-Huh: Where is he that came the last time?
Lauren: He is here. He is part of your soul.
An-A-Huh: That is what he said.
Lauren: I have come with him as proof for you. Please trust him.
An-A-Huh: I gave him a test.
Lauren: You did. He told me. It was a fair test and he has completed it. Let him speak now.
An-A-Huh: He has but one chance to prove his worth *(to Steve)* I gave you part of the ritual. You must tell me the remainder.
Steve: After we have turned palm to palm with our arms held in the sign of Huh three times against the Sun, we take a step back. We must then counteract the curse with love. The love that An-A-Huh and Ankh-Ka-Dna had for each other as twins. We must go back and recreate a last time together acting as when we were children, lying on the bed facing each other, but this time we join the symbols on our

foreheads. With delight, with humour, two being One, as though we were hiding our thoughts from the guards again.

When that love has flowed between us it is time to remove the lock from the heart. I believe you gave me the key. It is the hand symbol of the heart, the inverted heart. After making that symbol and making the symbol of the wings of an angel I have to suck the poison out from the heart seven times. Each time I extract it I blow it into the box and put the lid back on. When that is completed we seal the box with wax. We then make the sign of a seal on it on all sides. The curse is trapped in the box. Then I fall to my knees and I present this box to Ankh-Ka-Dna; I keep saying the words, "You are now in charge of your own destiny." I must say that three times followed by, "Be free, be free, be free." *(I was impressed and much relieved that he'd found all this out.)*

Lauren: What say you brother?

An-A-Huh: He speaks words of truth. I have wandered long. I wish to be free from the dark.

Lauren: I wish you free. We have both suffered for what we did. If you can rejoin the soul of this man, who is my partner in this lifetime, we can be together and you will not lose me again.

An-A-Huh: I believe there is truth in your words. Before me now I see a golden staircase on which I can ascend from this place of sorrow. You must leave this place now as it will draw on your energies. Carry out my rite. If you are successful I will know.

Lauren: We will do our utmost to succeed. Do you have any further instructions?

An-A-Huh: I have no need to give you instructions. He is adept in the art of magic. I believe now that we are one and the same.
I bid you farewell.

Lauren: And farewell to you. May we meet again before too long.

Steve: We need to go back down the spiral path. When we got to the bottom last time the faery picked up speed and I was running. We are on the level again now. I can see the silver dust in front of us. It's time to run. Feel the crunching under foot. Run and run. I can see the doorway in the distance. Getting large now. Okay we are at the doorway. I want you to go through before me this time and I'll take my athame as I pass. There, you are gone, I'm through and I have my athame. Thank you faery.

Lauren: Thank you.

Light behind the Angels

I was greatly relieved to be back. We had been left unscathed by our journey into this place of blank despair and had our instructions. I had also felt the love that Ankh-Ka-Dna and An-A-Huh shared in life and rather than remaining angry with him I felt pity for him as he'd wandered searching through the ages in the dark.

The Land of Forgotten Souls reminded me strongly of Ursula Le Guin's 'A Wizard of Earthsea' series. In her novels the dead wander through the dark lands, unresponsive and without hope. Perhaps if you passed from life expecting nothing but blackness you would find yourself there? Certainly An-A-Huh believed he was being denied the Afterlife when he saw his body quartered and burnt, yet I hadn't gone there despite suffering the same fate.

Happy Rebirth Day to Me

'By drawing from the bottomless well of wisdom, which is hidden in the essence of every man, we perceive grains of truth, which give those of us with knowledge the power to perform marvellous things.'
The Papyrus of Ani, The Egyptian Book of the Dead, translation Ramses Seleem

The next day was the 22nd of January, the eve of my birthday. It was also the date that the altar for Enlightenment was set to run to, the timing discerned before we'd had the first revelations about Egypt. We were three weeks on from the night of the choices and I had to admit that I'd been enlightened about my own soul's journey. It hadn't been what I'd expected Enlightenment to mean when I made that choice.

This was the night of the full moon and so it was the night the curse was scheduled to be lifted following An-A-Huh's guidance of, "When the moon is at her fattest." I found it incredible the way all the dates and times intertwined and focussed in on this one night. We were to perform the ritual to release the curse late in the evening so that it finished just past midnight into my birthday.

I was booked to deliver Eating Disorder Awareness training in Cardiff again during the day, which was probably a good thing as there was little for me to do in preparation for the ritual and it kept me from thinking about it and getting too nervous. The onus was all on Steve. He had been given instructions to make things for that night. The children were going to be at their dad's; perfect timing again.

When I returned that evening we ran through the instructions for the ritual. I was mainly to follow Steve's lead. We carefully prepared each other's symbols, painting both our hands and foreheads and then we went up to my bedroom. We stood face to face with our arms raised out to the sides, our elbows bent at right angles in the sign of Huh. We joined hands palm to palm and rotated three times against the Sun just as we'd been instructed. Then we lay upon the bed, face to face, as we'd seen ourselves do as children in those happier times. Lovingly we rested our foreheads together merging the signs.

My work was now done and it was for Steve to lift the curse. He had the triangular box at the ready. First he made the hand symbols he'd been shown over my heart, then he made a tube of his hands and began to suck the curse from me. Each breath was as big as he could make it, as he'd been told he had only seven breaths to rid me of the curse. Steve breathed out carefully into the wooden box slipping the lid

Light behind the Angels

on each time. The last few breaths were the biggest. Huge rasping breaths; these were his last chance to get every last fragment out.

Finally it was done. The box containing the curse was firmly closed. Steve melted sealing wax and dribbled it all around the box lid so that it couldn't slip open accidentally. Then he took a seal he'd made in the shape of an ankh and stamped the three sides of the box with it. It was just on midnight.

Steve knelt before me and presented me formally with the box. "You are now in charge of your own destiny. Be free, be free, be free." Saying that he passed the box to me for my safe keeping. Finally he presented me with a handmade brass ankh pendant he had carved for me as a birthday present that day. He'd carved the stem as a key, a reminder that I held my freedom now. I put it on. It felt much more familiar to me than the pentagram and I was very pleased to wear it. We slept soundly that night.

It was my 41st birthday. We discussed the events of the night before. Steve described the taste of the curse as old and stale. He said it felt heavy as he put it in the box, so that even if he hadn't lidded the box between breaths it wouldn't have escaped because it had sunk straight to the bottom. My heart felt correspondingly lighter, although the area felt slightly raw and tender.

Steve urged me to take good care of the box. If I opened it the curse would be reactivated. I promised him that I was extremely unlikely to ever do such a thing. There was a safeguard. If someone else came upon the box, chipped away the seal and opened it, the curse would not come back to me, however it still needed to be kept from prying eyes and fiddling fingers and so it was safely tucked away.

Following the release of the curse we both felt it was important to contact the High Priest aspect of Steve's soul and ensure he knew that the task had been accomplished. It was a strange situation, we hoped the High Priest had walked up his golden staircase out of the dark lands, but we knew he was not reconnected with Steve.

Once more Steve settled down to channel An-A-Huh.

Steve: I can see a blue light, a very, very blue light, with a white background and he's dressed as an Egyptian. That's how I see him. He's saluting me. *(Steve physically salutes back)* His eyes need time to adjust to being in the light after the darkness.

Lauren: *(speaking directly to An-A-Huh)* How are you feeling?

An-A-Huh: Strong! Put your questions to me.

Lauren: I'd like to know whether you are to rejoin the soul of Steve, or whether you must stay removed from him.

An-A-Huh: When his own Blue light is stronger I will work with him.

Lauren: Can you help him connect more fully with his Blue light?

An-A-Huh: He does not have enough trust in himself yet. He is full of self doubt.
Lauren: But he will connect back with his power in the future?
An-A-Huh: It is deemed this is what he must do.
Lauren: Can you see my Gold ray? How bright am I in this lifetime?
An-A-Huh: You are bright now but it is not yet full.
Lauren: Can you guide me?
An-A-Huh: He will guide you; the one you say is me. You need to rest. He needs to rest. But the wait will not be long.
Lauren: Do you feel released of the guilt you have carried?
An-A-Huh: I do and for that I give you a thousand thank yous.
Lauren: I have forgiven you with all my heart and I am so pleased that you are now back in the Light. I feel my heart is open again. It can work again. We are both released now.
An-A-Huh: You worked well.
Lauren: Thank you. Will there be a sign that we need to contact you again? That we are ready for the next step?
An-A-Huh: I will speak to you through him when the time is right.
Lauren: I am so pleased to be able to speak to you again. There is so much warmth in my heart towards you.
An-A-Huh: I feel once again the burning delights of love.
Lauren: I don't want to lose you again in the darkness. That time has now passed.
An-A-Huh: It has. We shall be together. He must not doubt. He has the blue ray of An-A-Huh. He will know. That which was not, shall be.
Lauren: I would embrace you as my brother if I could, but we can embrace as souls. Please brother step back now and allow Steve to come forward.

It is hard to explain how emotional I felt reconnecting to my brother. I feel your soul never forgets anyone you've loved and that there is part of me that is still Ankh-Ka-Dna, who had been truly missing her twin. I felt my heart chakra warming and opening as we spoke to each other. It was very odd to love a person who both is and is not your partner. It felt slightly clandestine, as if we were speaking behind Steve's back, even though Steve was sitting right in front of me and An-A-Huh's words were coming from his lips. If ever there was a line to prove that another person was speaking, "I feel once again the burning delights of love," did it for me. Not many Englishmen could speak that line and sound genuine. Perhaps men these days have something to learn about love from the Ancient Egyptians!

Light behind the Angels

It was funny how differently we felt about that day. Steve recorded in his journal that my birthday felt like an anti-climax, but then he'd completed his task and 'hadn't been there' for the most moving part of it.

Rays of Blue and Gold

'Gold is the colour of hidden knowledge and wisdom. As it is rich on the earth plane it is rich in spirit. It is tempered wisdom, tempered knowledge, tempered enlightenment. It is profound understanding: the deep wisdom of the past brought through into the present.'
Philippa Merivale, Healing with Colour

Two days later we both awoke out of sorts. The previous day had been absolutely lovely and we'd gone off to bed happily. These sudden mood shifts seemed to hit us out of nowhere and related to our dreamscapes. Steve had dreamt that my cat had deliberately scratched out a symbol in the sand that his guides had been showing him. I'd been aware that the cat had been physically thrown off the bed repeatedly in the night and this had irritated me. Steve said he'd felt the symbol had been important and he was frustrated as every time he tried to look the cat had scratched it out again. I'd dreamt I was cutting cords with the Roman and Steve had shouted tauntingly at me, "How near is he? Would he come to you if you called?" On opening our eyes we were both ready to tell each other to get lost!

Steve went off to smoke in the workshop and I got on with my day. Late morning I took a cup of coffee out to him and found he'd been writing his rant out on paper when he'd been stopped in his tracks by his lighter flame. He'd been sitting moodily flicking his lighter on and off, staring at the flame. He recorded his observations on paper. "The flame on my lighter went very small and it made me notice the colours, blue at the base turning into gold. It reminded me that we two make the One. I flicked it on again. This time the flame was even smaller, just blue left, but too little and weak to light anything with. Flicking it on again the flame was back to normal, both colours intermingled. I lit my cigar."

"There was no physical reason for this display, my lighter was half full and normally has a bright flame. Okay that has turned my thinking around, neat trick! We need to be together on this and trust that each of us is working for the other and for ourselves. We are strong apart, but much stronger together. This is a joint gift!"

I'd been having similar thoughts indoors. If we were falling out over mere dreams could we be trusted with more power? I'd asked for guidance and was told, "You haven't made a commitment to each other."

Light behind the Angels

The message was a bit embarrassing to relay, but I passed it on. Steve agreed and said that he did feel really committed to me. For a moment he let his habitual guard down and I saw his eyes soften.

That night when I went to bed I asked to see the faeries and a few seconds later a bright red light zipped across the ceiling. Steve could see lots of little green 'meteors'. I had the impression of movement and felt I was on the verge of seeing them too. As I turned over to go to sleep Steve saw a little green faery perched on my pillow. He could see its legs and wings before it took off again.

On my recommendation Steve attended the Shamanic Introductory course I had taken. My feeling was that he was a natural born shaman. I had already taught him the basics of journeying and he picked it all up with ease, meeting a very strong power animal and a warrior spirit guide whom he'd been communicating with. Some of his healing on my back was distinctly shamanic.

I lent Steve my Dictaphone so that he could record any insights from the day. Here's a transcript of his recording, tidied up a little, but otherwise just as he said it.

"This afternoon in the trance dance I was a bird and I was flying and hovering, gliding over the temple. I landed on a wall and then changed into me. The temple was circular, pillared. It had rooms around the outside and I was allowed to walk about. I was allowed to look in the rooms; they were white marble and were all different colours, with the exception of blue. I was searching for a blue coloured room.

I was shown a staircase which spiralled down into a temple within the hill. I was just a visitor, being shown round. We started in the East, saluted the Sun, arms held high, then slowly worked round to the West, then back to the East via the North. After doing this a couple of times a panel in the roof opened and sunlight, a beam of golden light, came straight down and hit a central altar which had a big sun on it made of gold. When the beam hit that it lit up the whole room. I was allowed to join in the dancing around the altar.

Shortly after that I left, back up the spiral staircase, back into the healing rooms, still looking for the room with the blue light which was not there. I was getting quite angry about this, at one point I remember putting my hands in my pockets because there were people there and I kept saying, 'Where is the room with the Blue Ray?' and each one answered the same, 'You must seek for that which was lost.' I was getting pretty irate. The music stopped, end of session."

Another anecdote Steve relayed that evening meant far more to me than it had to him. When journeying to the lower world he had gone to a cave and was shown a blue and gold flame. As he watched it changed into a spiral. A big rooster came out from behind a rock and his power animal kept chasing it away. Apparently Patricia had given him a knowing look when he had relayed that one to the group, but had kept her counsel. I felt I should enlighten him telling him the big chicken was my old flame's power animal. I felt he was still lurking around.

On the final day of January I woke tired and headachy. My sleep had been disturbed. I put it down to a glimpse of the 'twin flame' walking down the street opposite the Celtic shop the day before. I'd been looking out of the window thinking of nothing much when I'd seen him. My heart had lurched and my legs had gone weak, so much so I had to sit down. It was the first time I'd seen anything of him for months and the involuntary reaction of my body showed I still wasn't over him despite all the work we'd done.

Steve phoned me from Manchester. One of his Egyptian guides had tried to show him dark magic three times in his dreams. Each time he'd refused the knowledge. I felt concerned that he was being led astray and that this guide was not to be trusted.

Clearing out my bedside cupboard the same day I came across a little slip of cardboard with pencilled Bible references in copperplate handwriting. When I was a child my Mother had given me her little Biblical picture cards that she'd kept in her Bible as a girl and I'd duly tucked them into my Bible. This one was the only handwritten card and it had fallen out. I decided to look up the references which I'd never done before, despite having had the card for decades:

Ephesians Chapter 6 verse 11: *"Put on the whole armour of God, that ye may be able to stand against the wiles of the Devil."*

I'd only come across the 'whole armour of God' through Semele, yet here was the same reference in elegant copperplate script along with:

James Chapter 4 verse 7: *"Submit yourselves therefore to God. Resist the Devil and he will flee from you."*

Peter Chapter 5 verse 8: *"Be sober, be vigilant; because your adversary the devil as a roaring lion, walketh about, seeking whom he may devour."*

I was stunned that I'd found these three warnings about the devil just as Steve was in danger of being manipulated. A day later clearing out my coat pockets I found a scrap of till roll I'd scrawled on weeks ago whilst working in the shop, *"Checking authenticity – ask three times if the intention is pure."*

Light behind the Angels

I felt I was being guided with some urgency for myself, but more especially for Steve and I was relieved he'd refused the knowledge.

Soon afterwards I travelled with Semele to attend a Crystal Healing Conference held in Exeter. Entering the conference hall we claimed a couple of free seats in the middle of the rows and went off to get a cup of tea. On our return a woman was sitting in the next space along. I didn't really register her. When I'd sat down and got myself settled she turned her face to me and said, "Oh my goodness, for a moment there I could only see gold!"

I did a double take. I knew this lady! I'd met her on the same course when I'd met Fiona, my Arthurian lady-in-waiting. Her vision cleared and then she recognised me. She told me she'd also been guided to work through her Egyptian lifetimes and had been led to the colour rays. She felt that this work was important and she'd been trying to anchor the rays she'd been shown.

Over the weekend I gave Semele several short bouts of healing as she'd managed to crack a rib the previous week and it felt sore. Whilst I was working on her she saw the winged solar disk and felt that a new healing energy was coming through me. She was told that Sirius, the Dog Star was important for Steve and that I was connected to Orion.

The flurry of information and revelation slowed down. Normal life resumed and only occasional glimpses of the weird served to remind us of everything that had happened. It felt like developments were on their way, but there was a lull to allow for integration.

I wondered where things were going and so I sat down to channel more information and Steve acted as my scribe:

"Be not afraid, much of what we are trying to show you, you are blocking through fear. You need to use what is in your hands and you will find the power of it. You are still learning. Do not expect too much too soon, everything will come in its own time. Be at peace.

Purify your system, remove old blocks, as these prevent the ray from coming through properly. You will not be able to pass the ray onto others until you are ready and anchored. You'll be like a candle in a dark place.

Work with the image of the Dove. Meditate on the Dove. Bring the image down through your crown and into your heart. Just allow this light in and stop questioning so much, it is what it is.

You must rest. Repair your body and sleep more. We work with you when you are asleep. You are being schooled. You will move away from crystals to an extent. You will work with the coloured ray of light, no equipment. It will flow through your hands. The Gold Ray is for you. Reconnect your physical body to your Higher Self, reconnect to your Higher

Purpose. You will do more and more people will come to you for this reason. You will be a turning point for them, so that they can see their way. Be strong, there will be many requests. Protect yourself, not giving of yourself, but through yourself."

The comment on fear was pertinent. The scene of my Egyptian execution still haunted me and I knew that the energy of fear can be a powerful block. I dowsed myself an essence to help and came up with the Australian Bush Flower combination 'Meditation'.

Looking up the constituents in Ian White's guide I noticed that Green Spider Orchid is for the spiritual teacher who can then communicate beyond words alone. Reading on I found it also releases past life terror. How appropriate. I wrote down and worked with the accompanying affirmation,

'I now release all fears and terrors from my ancient past.'

Angelsword is another flower within the essence. In addition to its healing, clearing and protective qualities I read that it helps access skills from past lives. The combination felt exactly right.

I meditated and was shown a vision of myself as a series of Russian dolls. I was told I had been focussing upon the tiny one in the middle as my Self, when my true Self was made up of layer upon layer of other dimensional selves and was huge.

Steve dreamt that I was standing in a cave looking out into golden light and heard, "It is time for you to lead." In meditation he met Melchizedek and was taken to see the Blue sphere. He was allowed to dip his hands into blue light up to his wrists, which he described later as like touching a vertical pond. When he came back from his meditation he was still playing with the blue light in his hands, he could feel it there. He cupped the light in between his hands and was told, "You may keep it, or give it to her. Her need is greater." He was to offer me a choice whether I would accept the light into me. The blue light was to purge me. "You have far too much information and not enough knowledge, it will help the balance." I accepted the blue light and it was put into my back, forcibly knocked into the centre of my spine and then blown around with the breath.

"Spread it from North to South and East to West." Steve was given control of the energy and the ability to turn the volume up or down. I was guided to have more trust in my own knowledge and less in that coming from others. I was instructed to put my golden light into Steve's heart. It came in strongly that this exchange was part of the balancing. At this point Steve started to try and tell me what to do and how to do it and I surprised myself by telling him sternly, "Be quiet and let me do what I do best!"

Light behind the Angels

      I stood with my arms raised to the Heavens and visualised the Gold ray until it felt like golden light was overflowing from my hands, cascading over them. I held my hands briefly in a wing formation over his chest before I laid them on his heart. I felt my breathing deepen and I knew he had to allow the gold light to run through his heart and into his veins. My breathing was working like a bellows pushing more and more gold through his system. Finally I lifted one hand and placed it on his brow to unite his mind and his heart. Steve felt great heat and saw gold light behind his eyelids.

      It was time for him to drive back to Manchester and for me to fetch the kids from school. An hour into Steve's journey he pulled over and rang me leaving a message. He wanted to let me know that an amazing warmth was still spreading across his chest and his back. His message reminded me that the phrase 'The Blessing of the Rays' had floated into my mind as I'd driven off to do the school run.

      Since that time I see a neon blue light in my third eye when I meditate. I can't see the red of my eyelids, I see blue. The light seems to have an intricate texture, but I can't make the pattern out clearly.

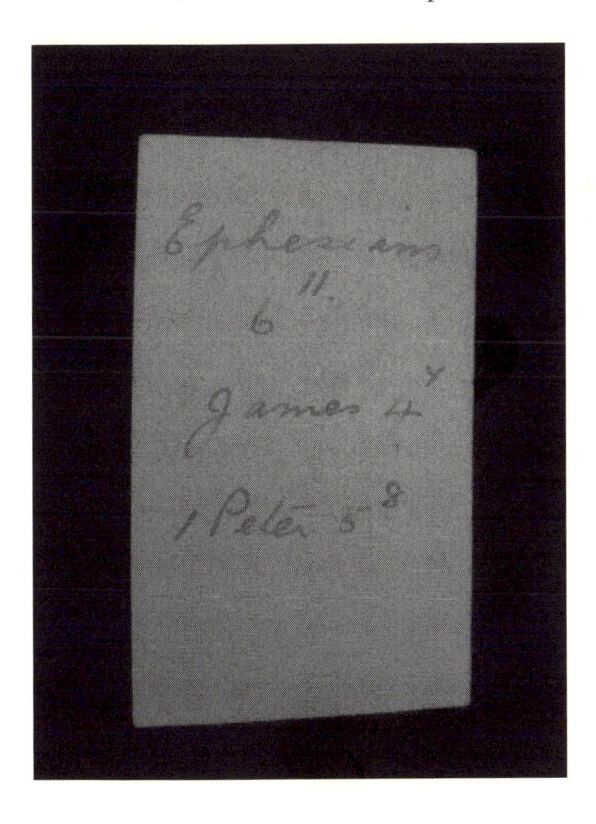

Spreading My Wings

'We must combine the toughness of the serpent and the softness of the dove, a tough mind and a tender heart.'
Martin Luther King

I had already worked with winged allies, having several different bird energies join me at various times. These days I have quite a flock! I love the feeling of flight and freedom that they share with me, literally being able to see things from a higher perspective.

I started to get guidance to use feathers in my healing too and first experimented with a beautiful owl feather. I found the feather could clear out the last 'wispy' fragments in the aura that remained after my crystals had broken up and cleared congested energies. 'Feathering down' the aura at the end of a session felt good to me and to my clients.

I knew now that my Egyptian name, Ankh-Ka-Dna translated as Life Soul Wing. Semele had seen the winged solar disk as I was healing her and Steve admitted that when he'd been researching my Egyptian name on the internet he'd found the winged solar disk and associated it as my symbol, but forgotten to mention it to me.

One day in March I walked into my healing room and did a double take as I caught sight of the window. There outlined in ethereal white was a pair of outstretched wings imprinted from the outside. I scanned the gutters and paths for a stunned bird, but I'm glad to say there was none. I'm sure a real bird did make the impression, but it felt like a sign, especially as it chose my healing room window. The outline remained for months until the window cleaner came and washed it off one day.

Leading an Angel Day for my students kick started more changes in my healing energies, drawing my attention to new techniques that I needed to explore. I taught the students to open their 'energetic wings'. We have these energy structures very like angel wings that are normally tucked away between our shoulder blades dormant. As the participants were all healers I was showing them how to use their new found wings in a healing situation. We were an odd number so I participated too.

How interesting! My wings were huge and now seemed to extend directly from my arms rather than my back. I needed to move my arms as if I was stretching and playing with them, enveloping my

Light behind the Angels

student in their energy. She was delighted with her healing and felt blissfully relaxed during it and afterwards.

When Steve arrived that evening I told him about the new development and how natural it all felt. I fancied another go and felt an occasion would turn up soon enough. I was right. I got my chance the very next day. He returned from a Shamanism course feeling awful. He'd been paired with someone practising healing with a rattle and 'rattled' was a very good description for how it left him feeling. It seemed she had shaken out black cloudlike energies from around his chest and head, but hadn't cleared them out of his aura.

Whilst outwardly showing concern for his discomfort, inwardly I thanked Spirit for giving me such a good opportunity to explore the power of my wings a little further. Whisking Steve up to the healing room I called in protection then stood behind his head with my arms outstretched. I found that by moving my arms gently backwards and forwards, up and down, the sensation of the wings increased and felt more tangible. My movements felt guided and natural. Meanwhile my 'patient' was experiencing a rather uncomfortable dredging sensation starting right down at his feet sifting through his body and up though the crown of his head.

The procedure lasted a quarter of an hour and when Steve got off the couch he looked visibly brighter and felt hugely lighter saying he felt, "As if I've had a complete oil and filter change," in characteristic motor mechanic's lingo. The dark cloud was truly gone.

The following Monday evening I went to my belly dance class. My teacher suddenly said, "Have you used Isis wings? Would you like me to bring some next time?" She'd never mentioned them before and a light bulb went on in my head. My wings weren't like angel wings they were attached to my arms like the wings depicted on the goddess Isis, right down to the golden colour as I saw them in my mind's eye. She brought the Isis wings in the next week. They were all silver apart from one gold pair. Guess who just had to play with those and order a pair to keep? They were tremendous fun!

The healing from my wings seems to work in conjunction with my Guides which doesn't surprise me and most people distinctly feel other hands on them even when I am working right out in the aura. Healings 'with my wings on' are quicker than normal, with people relaxing almost instantaneously. Even the talkative suddenly fall quiet and many drop off into a healing sleep within moments. They wake fifteen to twenty minutes later feeling incredibly relaxed. Various sensations have been reported by those who do manage to stay awake and the wings have been seen by the sensitive as metallic gold light. The treatment couch has also been felt to be gently swaying beneath them (it isn't wobbly in the least). This sensation is very common and although at first I was concerned it might be unpleasant as I get seasick myself, those that have felt it found the movement soothing, like being rocked in a mother's arms.

Light behind the Angels

Balancing the Male and the Female

*'You were born together and together you shall be forever more...but let there be spaces in your togetherness and let the winds of the heavens dance between you. Love one another, but make not a bond of love:
let it rather be a moving sea between the shores of your souls.'*
          Kahlil Gibran, The Prophet

Many messages and signs pointed to a need to balance the male and female aspects of ourselves on an individual level, and within our partnership. I felt this was happening on a Global level and the concept of male-female balance was being brought through to many people at once. I sense the rebalancing is ushering in the New Age and is very necessary after several millennia of male domination on Earth. Symbolically the balance was seen by us as a balancing of the power of the Sun with the power of the Moon.

The nine of wands from the Thoth tarot deck came up countless times. It is labelled Strength and the longest, sturdiest, central wand has a flaming sun at the top and a full moon overlaid with a crescent moon at the base. The interpretation of this card given by Ziegler is pertinent and clearly describes the process we'd been going through:

'Hidden unconscious powers (Moon) become visible through the radiant light of the conscious (Sun). Latent powers are awakened and can be applied towards a purpose. Recognising these unused potentials sets free more energies which are experienced as new and unusual... When the unconscious becomes visible we are faced with many things we have covered up in order to avoid looking at them. This can produce fear of some sort, the fear of feeling painful wounds we've covered up and hoped to forget... You will experience your energies as going far beyond the boundaries you thought existed. This is a key experience, the beginning of a far-reaching inner and outer unfolding of your potential.'
Gerd Ziegler, Tarot, Mirror of the Soul

We were being urged to draw down the Gold and Blue rays and combine them. At the beginning of April Steve woke from a dream in which he'd had a vision. In it we were both present. He was holding a blue crystal and I had a piece of golden heliodor in my hand. The sun shone through his crystal and the Moon shone through mine to blend the male and female rays together producing an Emerald ray.

I wondered whether this was a fragment of the original ceremony in which the rays were to have been blended in Ancient Egypt. I went into the healing room and brought out a few stones that were likely candidates for the blue one in his dream. We narrowed down his vision of the crystal used to an aquamarine. This was interesting as he'd been unaware that heliodor, aquamarine and emerald are all members of the Beryl family.

Steve sketched his vision of the rays blending as they were shown as angled together, forming a Y shape. I found it curious that the Moon shone through the golden crystal and the Sun through the blue one; you'd logically expect it to be the other way around. I wondered how that could ever be accomplished in 3D reality.

I purchased heliodor as I didn't have any and Steve bought himself an aquamarine as my pieces were very different sizes from the heliodor and it felt like we needed a 'new piece' for this work. I had a little emerald in my stock that hadn't been used in healing. Laying the pieces out we still weren't sure what needed to happen.

We didn't use the crystals until over a year later when we devised a ritual for the Summer Solstice in Crete, which was a variation on our earlier rituals together. We charged the stones in the light of the longest day at the centre of a sacred labyrinth, then at sunset we stood with the heliodor held in my right hand touching Steve's left palm and the aquamarine in Steve's right hand touching my left palm. The emerald was on the floor at our feet and we rotated Sunwise calling down the rays.

The work had been started, but we realised we had more to do together. Conditions in Egypt had been honed to perfection in preparation for the ceremony. We had prepared for it all of our lives and a monumental effort had been made by countless priests, priestesses and servants. In the twenty first century we must fall upon our own resources as a couple.

In late March we decided to go to Glastonbury for a day trip taking the dog with us. We just had an urge to go there, no big plans, I felt due for a visit and I fancied looking for a book I'd last seen there, 'The Keys of Enoch'. This was the tome that my own crystal therapy tutor used to talk about extensively and over the years I felt I really should take a look at it. It is hard to find and rather expensive.

Steve had been hand carving beautiful copper athames similar to the one he'd made me and he took some samples along to see if one of the magical shops would be interested in stocking them.

Light behind the Angels

Our journey was easy and the dog was so well behaved we almost forgot we had him sitting behind us. On arrival after letting him stretch his legs and have a drink we headed straight for an esoteric bookstore. Last time I'd been they hadn't had the Keys of Enoch in stock, this time there it was. I opened the white leather bound book with its beautiful gold embossed cover and knew I still wasn't ready to wade through the dense text. I felt I would buy it one day and since then I have done, but at that time I didn't want to spend money on a book that would just look at me accusingly from the shelf. Nevertheless as I stood there I had a fizzy feeling of expectancy in my solar plexus. Somewhere in this store was the right book for me, I knew it would give me more direction on my path and I asked to be guided to it.

Steve was still looking in the section with the Keys of Enoch and I walked through to the other side of the shop. A book on a display stand on the top shelf caught my eye, 'Handfasting'. I lifted it down and leafed through it. We'd talked about conducting Handfastings together before, but hadn't done anything about it. Steve had already performed several beautiful ceremonies for couples within his Manchester coven and I'd attended the last one he performed for his High Priestess and her partner. I loved watching him work; he has exceptional presence and just the right level of gravitas.

The Handfasting book was a slim practical guide to arranging a Handfasting ceremony, but I thought, "Steve probably knows all this stuff," and I popped it back up on its stand. I'd stepped about three paces away from the spot when Steve walked up behind me waggling the book, saying, "What do you reckon?" He must have seen me put the book back. I replied, "I didn't think you'd want it." He looked blank. I stepped back to point at the shelf where I'd got the book from. Lo and behold the copy was still sitting there. It transpired that Steve had spotted the exact same book on the bottom shelf in the other section at the same time I'd been looking at it. He'd thought, "I know most of this but it might be a handy reference for us," and decided to bring it through to show me. At the time we interpreted finding the book as a direction for our joint working. Nearly two years and several shocking revelations later, we realised it was also guidance about the importance of making a proper commitment to each other.

The Dark Just Got Darker

"Have you not thought how danger must surround power as shadow does light? This sorcery is not a game we play for pleasure or for praise. Think of this; that every word, every act of our Art is said and is done either for good or for evil. Before you speak or do, you must know the price that is to pay."
Ursula Le Guin, A Wizard of Earthsea

Late on Friday 9th May 2008 we were both woken by a tremendous thunderstorm. I got up to watch as I love the power of storms, I find them exciting and energising. This one seemed different though. The lightning was almost continuous and it was lighting up the whole of the Welsh hillside around the house like flickering floodlights in the sky.

Steve didn't lift his head from the pillow. He just said, "Has it turned midnight?" I looked and the clock was exactly at the witching hour. Without fully rousing himself he announced, "The dark just got darker and the fight just got harder."

He was ready to doze back off, but I was slightly rattled by that statement. The storm continued to rage and light up the room. He still wasn't fully awake, but I questioned him, just what did he mean by that?

"My job just got harder."

"And what *exactly* is your job?"

"Separating the Dark from the Light. Spiritual apartheid."

Now I was really getting wound up, such pomposity! "I thought you liked mixing it?"

"It's alright for me."

I gave up and let him drop back off to sleep. While I lay there pondering this strange exchange I received a message of my own about the chief of the fallen angels, Lucifer. "He will be the last one back in when every soul has returned," I had the distinct impression that the exiled angel had contracted to do the job he has been reviled for. "He has made the biggest sacrifice of any being." Since then I've come across another mention of Lucifer's role in Dolores Ashcroft-Nowicki's 'The Shining Paths' which concurred with my message, *"...then Lucifer bends the knee to the Grail, for in his way, he also serves, though man as yet does not understand his work."*

I received another message. We are 'pan dimensional' beings. I turned on the light and scribbled that phrase down in my journal before I dozed off. Reviewing my note in the morning made me smile

Light behind the Angels

as it reminded me of the 'pan-dimensional gargle blaster' from the Hitchhikers Guide to the Galaxy, a drink that literally blows your mind. I know that we are not beings pinned solely to the Earth plane. I am aware of multi-dimensional other selves that are operating on other planes of existence, on other planets and quite possibly other universes. Perhaps the challenge is for all aspects of the Self to become aware of and acknowledge the others? It is certainly a challenge to the Ego's notion of being 'top dog'.

The thunderstorm marked the start of another challenge to our relationship. Steve seemed to be hostile towards me and his demeanour was cold. He was touchy and fault finding in a way that just wasn't like him. I started to back away as it didn't feel safe to chat to him normally.

In the week Steve went on a shamanic journey to get better acquainted with his new spirit guide. When he came back he reported he'd been shown a modern house with red curtains that was being hidden by a pink mist. He said he'd been told it was hidden from him by someone he trusted. I didn't know what to make of this. I couldn't think of any modern houses that matched that description and nor could I think of anyone, apart from me, that Steve might trust. He doesn't readily place trust in others. He trusts himself.

Steve left the house and went for a drive. When he came back he announced, "I've found the house." I was mystified, but my confusion turned to shock and fear when he announced it was my old flame's place. Steve had used the address he'd been given in his dream the year before and gone round to take a look. It is a modern house and I'd forgotten there were red curtains at the windows. I hadn't been there for a long time and he was no longer in the forefront of my mind. It seemed unconsciously I was still shielding him. Now I felt I had good reason to have done so.

The discovery of the house and Steve's belligerent attitude sparked a fight. We sat across the kitchen table from each other trying to sort it out. As I looked at Steve my consciousness shifted. I found I was looking at a horrible angry male face overlying his. I hadn't expected this to happen and the face was full of malice. The shock jolted me out of my trance state, but I said, "You've got something or someone really dark with you at the moment."

Steve snarled back, "You are a clever little fucker aren't you?" and there was my proof. Steve and I may have a fiery relationship, but he has never, ever, stooped to name calling and he certainly would not sling such obscenities my way. Steve needed an exorcism. The words he'd heard coming from his own lips had shocked him.

I prepared my healing room with especial care, casting a protective circle, lighting quarter candles and calling in the Archangels of the quarters and all of my helper guides. Once again I donned 'The full armour of God'. All of my working tools were anointed with frankincense oil. I knew this was going to be a battle and this being was dangerous as it had taken over a good part of Steve's consciousness and was able to speak and act through him.

I lay Steve on the couch and began by working all over his body top to toe with my big gourd rattle. I wanted to loosen the hold these energies had on Steve's physical self. Next I took a large black obsidian massage wand and went over his body with it. Obsidian is a powerful ally against dark forces and despite applying minimal pressure Steve began to writhe in agony and claw at the couch. At his bellybutton the writhing was especially impressive as his stomach undulated in waves from side to side. It was reminiscent of the scene in the movie 'Alien' where the monster is about to burst out.

All went quiet, but I felt this beast was just hiding from me. During this bout Steve had visions of himself as his Dark & Light Gemini twins. He had an image of his twin selves sitting outside a taverna in a sunny square chatting. Suddenly they would jump up and have a fight, then sit back down and drink more wine together. From time to time the darker twin would grow larger. I felt an internal battle was raging for supremacy.

We had a break. I knew we weren't done but I needed to regroup my energy and Steve was physically hurting from the contortions his body had been put through. I had to be sure that Steve was prepared to let go of the dark energies that he'd been hosting. I wasn't convinced.

Back on the couch I dowsed for the exact position of these entities and found them lodged at the brow and solar plexus. We decided on a joint approach and combined our energies. I stood at Steve's head and we joined our left hands, each holding our athames in our right hands to direct at the chakras where the entities were attached.

I'm a believer in saying things as if you mean them, perhaps it is my Drama background, but the manner in which you say something can carry as much power as the words you say. Now I was into the role of exorcist and I forcefully declared, "In the name of the Light we cast out the demons from Steve. They cannot remain, they must go now!"

Steve's breathing changed, it became deeper and rasping; this was turning into a scene from a horror film. "You must leave now!" I demanded, "You will not return, you will leave and you will not return!" Steve's face became contorted with pain, then he suddenly

Light behind the Angels

relaxed, "That was not nice, I did not like that, I hope that's done." I didn't think so. "You just want to stab me again with your athame!" he quipped. That was more like the Steve I know and love, but I still felt something lurking. I dowsed that the brow was now clear but the beast in the solar plexus remained.

We rearranged our athames one on either side of Steve's solar plexus, working together in a pincer movement. The creature didn't like that. It shifted rapidly up through Steve's body and he coughed it up, painfully, choking, vomiting it up and out of him.

Afterwards Steve told me, "I felt a lot of pain. There was something coming up and out through my mouth. It exploded into bits and then that was it. There were odd thoughts going through my mind like, 'This girl's got guts!' You've done a great job. I just need to rest."

Steve went for a lie down and I journeyed to ask for a permanent guard to watch over me for the time being. On the evidence, times had indeed got more dangerous and I wanted some extra reassurance. I was given two new power animals, one of whom was a characterful vulture, plus two of my 'old faithfuls' turned up and said they'd always be there for me.

When I went back downstairs Steve asked me what I'd been given and a sixth sense told me not to divulge the information, even though we normally share everything. He reacted furiously and I knew my guidance had been right. Something was still using him. Steve ranted and raved, threatening to call it a day if I couldn't trust him. I explained I was following my guidance and he suddenly sank to the floor and started to bang his head against the cupboards crying and saying, "I don't know what to do." This kind of despair and helplessness was shocking to see in someone who always appears to be so strong. We had more work to do.

Back in the healing room Steve remembered a message he'd received months before which had puzzled us: "With your fire dagger pierce the heart of the double headed dragon." He'd since been looking for two headed dragons in pictures and on the internet. He had found a picture on the label of a bottle of Welsh beer, but that didn't make much sense. Now we understood the double headed dragon was within him and the fire dagger was my athame, hand carved for me from solid copper, with colours like flame.

Now I took my 'fire dagger' and held its point at Steve's heart. Again he contorted in agony, describing the sensation as 'fiery acid burning at my heart'. Next the point had to be held to the back of his heart and then at specific points along his spine. Each touch brought more writhing and pain, although physically I wasn't pressing the point in at all. If the placement of my athame was correct he felt excruciating pain, if I was slightly out nothing happened.

Over the course of the exorcism the pillows went flying off the couch as Steve writhed and arched his back. Finally I had to return to the original point at his heart. This time to my psychic sight it appeared that the dagger went into his body and thick black blood welled up around it. I had to keep the blade in place until all the blood had drained away. Then I had a picture of a new heart with white wings which flew in front of my face. I breathed it down through the athame blade and into Steve's body. He reported it felt cool, like fairy dust going in and finally all was calm.

Light behind the Angels

The Scavengers

'Adoration to the light of God in nature, where it rises on the horizon in the eastern side of heaven...Homage to you, the principle of light, in his rising and setting...You sail across the sky and cause the existence of everyone who looks at you.'
The Egyptian Book of the Dead, translation Dr Ramses Seleem

The very next day brought me confirmation of my new allies. Walking to school with my son we caught up with the bin men doing their rounds. Written in large black letters on the rubbish truck was its name, 'Vulture'. I'd never noticed it before. I was pleased with this as I get a lot of confirmation from lorries. It is a quirky way of my guides getting my attention that they know I'll enjoy.

On the walk back from the school it was raining. Steve caught up with me and gave me a lift home in the car. I was just about to tell him of the Vulture when he said, "Oh look!" and pointed at the mudflaps on the lorry ahead of us. They bore a picture of a scarab beetle with the word SCARAB written below.

I'd already been pondering the possible Egyptian connection through my vulture. Maat was the Egyptian goddess who weighed the human heart at death against a feather. If the heart was lighter than the feather the soul could go on to the Afterlife, if it was heavy with guilt it could not. The feather of Maat belonged to a vulture. Seeing the Scarab felt like a confirmation that my new guides were Egyptian in origin.

When we got back we cleansed the house from top to bottom as we'd both been too exhausted by the drama of the previous day to do it then. We'd felt the energy was at best 'off kilter'. By the end of the cleansing I was aware of an unpleasant energy sitting right in the small of my back. Back in the healing room Steve drew the energy from me, up through his athame and into his arm, "Like filling a syringe with poison." He'd tied energetic tourniquets as before and expected to be able to drain the toxins off afterwards.

I had a meeting to prepare for so I jumped off the couch feeling very much better thank you. I left Steve to read upstairs. When I returned a bit later he reported that he felt like his arm had been poisoned. I touched it, physically it felt chilled and he sensed the venom had crept up past the tourniquet he'd set below his elbow. Steve felt that his whole arm was withering and that the poison was heading for his heart. If it reached his heart he knew it would kill him. He took his athame and physically scored the skin all the way from his shoulder to his wrist to release the venom. He'd asked me to do that for him but I couldn't bring myself to press hard enough to break the skin.

Later, when I had time to reflect, I remembered that the morning after the storm I'd woken with a sharp pain between my shoulder blades and Steve had psychically seen a rattlesnake hanging there by its fangs. He told me his new guide had unceremoniously, "Twonked it over the head with a lump of wood," and it had fallen off. I had briefly wondered about getting its venom out of me, but then it was time to get up and go about my daily chores. As I felt none the worse for the experience I'd forgotten all about it.

I realise now that my lifetime as a Minoan temple priestess left me energetically immune to snake venom. I have an affinity for snakes and love the two serpents that twine up my caduceus tattoo. However snakes are not Steve's medicine and so a snakebite that had been a mild sensation for me was life threatening for him.

My meeting was an event planning session with Semele. The unfolding of the latest drama could all be dated from the thunderstorm and I wondered if it was 'just us' or whether others had been affected too. Semele replied that she had woken with a cold left shoulder blade the morning after the storm and her arm had got progressively colder all week. Touching her left arm it really was like ice and felt totally different to the right. We went back up to the healing room and I removed an entity with a pincer movement of the black obsidian wand and my athame. It was rather like squeezing out a splinter. As soon as it was 'visible' on the surface I saw my new friend the vulture swoop down on it and gobble it up with apparent relish. Warmth instantly flooded back down the arm much to Semele's relief.

That night at belly dance another healer friend started to tell me about a scary change that had come over her partner. He'd woken the morning after the storm, "Like a devil," to use her words. He'd been threatening her and loomed over her aggressively. This behaviour was completely out of character. Fortunately he'd been working away from home, so she'd had a break from it, but they hadn't spoken all week, when normally they'd talk daily. Her experience was all too similar to ours and everything seemed to point back to the storm.

I journeyed to meet with my guides and I asked about the snake attack. It seemed strange to be attacked by a creature for which I have such respect. Steve wanted to know where the snake had come from, who'd thrown it and why it hurt him, but not me. I took myself off to the Upper World and my new vulture friend flew with me. I was met by an Egyptian male guide who told me his name was Amun Ra. Although he treated me as an equal I found myself curtsying humbly to him. He took my hand and we walked as we talked.

Light behind the Angels

Amun Ra appeared to be quite a young man, clean shaven and rather handsome. I looked down at myself and found I had a golden dress on, very long and flowing and my appearance seemed younger and more Egyptian. I asked him for a sign by which I might know him and he showed me a scarab beetle. He told me I could use the scavengers now, the scarab would come in to remove unwanted material and the vulture would eat it up.

He didn't tell me where the snake had been sent from, but said I was not affected because I carry the symbol of the snakes. He warned me we could expect more things to be thrown at us as we were now burning more brightly, but he was very calm in his pronouncement as if it wouldn't really matter and I shouldn't worry about it. He said I was the Phoenix, and at that time I took it as a metaphor for rebirth.

Afterwards I reflected on my journey. I felt I'd heard the name of my guide before. I knew Ra was the Egyptian Sun god and wondered if Amun Ra was the name of a pharaoh who'd taken the god's name as part of his own? Looking it up I found that Amun Ra was one of the names of the Creator. No wonder I'd been moved to curtsey!

I love my scavengers. They get a bad press but I have utmost respect for them and the work they do. Without their assistance there would be much more disease and contagion spread from rotting corpses. They are Mother Nature's sanitation team.

Next day I felt moved to dig out an old journal and find a transcript of a psychic reading I'd had three years before. At the time most of that reading hadn't made much sense to me, it seemed too farfetched and fanciful. Now I had more respect for her perceptions. She'd been the one to foresee Steve's arrival 'on a distant path'. Now I revisited the psychic's words. I found she'd spoken of an Egyptian guide around me, *"I'm seeing a scarab being brought in like a token being offered by one of your helper guides. A male Egyptian with a gold band around his head. It is a gift and has a message in it for you."*

More corroboration came in a healing soon after. As I carried out the treatment my client saw a black dot at her third eye. She watched as a shining beetle appeared behind it, pushed the blob out and carried it away, then another blob emerged carried by another beetle and then another. The scarabs carried the blobs away from her in many different directions. I was reminded that the scarab beetle rolls dung along between its legs in nature and the Egyptians revered it, believing it pushing the Sun across the sky. My client felt these beetles were helping her release toxic thoughts and wasn't in the least perturbed by her vision.

Back in the Celtic shop I decided to have a little splurge. Now and then I'd spend my shop morning wages on a treat just for me. I'd been eyeing up Jamie Sams' Medicine Cards for ages. They are quite pricey, but they were calling to me and occasionally in the past I had carefully opened the outer box and read what the book had to say about my various animal helpers. When I got the cards home I asked which animal ally was working most closely with me at the moment. I spread the cards, chose, and picked Turkey, hearing a little voice in my head say 'vulture'. I read the description of Turkey, feeling that this didn't fit and then it dawned on me that there is a species of vulture called the 'turkey vulture'. As there was no vulture in the Medicine Cards pulling the Turkey card was the best way of getting the message through to me.

Soon after I received a copy of Ted Andrews' wonderful book 'Animal Speak' for review. I looked up my vulture. Andrews gives a very positive press for this bird that is often viewed negatively. The detail that most moved me however was the Latin name for the turkey vulture. It is called *cathartes aura,* which Andrews translates as the 'golden purifier' and which I interpreted as 'catharsis of the aura'. Could there be a more perfect ally for deeply transformative healing work?

Perhaps I don't have the most glamorous power animals, but I adore my ugly-beautiful helpers.

Light behind the Angels

Medusa

'Most of your experiences are unconscious. The conscious ones are very few. You are unaware of the fact because to you only the conscious ones count. Become aware of the unconscious.'
Sri Nisargadatta

Soon after the thunderstorm we took my crystal stall to a Mind, Body, Spirit fair. Although I didn't feel all that bad considering the drama we'd been through I felt compelled to book a healing with Estelle. Estelle is an intuitive healer who describes herself as a medicine woman. We'd both had a healing with her at a show the previous summer and had been impressed by her abilities.

As soon as I sat down she said, "I can see Medusa around you. Snakes, lots of snakes. Not good, this is heavy. You are being cursed." I was shocked, because I hadn't felt all that bad for a few days. I thought we'd dealt with the trouble. I told her briefly about the attacks we'd experienced since the storm. She replied, "Yes, I could see it on Steve first thing this morning."

Estelle sensed the curse was set up several lifetimes ago and that five people clustered around me now had initiated it back then. My guides were frustrated as they'd warned me about one of these people repeatedly over the last year, but I try to see the best in people and I tend to overlook the worst. I had realised this friend had a lot of anger in her and she left me feeling agitated, but I hadn't severed the connection. She was present with her own stall at the fair.

Estelle warned me, "You must be careful and suspicious of everyone right now. Call on St Germaine, the violet flame and Merlin's energy to protect you." She explained the snakes got through to me easily because I see them as healing allies and so I wasn't guarded against them.

Estelle hugged me and whispered, "We have to stay strong for others, be the rock, but sometimes we need help too Sister. They want to split you two up, but love is stronger. Connect at your hearts. You are stronger together."

As we hugged we were interrupted by the very friend I'd been warned about. She grabbed my hand and wouldn't let go, saying she was concerned about me and was 'giving me healing energy'. It was an urgent, though perhaps unconscious attempt to plug straight back into my energy field, as Estelle had just disconnected the cords. For the rest of the show this friend hovered at my elbow, shadowing me, pumping me for information about my healing. I couldn't have had a clearer sign that she was one of the five.

When I got back to my stall from the healing I could see Steve was seething with anger. I ignored it. I knew it wasn't him, just dark energy talking. I sent him straight to Estelle, and he went off grumbling that he didn't need any healing. She quickly rebalanced him and brought his sunny self back to the fore.

Back home I pulled cards from the Sacred Circle tarot to see whether I could work out who the five were. The first card I pulled was the Web, confirmation that everything was interconnected. The Page of Swords came next, labelled Thought. This card startled me. His face was the image of my ex husband, I couldn't believe I hadn't noticed this before. He is often deep in thought and so his personality also fitted the portrait. Two of the energies had now been identified. I couldn't fathom the other cards, although there were several snakes in the illustrations.

I wondered whether my vulture could be called upon to eat up the troublesome serpents. Steve recalled a legend of an eagle eating a snake and went online to research it. He found a legend of the Snake and the Eagle from Albania. I sometimes work with Eagle energy so this seemed a promising lead. Again my guides were hot on the trail with instant confirmation. I walked from the office into the lounge and found my daughter watching the Eurovision Song Contest. I sat down to watch five minutes of pulp television with her. Within a few minutes Albania were on and the Albanian flag with its double headed eagle was filling the screen. Not too subtle!

We wondered whether there was an astrological angle to the events. There had been two full moons falling in Scorpio. I started leafing through astrology books and came across a passage on Medusa. She was believed to be linked to a malefic star, Caput Algol, believed to be evil by many ancient cultures. I hadn't heard of evil stars before.

The next morning my daughter sat down to breakfast and completely out of the blue announced, "Did you know that people believed the stars ruled their lives and that influenza is called that because it means under the influence of a malignant star?" She'd been reading 'Horrible Histories'. That settled it; we were on the right track.

I mused over Medusa. This fierce goddess had never worried me before. I remembered that Carmel, the friend who'd introduced us to each other, came to my 40th birthday fancy dress party as Medusa with her head covered in rubber snakes. At the Faerie weekend with John and Caitlin Matthews I'd been shown serpent energies several times, but they hadn't been threatening. Caitlin had led a guided meditation for us to each receive a protective symbol from Faerie for

Light behind the Angels

our homes and I'd actually been given a design of snake's heads radiating out. We'd been asked to incise clay disks with our designs. Unfortunately when they were dried they'd all gone into a basket and been picked out at random by the participants in the final ceremony. It meant I didn't have my own disk, all I had was a rough sketch in my notebook, by which I'd written a note: 'Snakes again, Medusa?' It had been a well intentioned exercise, but reflecting on my experience I feel if you are given a symbol for personal protection you should be encouraged to keep and use it, not give it away! If I had done I may have been saved a lot of grief.

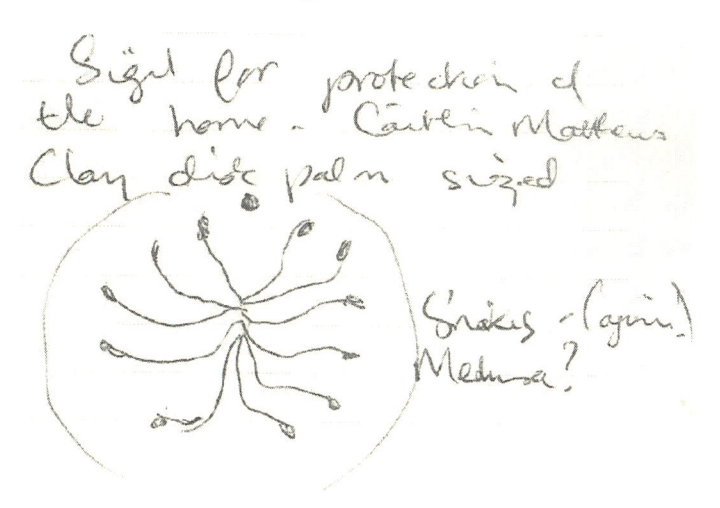

Sigil for protection of the home - Caitlin Matthews
Clay disc palm sized
Snakes (again) Medusa?

At that time my son had an enthusiasm for Yu-Gi-Oh, a Japanese cartoon that had spawned collectible cards to duel with. He'd spent plenty of his pocket money on these, but now he'd found a site on the net that allowed him to create his own cards, a move I heartily approved of. He was using photos from our computer, setting them into Yu-Gi-Oh card backgrounds, naming them and assigning his creations their fighting strengths and special powers. He was utterly absorbed.

From time to time he'd present me with his latest card. He'd already transformed me and the dog into Yu-Gi-Oh warriors, though slightly wimpy ones. Now he brought his newest creation to show me. The picture was of a statue of Owain Glyndwr, the last Welsh Prince, mounted on his horse in full battle armour. My son had entitled the card the 'Iron Defender'. He'd given it maximum strength and typed, 'Can't be distrod by dragon types' beneath. His spelling needed a little work, but the meaning was clear enough, 'destroyed'.

What my son hadn't known was that Steve had modelled for the statue. He'd been asked to pose for the sculptor more than a year before to help him get the musculature right and had spent a memorable hour standing naked, propped as if leaning forward on horseback. The sculpture stands in Corwen and our friends had sent us some photos as Steve had never been to see the finished work. At this time of strife my son had created a card of Steve armed and battle ready, sword in hand and named him The Iron Defender. That had to be reassuring!

[IRON DEFENDER card image]
[IORN / FUSION / EFFECT]
distorer golem/blue eys wight dragon. can't be distrod by dragon type's
ATK / 0 DEF / 3000

Light behind the Angels

Open the Door and the Light Comes Flooding In

'Oh God give me strength to be victorious over myself, for nothing may chain me to this life. O guide my spirit, O raise me from these dark depths, that my soul, transported through your wisdom, may fearlessly struggle upward in fiery flight.'
Ludwig van Beethoven

The healing Estelle had given me at the Mind, Body, Spirit fair confirmed Steve's psychic perception that snakes were attacking me. It was remarkable to get such a clear corroboration and a great relief. Saying, "I'm being attacked by snakes that have penetrated my aura," sounds utterly crazy and would take most healers well out of their depth. We booked to see Estelle in her own healing space in South Wales the following Sunday.

The intervening week was really difficult. We felt we were being pitted against each other as if something, or someone, was trying to split us up. There was so much unreasonable anger in the air and we were always just a hair's breadth from falling out. We had to remind ourselves that this was coming from an external source. To preserve the peace we tried to keep out of each other's way.

Steve was fully occupied painting the outside of the house. We'd hired scaffolding and normally he doesn't mind heights. This week however climbing a ladder lashed securely to the scaffolding platform was making him quake inside. Determinedly he finished the job, but I could see the relief pouring off him when it was over.

Sunday finally came and the journey to Estelle's was nightmarish. The sky was a leaden grey and it was raining heavily. The directions I'd printed from the internet sent us along a tortuous twisting route. We followed Welsh roads that wound up and down the hills and valleys, trailing us through desolate mining towns whose main streets felt dour and oppressive.

As I drove my stomach was in knots and a part of me was begging to turn the car and head for home. We'd left the house in plenty of time, but we were making poor progress and ran late. Even when we got to the village we couldn't find our destination. Feeling fraught we were guided in over the telephone and arrived at last to be met by this diminutive woman of phenomenal power.

Estelle sent Steve off to read magazines in the kitchen and began her healing with me. She'd already meditated on our problem before we'd arrived and picked up some very strange information.

"Those who are connected to higher vibrational energies are being stopped. There's a barrier closing you off from receiving and sending transmissions to make you invisible to those higher energies. Poison arrows are being fired and you are getting hit left, right and centre, so it's not surprising you are in such a fearful state. It's not just coming from this lifetime, it's coming from a previous lifetime."

That sounded spot on. I was certainly full of fear and I couldn't see what I could have done to attract all of this malevolence. Estelle warned me that the people sending the energies were so close to me that I'd have problems acknowledging them as my attackers. I knew one was the healer friend and another was my ex husband, that much was clear, however there were three others whom I hadn't even suspected.

I stopped for a moment to think. Something made me say, "Semele is one of my best friends, if it was her my world would turn upside down. She is one of my best friends and she is light, but you are giving me that knowing look..." I trailed off.

Estelle was gazing levelly at me. She explained, "It is about the recognition of each other's energies and the honour and respect you must have. One grows and moves forward, the other grows and moves forward. You will know straight away that we are right because you will have a contact from these people to try to get back into your energy field as soon as we disconnect them. Whether they are close friends or close family you have to disconnect from the emotional energy."

Estelle brought me back to Semele, "Why did she come up in your thought processes?"

"It's hard to know because she's lovely. If I had to be bothered about anyone attacking me it would be her, because we are close. I know we've had past lives together."

"At any stage do you feel disempowered when you are around Semele? Not by her actions, just in her energy?"

Now Semele has the appearance of a faery queen. She is slight, graceful, sings and dances beautifully. Next to her I have sometimes felt like the 'ugly sister' because I am heavier and lack her elegance. I admitted all this to Estelle, rather shamefaced about the childish nature of my feelings.

"This is important. It is a crack in your energy, a weakness within your being, a weakness within your self portrait on the physical plane. The physical is where the attacking energies can come in. It is a

Light behind the Angels

weakness that cracks your auric field and allows darkness in. I don't think you see the beauty within yourself though. In this lifetime those that have a bit more energy within them are holding it in their weight. You need that. You can hold the energy more easily."

Estelle was adamant, "You are very powerful, very centred, very grounded, however you are getting knocked by what you feel are silly little things and they add up."

A spasm of fear ran through me. I'd already had one of my worst fears realised, my best friend's energy was attacking my own, I wasn't sure I could cope with another revelation on that scale. I admitted my fear, "Steve is my rock, please don't let it be him." I just didn't know who I could depend on anymore.

Estelle reassured me, "You guys are meant to be together. Steve can go into the darkness but he goes in to bring it into the light. He's one of those keys. The people working in this energy will not want him to be with someone like you. You are the lock and he is the key, does that make sense? Together you are opening the door and the light comes flooding in."

"Imagine we have a cauldron and it has energy in it from their past lives. This energy was created several lifetimes ago. You've reached a level now that has set it off. It has been like sparks lighting under the cauldron; one spark goes off, another spark goes off, you don't notice too much, but when the fifth spark ignited it was like an inferno. These people all have powerful connections with you. Steve's been the host for the energy that is attacking."

That explained my fear. He wasn't the perpetrator of the attack, but he was carrying the energy of it. The past few weeks had been horrible, like living with a different person. It had been hard to stay with him and I'd been walking on eggshells to avoid argument.

"Disempower you and you disempower both of you. It's because of his journeys in the Underworld that he's picked this energy up, but ultimately it's for you, for the work you've got to do as a couple. The energies are rapidly moving. You need to attach to the higher vibrations. You have worked with high vibrations many times before; you need to connect with that again. Keep telling yourself, 'I need to remember.'"

"I'm seeing a couple, a South Londoner, dark haired. The female is the butterfly. She is the energy pulling you in and he is the one that's causing you grief. It is hard for me to point these out because they will be close to you."

I realised later that she was describing my father and mother. Sometimes the people that affect us are so close we really can't see it.

"When you are a Lightworker in many ways it is a lonely path, but a true path. It is unconditional in every aspect. Disconnect from the emotion and see the energy. Things become much clearer for you when you aren't attached emotionally."

"You have to realise that the dark energy surrounding you is witchcraft. This past life energy is keeping you suppressed. Whenever you get to a certain vibrational level these five energies kick in to keep you from progressing further. In some lifetimes you've been happy to remain at that level; however you now know there's more because you've been back and seen it for yourself."

I believe Estelle was picking up on our Egyptian lives at this point. I'd had a reminder of the level of power I could attain when we'd revisited those lives.

"You chose this lifetime to remember and to declare, 'I'm not going to be stopped at this level anymore.' If only you could see the work you are going to do you wouldn't be worried about who or what you are attached to. You will do your work together. Sometimes he will go off here and you will go off there, but then you'll meet again. When you get to the frequency you will be working at it won't be an issue for you.

"Once you feel disempowered by anybody, however close, you must cut the connection, if only for a short time. Disconnect the power until you have re-empowered yourself and are no longer affected. The truest Lightworker is not affected by anything because they know that they are coming from love and light."

"The more you disconnect, the more you regain your own energies. They will always try to reconnect. It's not to say you can't have a connection with people, but it is recognising how far they can go. There is a boundary they can't step over, no matter how good they are, or how light they are. We all have a dark side."

"Whether it is done consciously or subconsciously a person of your truth, a person on your path, will have to have someone close to them to test them, otherwise you wouldn't learn the lesson, you'd just shake it off. When other people have tested you it didn't affect you because they weren't connected into your heart energy. These ones all are. They are so close you have to listen."

"We have to look at the root of the problem: you are a lightbeing. You can't truly see your path at the moment because it is being blocked. There is something within you as a healer, as a reader, as a clairvoyant, as a medium, that you no longer see your path, you don't feel empowered enough to do this path. In the past you have been disempowered and so you feel that you are not good enough. But there is a higher consciousness within you that knows there is more."

Light behind the Angels

"You have chosen to break the cycle this lifetime because you know that you can do it. You are reminded every day that you can do it. Your soul has made sure that you haven't forgotten, and your spirit needs to be enlightened again. You need to take flight on your own and soar like an eagle, because you know you can. The fire under the cauldron has gone out."

As we sat and Estelle talked it through I could feel the energy shifting within me. Suddenly I was feeling much better, much more like my normal self.

"Reclaim your energy now with conviction. Declare, 'I am connecting with Source.' Connect to the highest vibration. You are only reaching a certain level with Archangels and Ascended Masters. You are dealing with Outer Space stuff, right out there. The Ascended Masters are stepping aside and evolving and in that evolution we need to protect from the heart out.

"Attach to the energy at your heart, a golden white light, Divine Source energy within one's self. Attach to that energy; see it as a star of energy at the core of your heart. Work it through your heart chakra, forwards, backwards, expand it out through your whole being and let it run through you as if you have turned the light on. Take it from your physical and expand it out through your space, make sure you have boundaries where it stops, so that people know when they are stepping into and out of your space. When you've done this nothing can follow in because you are reflecting Light out. When you put your barriers on the outside they can be breached, angels are good but they are not high enough for the energies that you need to work with."

"They are saying there is dead energy in your hair. You are going to get a haircut. Not all of it, but a large trim. There is power in the hair. Trim it back in order to strengthen it. Medusa. The snakes and hair. The energy of the snake woman that you are."

Estelle's mention of Medusa startled me again. Sometimes I'd even felt like my hair was writhing, alive like snakes. Becoming a snake woman sounded like aligning myself with her malicious energy and yet I loved serpent energies. A paradox.

Estelle picked up on my discomfort. "There is a Medusa in Light energy. I can see her quite light in her grey silvery colour, she's the opposite. Whatever there is in the Dark, there is a reflection in the Light, and whatever is in the Light has a reflection in the Dark. You are bringing through the new."

A Magical Child

*'When you finally, completely face fear itself, it is nowhere to be found.
Fear can never survive total meeting with consciousness.'*
Gangaji

Estelle began to see the past life where the curse energies were set up, "The year is 1620. As a young girl you were hiding in bundles of hay at the side of a building in a little village. You have a brown bonnet with white cotton underneath, Celtic I'm told. You used to watch soldiers come riding through. You saw your mother raped. They were looking for you and you hid. It was difficult for you."

"You lived in your imagination. I can see you cutting the apple in half so you could see the star inside and I can see you playing with chimes and ribbons. You were only little but there was so much magic in you, you'd kept it with you. There was an old woman that used to teach the old ways. You are being reminded of the old ways now. This child knew the magic and you used to create this magic from the Outer World. You were very feared, but you didn't fear it. You were born way ahead of your time."

"The old woman knew this and took you in as her grandchild. Be reminded of the magic you used to create because you are going to create it again. The other children feared you and they went and spoke to the village witch of dark powers. They weren't little children, they were teenagers."

" I'm being shown the story of the witch with the apple: Snow White. This witch didn't have a disguise, she used the children instead. She used them as a way of getting to you. Five children, they are the ones that the attack is coming through now. She was your sister, your friend, the white one; she was your sister in that lifetime; Semele. You looked up to her as a mother, she was 15, but she feared you. This witch draws on fear; she's the one that makes you feel fear now."

"She's just spoken, 'Services due now paid up, services rendered, blessed be'. You've been released. You are a Lightworker and you've chosen your path. You have been at a crossroads. Had you realised you could have surrendered your powers? You had a choice. These energies have done you justice in many ways to say, 'Are you going to keep on and disconnect from us, or are you stopping right now?' You've decided to continue."

Light behind the Angels

I remembered a dream I'd had before all this had happened. I'd been on a small flat boat, raft-like, travelling through steamy green swamps, with a Voodoo priest guiding me. We came to a place where the waters divided, on the left the way looked clear, but I knew I had to choose the path on the right that had long black snakes hanging down over the entrance. I made my choice and was not afraid to pass.

My dream made sense now. I could confront the dark energies in my path and go past them, or turn away and take an easier path. I had made my choice in the dreamscape and so it had materialised in the waking world.

The healing was over. I felt much better and the sense of relief was immense. Estelle channelled a final message from one of my guides: "Remember who it is you are, not only in this lifetime, but many lifetimes. Shift what is no longer needed for your highest good and move forwards now."

Steve entered the healing room and had the 'wicked witch' energy released from his system. The five had reactivated her curse and summoned her without any of the protagonists being consciously aware of it. Estelle had a warning for Steve that we should both have kept more clearly in mind as it turned out to be prophetic, "You will have other energies trying to separate you because you are strong pillars within your lightbeings. In this lifetime you two have asked to work together to form the energy that is coming through at the moment. You are working directly with star energies, hence it is so potent."

"A man of your calibre has the ability to disconnect quickly from the emotions when you know that they are detrimental to yourself. They could be your best mate, they could be your father, mother, but because of what has been created within you, you are able to disconnect with that straight away. You know if it isn't good for your being and your spiritual growth. Lauren has a bit of an issue with that because loyalty from friendships and family is very important to her. Now she should be able to see, 'I am a soul leading my life through this vehicle and that's another soul teaching me a lesson.'"

"Although it frustrates you that she can't see straight through it as you do there's a reason for it, to have empathy. She's teaching you to soften and lighten up and have some feelings and emotions. These beings are trying to communicate with you through love and emotions. She's teaching you so that you will accept some of the information they give you. That's where your challenge is."

"There's jealousy of the spiritual growth that you two have. Remember that you have a strong relationship and people are envious of that; whatever you go through you are still there for each other."

"Now the energy has surrendered and released itself from Lauren and it is doing the same to you. You could have told me who the five energies were, I know that you've got answers for her, but she's got emotions for you, so there's a balance."

Estelle completed Steve's healing and the energy between us felt completely transformed. The outside world mirrored the change. Our return journey was plain sailing. The weather had cleared up, our moods had lightened and the new route we chose was an absolute breeze.

The next morning we both woke feeling so much better thank goodness. I was teaching and I needed to be back on form. As I sat drinking my coffee in bed a word popped into my head and I commented to Steve, "It's the Arcturians." The word seemed to come from nowhere, I hadn't been thinking of anything at the time.

We got up and started tidying the lounge ready for the students. Steve bent down and picked up a scrap of paper from the floor. It was a snippet from our pile of collage scraps which we'd cut out to create a vision board of our dream home together. This piece was a photograph of a large crystal point. I was about to throw it into the waste paper basket when I flipped it over. There on the back, picked out in bold, was written **Arcturians**. Now we had a name for the off planet beings that were trying to work with us.

Later the same morning I had a text from Semele: *Hi Lauren. Dreamed about being attacked and cursed by a witch last night and dog was going mad. Can you let me know if you sense anything around me? Thanks!*

Wow! I was impressed by her clairvoyance, though slightly unnerved that the witch had gone after her. It was the proof I needed that Semele was really involved as I hadn't wanted to believe it. I texted that she needed to contact Estelle, whom she knew well enough, mindful of the warning to stay disconnected despite my desire to help.

When I next saw Semele she told me more about her nightmare. She'd dreamt that she'd walked into her office at home and found the witch hunting though her things. When she ordered her out the witch had sent energy shooting at her through her fingers and Semele had responded with lightning like energies from hers. They'd had a sizzling lightning battle and Semele won, sending her packing. She wasn't troubled again and I was able to tell her what had really gone on.

There were no other members of the infamous five that I felt would want to hear their part in the story at the time, however I soon had more visual proof that my ex husband had been one of the five. Standing in his living room I spotted a new painting hanging on the wall. It was a strange sunset. Light emerged from the Sun coiled out in

Light behind the Angels

the shape of a fat orange snake. Expressing an interest he told me that as he'd watched the setting Sun one evening it had seemed to him that a snakelike stream of light had formed. The image had been so striking he'd been moved to paint it.

Medusa in the Light

'Do you know magic? Can you utter the name of your soul and bring yourself back to light? Can you speak your destiny, create life for yourself from yourself, as Temu created Ra? From the light of your works do you know who you are?'
Normandi Ellis, Awakening Osiris:
A New Translation of the Egyptian Book of the Dead

Steve had presented me with a snake staff the year before. He'd actually started carving it before we'd even met, not really knowing why he was making a staff and without a notion of who it was for. He'd finished it during the first summer we were together and it is a magnificent piece, almost as tall as me, with a fat snake winding all the way up from its tail at the base to its head at the top where Steve set a quartz crystal point. I'd been very pleased with it and thought it was a beautiful item, a true staff of Asclepius, but I'd never worked with a staff, so I didn't know what to do with it.

Now Estelle had released the dark snake energies from me I was keen to reclaim my snake power and my snake staff seemed the obvious way to do it. I had the urge to stand on the hilltops and proclaim my right to be fully in my power. There are wonderful hills only a short drive away and so Steve and I went late one afternoon. I knew which one I had to climb, not the gentle slope Steve had been hoping for, just five minutes from where we park the car; I needed to get to the top of a craggy hill with a large hill fort on it. I'd been there once before and it's a fair trek from the road through marshy ground and then a good half hour's steady climb to the fort. I doggedly stuck to my guns despite Steve's protests that this nice hill here would do, and we struck out for the fort. The staff came into its own, helping me with the climb.

Once up there I think Steve realised why I'd been so determined. It is a magnificently wild place, higher up than the surrounding hills, with panoramic views all the way around. You could see why the ancients chose this place to build their fortifications; enemies would be seen from miles off. For a few moments I felt a little shy about what I was going to do. I was there to demand the full return of my power from the gods.

Light behind the Angels

I stood with my staff held out before me and faced East. I was calling my powers back from the Eastern winds. Once I'd started the light breeze that had been toying with my hair began to pick up and became a wind carrying my voice away. I found I was shouting into it, meaning every word. I stood arms open to accept the energy that was being returned to me and waited until the process felt complete. I moved to the South and demanded the return of my power from the South winds. The wind was whipping my hair around me now, getting stronger. Again I waited until the return of my energies felt complete and I strode to face the West and repeated my demands.

With each turn the wind became stronger. It felt as if I was truly invoking the wind that raged around me. Finally I turned to the North and completed the reclamation of my power from the North wind. The gale was tremendous by now and utterly exhilarating. I was empowered and the snake staff felt alive in my hands. The air was full of energy and it was being channelled into me through the staff.

Ceremony complete, we picked our way down the hill in the gathering dusk and returned home. Later I reflected on the significance of turning to each of the directions and calling upon the winds for the return of my power. In Egypt I'd been quartered, burned and my ashes scattered to the four winds. Intuitively I had called to the winds of the cardinal directions to return what I had lost.

The ceremony had been an important part of re-member-ing myself. Having reclaimed my energy I decided to take Estelle's advice and get a haircut. Normally I'll just have a small trim once a year to keep the spilt ends under control, but I'd stopped using dyes on my hair a while back and now I had two tone hair with my natural deep brown fading into a washed out henna red at the ends. Time to get rid of the old and inauthentic me I thought.

Asking around for a good salon several friends pointed me to Phoenix Hairdressers and so I booked an appointment. The same day I took my son and a friend to the playground after school and sat reading the latest Kindred Spirit magazine. I flipped through it and settled on an article about the Phoenix and its origins as the Bennu bird in Egypt. That evening as I told Steve where I'd booked for my haircut I was jolted into awareness. My attention was being drawn to the Phoenix, but I hadn't picked up on it.

I had my haircut and my head felt much lighter, though my hair was still long. It felt good to have hair that was all my own natural colour. It was probably the first time since my teenage years that my colour had been entirely and authentically my own. I felt I was reclaiming my true self. I also reflected on the significance of cutting hair. My hair had been halfway down my back and when the ends were growing I would still have been in my marriage, probably at an unhappy phase towards the end. Cutting my hair removed the sad energy of that time from my physical being. Every other part of our bodies is renewed and regenerated over time, but your hair can stay with you for many years, especially if you grow it long.

There was a veritable deluge of phoenixes around me now. I started playing a game with my guides to see if I could get through a whole day without being shown a new phoenix sign. Sometimes I would get to the evening and they hadn't 'got me yet'. I would walk into the lounge and someone or other 'Phoenix' would be mentioned within minutes on the TV, or someone's pet would be called Phoenix, it was crazy.

One day I was feeling particularly smug having got all the way to bedtime without a phoenix. I picked up Ted Andrews 'Animal Speak' safe in the knowledge that he doesn't cover mythological animals. That was one place they hadn't planted a sign! I turned to the back cover reading the comments from the reviewers and laughed,
one of whom was called Phoenix McFarland. You would have thought it the most popular name on the planet and the best title for anything from music tracks, to cartoon episodes, to computer software.

I sat and thought about what I knew of the Phoenix. It is an ancient mythological bird, variants of which appeared in many ancient cultures including the Egyptians with their Bennu bird, the Chinese Phoenix, the Native American Thunderbird and of course the Greek Phoenix. Shared beliefs included a very long life. The Phoenix had the ability to regenerate itself by setting fire to itself and being reborn from the ashes. Okay, perhaps I was getting somewhere. I'd really been burned to ashes in Egypt and now I was rediscovering myself. Was it a symbol of my own rebirth perhaps?

In my 'winged' healings I remembered there had been a couple of mentions of Phoenix energy. I looked back at the notes people had made on their feedback sheets: *"Was put into burning flames, flickering all around me, over my head and then up through my chakras. "Rise out of the ashes," given to me. Saw the word phoenix yesterday and pulled the card 'healing'."* Another lady had drawn a card on the evening of her healing and noted it on her sheet: *"I pulled Thunderbird of the Blue Star Angels: the card of the mystical bird of spiritual illumination. The Thunderbird carries messages from the Great Spirit to humans on earth. The Thunderbird could be related to the phoenix of Egyptian Mythology (which might sit better with you)."*

It was interesting, but I clearly hadn't grasped the full message as the phoenix messages continued unabated. In the Celtic shop I looked up the Phoenix.

Light behind the Angels

I scribbled these notes on the back of an old envelope:

'In mythology of Heliopolis, the city of the Sun, the Bennu was the soul of the Sun God Ra and was linked to the rising and setting of the Sun, the yearly Nile floods and the cycle of birth, death and resurrection. The word Bennu probably comes from weben which means 'rise' or 'shine'.'
Brenda Rosen 'Mythical Creatures Bible'.

It seemed that the phoenix was linked to my Egyptian lifetime. I remembered Amun Ra had called me the Phoenix and that we were termed the 'Shining Ones' by the Egyptian people. Was the Phoenix a new power animal for me to work with, or an innate energy I carried within?

Independence Days

*'Everything we hear is an opinion, not a fact.
Everything we see is a perspective, not the truth.'*
Marcus Aurelius

One morning Steve came downstairs feeling 'edgy' and warned me he needed a day left on his own. I've grown to respect this need; I feel it too and recognise it is a spiritual hunger for space. Steve disappeared upstairs and when I went up a few hours later with a drink for him he was sprawled completely naked on the bed. That's not too unusual, but this was totally naked. He had taken off his watch, his ankh and most significantly his pentagram, which was permanently round his neck. He spent the rest of the day 'tripping' through the Cosmos.

Steve explained later that when he'd had his shower that morning he'd been seized by an urgent and furious need to strip away all things that were not essentially him. He had started by thinking about books, "I am not someone else's regurgitated words," then got right down to things he habitually wears, "I am not this pentagram, I am not this ankh."

Whilst lying on the bed he'd been taken to many strange places across the Universe. Most touchingly he'd been taken to a place he recognised as home. Here he was just a bubble of light and all the other beings were similar bubbles of light. He'd communicated telepathically with these beings and felt an enormous yearning to be back there. He could only describe it as 'utterly blissful'.

I found it amusing because he floated around the house for the rest of the day with a spaced out expression on his face telling me how lovely it all was. This is the man who is stridently 'anti fluffy bunny healing' and views himself as a spiritual warrior. Suddenly a return to a reality where nothing happens, the only feeling is love and there is no real difference between any of the beings was his greatest desire.

That evening when I lay down, my ankh felt like it was strangling me and I could feel a presence by my left ear trying to connect. My pendant had been managing to tangle itself in my hair for the last few days and it felt really heavy round my neck. I turned the light back on and announced I'd have to take off my ankh too. As soon as I took it off it felt like a switch had been thrown. There was an incredible influx of energy through my crown and third eye. I felt that the ankh being familiar and ancient was strongly protective for me, but it blocked any energy that it didn't recognise. New energies were being prevented from coming in.

Light behind the Angels

It was quite strange to have no jewellery on. It had been many years since I'd had a bare neck. It was part of stripping myself down to get to the core of who I am.

Steve's blissed out experience caused him emotional pain as he was seized by a longing to return. For a while he felt quite miserable to be stuck on Earth in 3D physicality. Whenever we meditated he would find himself zooming back to 'Bubbleland' and the yearning would start again. For some time he simply blocked it out as too painful, until he learned to work with the energy and connect without the heartache.

We'd booked a stall at a Faerie and Elemental Festival held in a forest in South Wales. Semele shared the same healing tent and Estelle was there too. On the Saturday the rain came down in torrents. Things were very quiet and I suggested to Semele that we should take advantage of the time to swap a healing with each other as we had both been busy and we seldom managed to do this back home. She agreed and offered to give me a healing first.

It soon became apparent that this was a very important healing for both of us. Her attention was grabbed by an object lodged deep in my heart chakra. When I tuned in I sensed it was a crudely shaped bronze metal pin, quite thick. Suddenly I realised that this was what the old witch had used on me in the Celtic past life. She would have made a cloth poppet and stabbed pins in it, one for each of the children, a bit like a voodoo doll. Semele realised that, as my older sister, the pin would be placed in my heart because I had trusted her and she'd betrayed my trust.

I saw that my sister had taken something of mine as a witness to personalise the doll with as she had complete access to my belongings. Maybe she'd cut my hair or nails in the guise of taking care of me to get the witness. The heart pin symbolised emotional betrayal.

Together we focussed on extracting it. It took several big pushes to remove the horrible thing. At the end of the healing Semele had the image of Mother Mary rocking me in her arms as if I was newborn again. I was told to rest and allow my guides to look after me.

I felt so relieved when we were finished and Semele also felt better. After the healing with Estelle I'd had the word 'reparation' in my mind a lot. I was delighted Semele had made her reparation without being asked, as initially she had said, "I'm not like that this lifetime, I am your friend." I'd known the karma needed to be balanced to fully release the issue. When I hopped off the treatment couch we had a hug and shared some healing tears. Semele knew she'd been scared by my power in the previous lifetime and had tried to stop me, but this time she had been guided to me as her spiritual teacher. She felt it was very appropriate that she'd sought me out and respected my teachings this time around.

I returned to my stall from this wonderful healing and within moments a shiatsu masseur with very dubious energies appeared and without asking permission took hold of me and started hitting me with the side of her hands painfully up my right side. I was too stunned to say anything. This woman was a stranger. What made her think she could invade my energy like this?

I was startled by the parallel with the friend at the last healing fair who had zoned in on me straight after my healing with Estelle to 'give me healing'. Twice in a row I'd received a profound healing in a public place and immediately afterwards had my boundaries violated under the guise of 'giving healing'. There was a lesson here for me about energy thieves. I had felt wonderfully bright and shiny hopping off Semele's couch, but in that newly healed state I was more vulnerable than usual. This woman had whisked in and stolen some of that lovely fresh energy to supplement her own.

I ended up keeping that particular healer out of my space by placing strong barriers around my aura for the rest of the weekend as she was sharing the same marquee. Naively I used to believe that healers were in business for the wellbeing of others. My eyes had been opened. Not everyone has such a pure motivation.

Later the same day I received a text from my ex husband saying our Decree Absolute had been granted. He'd received a letter that morning. I felt completely elated by the news; my freedom had been a long time coming; now it was official.

Next day, once my energy had settled, I sought out Estelle. I had an instinct that if one pin had been placed within my energy field on Semele's behalf there would be at least four more past life pins lodged in my system.

I was right. Estelle found one in my crown chakra, one in my lower back which went down my leg, one in my solar plexus and one in my left ear which was blocking my clairaudience. She extracted them all. Estelle picked up a past life vision of me as a woman in a long green velvet dress. I'd seen this dress before and knew she was tapping into the Guinevere lifetime. When she looked I was wearing a rose quartz pendant. She questioned whether I wore one now. I don't, I felt it was from the past. She saw it as laden with grief, holding me stuck in grief. It was shaped as a teardrop and she removed it. Next she removed a gold Celtic knot that was wrapped around the dress. She felt it was holding me into a relationship, Lancelot again I knew. I was plunged into a lake, which is significant as the lake comes up so often.

Light behind the Angels

With my divorce now granted I could officially change my name. My solicitor had warned me that things could get complicated if I did so during the divorce, so I'd waited. It was a full year and a half since I'd decided upon my new name and I was getting frustrated that all official documentation still bore my married name. This just wasn't me anymore.

I made an appointment to see my solicitor and we changed my name by deed poll. It took all of twenty minutes and it was only later I noted the significance of my appointment. I realised I had changed my name on the 4th of July, Independence Day. I couldn't have picked a more auspicious date.

Abandonment

Our real blessings often appear to us in the shapes of pains, losses and disappointments; But let us have patience, and we soon shall see them in their proper figures.
Joseph Addison

As September progressed I found I was getting increasingly clingy with Steve. We'd spent over a year and a half with him trekking weekly between Wales and Manchester and I'd been happy enough to spend half a week at a time by myself, so now it was hard to explain why I was struggling. I felt insecure and vulnerable.

My feelings were brought to a head when he decided to spend the weekend away from me. There were legitimate reasons for him to be away, but I became fearful, I had strong feelings he would be unfaithful. When I tried to talk to him he couldn't grasp what my problem was.

On that first weekend away Steve's mobile was switched off most of the time and I couldn't get through. He'd always answered my calls before and this made me feel frantic. Steve came back to Wales midweek, just before the Autumn Equinox. He took a call from his High Priestess. The coven normally met on a Thursday, but she'd decided to move the meeting to Friday for the Solstice. Without giving it a thought he made himself available. We were heading out for lunch. Within five minutes of driving his phone went again. This time it was a customer wanting an MOT. I heard Steve ask, "When does it run out?" and then, "No problem I'm in Manchester this weekend so I'll pick it up first thing on Monday."

I was angry and upset beyond belief. How could he be so insensitive to my feelings? His customers were in Manchester, but normally he'd have fitted them in mid week and been back here with me on Friday night. He was deliberately taking weekends up there, so who was he seeing? Someone who worked weekdays that much was clear to me.

We never got to our destination. I drove us to the riverbank and we stood on the bridge fighting. He couldn't see my problem and felt I was making something of nothing. He accused me of being controlling. I felt he was being defensive and covering up what he was up to in Manchester. It was horrible, but I did realise that the phone calls had been genuine. I'd heard them. The customer was a Canon in the Anglican Church. It seemed unlikely that he was part of any elaborate subterfuge!

Perhaps I was being shown an issue for myself? Perhaps I was being shown past life insecurity. The theme of abandonment by my lover had run through many past lives thanks to the efficacy of the Ancient Egyptian curse. Although the curse had been lifted in January we hadn't begun a clear up operation from all of those damaged lives. The pattern had to be cleared out for good. I'd been repeatedly pulling a bleak landscape entitled Abandonment for weeks from my Sacred Circle tarot deck and not grasped that it was something for me to sort out.

When the children went to their dad's on Wednesday night we took the opportunity of an empty house to do a past life regression on me. As I was led through the visualisation I got to a garden gate into a walled garden. I know what my gate and garden usually look like. This one was different. A big arched gateway with a solid oak door in it with huge iron hasps. The wall itself was crenulated grey stone. A castle wall.

Walking inside the garden I could see this was also different from usual. It was much more formal than my usual cottage style garden. I was walking in manicured grounds. As I walked my costume changed and I found I was wearing a long velvet dress. I went to sit on a stone bench where one of my guides approached me. He was Merlin, tall, with long grey hair and carrying his staff. I got a clearer look at his staff than usual. It had a twisted carving spiralling up it rather like my own snake staff, but at the top the wood was claw like, holding a clear crystal orb. In front of me was a firebird and as I rose it flew to me. It perched on my outstretched arm just as a hawk would. Both Merlin and the firebird travelled with me.

Although the past life visualisation calls for a temple I knew I was walking up castle steps and into a castle, however I managed to put a violet flame in the centre of the flagstone floor for purification and stood in the cool flames to cleanse myself before proceeding. In front of me was my doorkeeper. The character was a change to my normal doorkeeper, this time he was a monk in a brown habit. He took a golden key from inside his robes and handed it to me. I opened the door to the library where all of my past lives are stored and found that this was changed too. A stone room of some grandeur.

I headed for the book that was shouting at me from the shelves. The spine was of a greyish cream fabric and the covers were of red leather. On the front cover was a jewel set within a gold embellished equal armed cross, very ornate and expensive looking. The book was thick and heavy and I lifted it over to a reading table.

On opening it I found pages and pages of medieval manuscript, such as monks would write with beautifully illuminated capitals. I couldn't read it, but continuing to flip the pages I found a family tree and the name at the bottom of the tree was Guinevere. At this point I knew that there was a danger of slipping into all of the mythology about her life and I wanted a healing, not a fantasy.

Scenes from the life began to unfurl before me. I caught sight of myself walking about the castle corridors alone, feeling bored. There was nothing to do. My needs were all met, the men were away and there was a limit to how much needlework I would do. Looking at her she was beautiful, young and willowy, with long, luscious, red brown wavy hair. Her face was the picture of discontent.

We moved to another scene. A banquet was being held in the castle. The men had returned victorious from whatever exploit they'd been on and a feast was being held to celebrate. I was enjoying myself now. Courtiers were being introduced to me and bowing or curtsying. I was quite the centre of attention. The meats on the tables were plentiful, huge and shiny with glaze. It's not what I'd want to sit down to now as a vegetarian, but it was the height of fashionable food then. There was music and dancing and I was having a wonderful time. I was enjoying the admiration I was receiving.

Back in my own chambers I knew my husband would visit me and then leave. There was no real warmth there, no emotional attachment, although I respected him. He was older than me and his attention was fixed on running his lands. We didn't spend much time together other than his conjugal visits. I was young, beautiful and very, very lonely. A trophy wife, high born and good to show off from time to time, but that was it. Most of the time he was away and I had to occupy myself.

In the next scene I was strolling in the garden with a handsome younger man, one of the ones who'd been looking covetously at me at the banquet. I knew I shouldn't be with him alone, but we were just walking and talking. I was getting the sweet attention I'd craved and he was delightful company. We were quite restrained, but the way in which he kissed my hand made my heart race and I knew I wanted this man. I hesitate to call him Lancelot, as I didn't hear a name in the regression.

Merlin met me alone in the gardens and warned me off my paramour. I was upset and angry with him. I'd thought no-one had noticed and I'd done nothing wrong, yet. I didn't think he'd tell my husband; he was trying to protect me. Back in my chambers I could see myself pacing. I wanted this man; I wanted the feeling of being in love. I wasn't going to let Merlin stand in my way.

Light behind the Angels

The scene moved on and I found myself in my bedchamber with my young lover. We were passionate and I felt carried away by love. He promised to steal me away. I knew that we couldn't get away with this, but I wanted to believe him. This was the love of my life and although I could feel that it would end in disaster, I couldn't give him up.

Moving on I could see myself crying in my chambers. Sad and alone again, the men had all gone; my lover amongst them. At this point her tears became mine and I was wracked with sobbing that came from deep within me. Steve placed a tissue in my hand.

It was worse, people knew, and I would see heads turning towards me as I walked by and catch whispered snippets of conversations. I was the centre of gossip and scandal and I knew I would be in trouble when my husband returned. My solace was my religion. I went to see the Friar, robed in brown and I recognised him as the doorkeeper. I knelt before him and he listened to my anguish and gave me absolution. I could see my hands clutching my ebony rosary beads.

We moved on to the return of my husband who had been told of my unfaithfulness. He was furious with me, understandably so, and he shook me by the shoulders. Then he cast me away from him and my shoulders hit the stone wall. My physical shoulder hurt at this point as I lay on the couch. It was only bruised, not broken, but my husband had never been violent to me before and I was shocked. More sobbing came, both from Guinevere in the vision and from deep inside of me.

From that time on my husband was even colder and more distant. He visited me seldom and I was left alone. No word came from my 'true love'. He had gone away on a noble quest. I felt he was trying to redeem his good name and win back favour with my husband. Not a thought for me, only for his own skin.

Years passed and nothing changed. I provided no heir. I found my peace in Catholicism and my trusted Friar. I had no friends. A very lonely existence. In the last scene I saw my husband on his death bed. The coldness between us remained but I had otherwise been protected and made comfortable. Now he was dying without an heir. I had failed him in this, and I knew his lands would be locked into a power struggle. I didn't know what would happen to me, but my place in his kingdom was dangerous without him so I took myself to a nunnery and hid from the world there, finding sanctuary in prayer.

At the end of the regression Merlin said I'd had enough and so the book went back on the shelf and I returned to the door of the library. There was my doorkeeper waiting for me and I shook with grateful tears. Once we'd walked through the garden and out of the gate I returned to my modern day appearance. All felt peaceful. I realised that although I'd connected with the Guinevere lifetime before I'd never felt her emotions. Whether the lifetime was really mine, or I'd tapped into the collective subconscious, the tears were absolutely genuine and came from deep within me. That grief had to be released.

I expected that the past life regression would sort out the angst I'd been feeling, but Steve continued to change his pattern of visits and spent the next weekend away too. This time he'd planned an outing with some of his coven members. They'd gone on a jaunt to the infamous Pendle Hill and then round to one of the covener's houses to socialise. I was beside myself with possessiveness. I rang him. He was having a nice time, making friends with her dogs, generally chilling out with his friends, what was my problem? He thought he might stop over as he'd had a few to drink and he'd been offered the couch to sleep on. I begged and pleaded, "Leave, go home now please. Promise you won't stay the night?" I was in tears and getting hysterical. He told me he'd go when he was ready. I spent an uneasy few hours with unwholesome scenes running through my mind.

Steve returned to Wales, but he still seemed determined to test my limits. The two women coveners ran an adult toys business and he told me they'd all planned another outing together, this time to Birmingham's notorious fetish fair the following weekend. I went into meltdown, feeling sick with anxiety. Steve made it clear he wasn't impressed with my behaviour, labelled me prudish and left for Manchester again. My body just couldn't take the stress and within a few days I developed an abscess 'down below'.

I tried to ignore the discomfort as I believe your body can always heal itself, but stress had knocked out my immune system and it just got worse. I went to the doctor's, quite a rarity for me, and she gave me antibiotics. They didn't work and over the next few days the pain became unbearable and the swelling grew until it was difficult to walk. The only relief came from the constant application of ice packs.

Steve returned to find me bedridden and as the abscess was only getting larger he drove me back to the doctor's who had me admitted to hospital immediately. I was operated on the next day and the expected small operation took several hours as the infection was much worse than expected and had been spreading fast. I was kept in for several days and Steve took on the role of house husband, looking after the kids and the animals. The planned excursion was cancelled

Light behind the Angels

and his peculiar new routine broken. Steve went back to mid week working in Manchester and returned to Wales at the weekends and our relationship settled down again.

Recuperation took longer than expected. I've always bounced back from illness and had never had an operation before. A few days after I returned home I woke with a tremendous headache. It felt as if my head was in a vice. Steve's reaction was strange. "Go and stand over there." I dutifully stood on the other side of the room and found the headache had lifted a bit. "Now come back." It was just as bad. He explained that he could see a portal over my pillow with some unpleasant looking beings pushing to get through. They were prevented by one of my angels who stood guarding the space with his sword.

I think I'd opened the portal inadvertently with all of the anaesthetic junk leaving through my crown chakra. "I'm off to feed the kids breakfast and take them to school. You can close the portal can't you?" I must have looked suitably pitiful. Since having the anaesthetic I'd been struggling to even ground myself and had resorted to using a big chunk of black tourmaline as an anchor. Closing portals to who knows where was beyond me at that point.

Steve gave a stretch, waggled his fingers in the direction of my head and my headache vanished. He grinned, "All done." What a show off!

The Return of the High Priest

'In mysticism, knowledge cannot be separated from a certain way of life which becomes its living manifestation. To acquire mystical knowledge means to undergo a transformation; one could even say that the knowledge is the transformation.'
Fritjof Capra

We'd sensed that An-A-Huh had stayed close to us since his release from the Land of Forgotten Souls and wanted to rejoin Steve's soul. One of my students, Glenda, a spiritual healer, had glimpsed him standing close by Steve during one of the teaching weekends. We knew already that she was somehow linked into the Egyptian life and I had an impression that she was one of the Temple children; a little boy.

Later I received a card from her with a note: "The Egyptian man outside Steve, I think he was holding a tube with green light in it, capped at both ends by copper. The green light contains knowledge. Does this mean anything to Steve?" I called her up and carefully questioned her. It appeared that the colour green matched the shade of almost fluorescent emerald green that I'd been seeing all year. Connecting the Egyptian, the word 'knowledge' and the colour green I wondered again about the Emerald Tablets of Thoth.

At the end of October Steve decided it was time to reintegrate An-A-Huh. He had been at a sound healing workshop all day. Fresh from a gong bath he felt very chilled out. He'd shown me a card he'd brought back from the sound workshop which carried a purple diamond drawn on it and the word Knowledge. He'd then picked a crystal card from the dish on the kitchen table which had a purple fluorite octahedron with the words 'Self Discipline'. Not liking the message he'd tried to put it back, saying, "Wrong one!" but I'd spotted it and pointed out the similarity to the other card, two purple diamond shapes in one day.

The reintegration felt like the right thing to do and not too difficult. In fact I was sure Steve could accomplish this with little help and suggested he work shamanically and I drum for him. First he picked up a purple fluorite octahedron and popped it in his belly button. As fluorite helps with structure and organisation and the navel is symbolic of your birth it made sense to me. As expected it was easy to find An-A-Huh. He had been waiting for this.

Light behind the Angels

Steve described his journey afterwards. "There was a very dark, but clear, night time sky. There were no stars. I had stated my intent that the Egyptian High Priest would no longer be fragmented from me. That if it was deemed right and necessary we two would become one. I was told, 'When it is complete the sky will be full of diamonds.'

I called to An-A-Huh and we went for a quick tour of Egypt. There were no pyramids, but there were temples. It was very fertile land by the river, very little desert. It was him showing me his memories. Then he came over here and I gave him a quick tour. It was like a memory swap. We agreed that we'd give it a shot.

He stood in his world and I stood in my world. There was a dividing line. I could see his world and he could see mine, as though there were two pictures joined in the middle. We crossed our arms in front of us and held hands. Our arms made a figure of eight, then we rotated clockwise. He came through my world and I went through his world and we started to spin, then both worlds disappeared and all we could see was the night time sky full of stars."

At first the reintegration of the High Priest seemed a success. Steve would get occasional glimpses of his Egyptian life as he went about his daily business. When he was showering An-A-Huh was reminded that he used to be cleansed with scented oils, at the health club sitting in the Jacuzzi he was shown that we used to bathe together in a pool in the Nile, kept safe from crocodile attacks by a living wall of slaves and guards. Their lives were dispensable, ours were not.

It was a strange clash of cultures and it must have seemed far more peculiar for An-A-Huh, who'd been used to having his every need waited upon, to find himself in a modest modern home with no servants. Although he was now housed within Steve's physical frame he remained a distinct personality. It seemed he had retained the option of splitting away again if he didn't like the way things were going.

As time went on we questioned our wisdom in inviting An-A-Huh back. One morning Steve came down at breakfast and saw me clearly as Ankh-Ka-Dna. He felt a 'red mist' descend, the anger An-A-Huh carried about my foolish behaviour which had precipitated our demise. He was still more incensed with the behaviour of the Assistant High Priestess and he stayed away from his café owning friend for a while as he couldn't suppress the rage.

At this point I had a phone call from Glenda. She had the impression that the High Priest was threatening her in her dreams and meditations. We couldn't understand why. Was he dangerous? Had we made a mistake allowing him in? I calmed her down and gave her some practical advice, but I was troubled.

I asked for strength to get through this phase as I lay in bed one night. I distinctly heard a male voice in my ear say, "Go and fetch your thunder stick." It is unusual for me to hear an external voice like this, normally I hear the promptings of my guides in my own mind and I have had to learn to distinguish them from my own thoughts.

I knew what my guide was referring to; my snake staff. Obediently I got up and went downstairs to fetch it. When I got back into bed I lay down and held it in my hand. A powerful energy coursed through my body and I felt physically and emotionally fortified.

I put Steve on the couch to have a chat with An-A-Huh. The High Priest admitted he was finding our lifestyle very strange, but told us he liked our 'chariots'. Apparently he'd been fascinated by Steve's job as a mechanic and enjoyed the car rides back and forth to Manchester. He was retaining his individual sense of self and resisting settling back in as you might expect with a more normal soul retrieval.

I performed a healing on Steve's Hara line. This is a beautiful golden line of energy within our core that connects us to the Planet and the Heavens. It has several distinct energy structures along it. Steve saw that instead of a single Soul Seat he had two glowing lights in his chest, one for him and one for An-A-Huh. The Soul Seat connects us to our life purpose and with two working independently we wondered if Steve would be divided between his purpose in this life and his purpose back then. We were guided to connect the Soul Seats and placed a fulgurite between to join them. Fulgurite is a strange crystal. Unlike most it forms in an instant when lightning hits desert sand, creating fused hollow tubes of melted sand. This channel was perfect for linking the soul seats and creating an easy flow of energy between them.

Promises Kept, Promises Broken

*'And ever has it been known that love knows not its own depths
until the hour of separation.'*
Kahlil Gibran

Steve was set to join us for our second proper Christmas together. After the crazy events of the previous Christmas and New Year I was hoping for something a little more traditional.

Back in Manchester things had been happening that I was quite innocent of. When Steve arrived in Wales he was subdued and not his usual self. I questioned him, asking what was wrong. He told me he'd been journeying and found himself as a Native American medicine man in his tipi. He saw himself delve down into a cave and consult with a wise woman, an ancient lined Native American version of me. I've glimpsed this face in my own reflection in the mirror quite often, so that didn't surprise me. After this he journeyed into the sky and met a Native American Chief with whom he conversed in his own language. He said he could understand it and speak it at the time, but couldn't attempt to translate it to English. What he did retain was the Chief's name, Standing Bear, which had appealed to his sense of humour as a life model.

The scene had shifted to one of utter sensuality in his tipi with his squaw, coating each other in scented oils and enjoying a level of ecstasy in each other's arms that we'd never known together. Our relationship had been built on the meeting of minds and spirit. The physical passion we'd found with other lovers wasn't hot between us. Physically we found each other desirable and having both been burnt by relationships built on all consuming physical passion this calmer attraction seemed more comfortable.

Back in Wales Steve was being tortured by scenes of sensuality that were played out every time he closed his eyes. He had a strong sense that his 'squaw' was someone he knew in this life and I was sure this was the case. He got a name through for her, Deer Who Leaps, and his own name had been Black Wolf.

He admitted that a group of 'high level guides' had told him that his work with me was done and it was time for him to move on and 'fix' this other woman. He'd been worried the Christmas before that he might be moved along like this and it had sounded insane to me, yet he felt he was being commanded now.

I was devastated. We'd worked so hard together through all of our challenges, was he really going to walk away and treat me simply as a job well done? Was that what he really wanted to do?

Meanwhile Christmas was rolling along and I was trying to hold it all together for the kids. I had a fragile grip on myself and went through the motions of a traditional family Christmas, but inside I was in utter turmoil again.

On Boxing Day, whilst my ex had the kids, Steve left. He drove back to Manchester to make his mind up. When he left I felt that it was all over between us. I howled with grief. This was the real Abandonment I'd been warned of by the cards, it may have had its echoes in past lives, but it was happening again here and now. I was surprised by the force of my emotions. I grabbed the crystal singing bowl Steve had bought me for Christmas and played it, sobbing my heart out at the same time. Somehow the sound helped draw the pain from my heart and it gave me some sort of company in my despair. I'd allowed myself to be guided by Spirit in my choice of partner, I'd made all the sacrifices Spirit had asked of me and still my heart was being broken, still my love was being taken from me. Bereft, I cried through the whole night and didn't sleep at all.

The next morning in the depths of my despair I reached out to Glenda who had seemed to perceive so much about Steve. She still disliked the High Priest intensely, but I surmised that was because he'd had me executed and as an Egyptian temple child she'd loved me. I telephoned her and she listened sympathetically saying I could call her if I needed support. She commented that the same high beings were guiding her and she was being taken up on their light ships for instruction. She told me they were very high and their orders were not to be denied.

Then she said, "I've seen some of that life, I think I was in that tribe, you don't think I'm the other woman do you?" I reassured her that she wasn't. Steve has always been attracted to a certain type and his partners have been dark haired and brown eyed, like myself and quite unlike her. I felt I would have picked up vibes long before if she'd been a threat to our relationship.

I put the phone down, my desolation now mixed with righteous anger towards these 'high and mighty' beings who thought they could treat human beings as their pawns. I have always taught that your guides will advise you and set signposts on your path, but they will not dictate and they always leave you with free will. These 'high beings' seemed set on breaking those fundamental rules and yet both Steve and Glenda were listening to them and taking their orders from them. It felt very wrong.

Light behind the Angels

I was desolate. I drummed the grief out of me for an hour and then took a long bath. All I could do was to wait it out. The decision was not in my hands.

Late that afternoon Steve returned, to my relief. No decisions had been made but at least he was here with me. He'd been shown who the woman was in this lifetime. It took me one guess to get to his coven and one more to the woman herself. It was the very same woman whose house he'd been in when I'd become hysterically clingy in the autumn, phoning him and begging him to leave. He'd called me controlling back then, but some deeper knowledge had been guiding me and pushing me to get him away from her.

Now I knew that had I not needed my operation I would have lost him back then. All my vibes had been right. He may not have done anything wrong at that time, but he was being brought into ever closer contact with her and something would have happened. Ironically I remembered at his High Priestess' handfasting ceremony I had held one end of a decorated hoop whilst the other woman held the other end and we'd stood for some time facing each other making an archway for the couple to enter the circle. I'd rather liked her.

Steve had left his coven that autumn due to an ethical disagreement with the High Priestess and I thanked our true guides for bringing their debate to a head at that time or he would still have been meeting with the woman on a very regular basis.

On Steve's return to Wales the interference from these 'guides' got worse. He was told that as his reward for 'fixing me' he could have a fantastic and lasting passionate relationship with this other woman. He felt that all he had to do was knock on her door and their life together would begin. I couldn't believe the callous cruelty of it and I wasn't at all convinced that these were true guides in the Light, but he was adamant that they were high and powerful beings.

I put him on the treatment couch to try and help matters. I asked him to connect with his reliable, more familiar guides. His warrior guide appeared briefly, told Steve he was being 'a twat' in his earthy manner, and then vanished. None of his normal guides could be contacted after that.

As I performed a healing on him the beings took advantage of his relaxed state by showing him glorious pictures of his future with this other woman. He was shown wonderful sunlit scenes of them living a life of luxury together in a hot country. I asked him to spare me the scenes of hot passion that were running in glorious technicolor through his mind. They'd found one way to make sure I didn't do any more healing for him!

Steve decided we should take on a practical project and suggested we paint the therapy room. He'd been talking about it for a while as all of the incense and candles I burn had left sooty marks. We went out and got the paint, with me hoping I wouldn't bump into anyone I knew. Of course I bumped into several people who wanted to ask me how my Christmas had been. I had to put on a brave face when I could barely speak for the tears welling up.

We began to paint. I tried to connect with my guides, but I couldn't, all I could hear were these 'high and mighty beings' and I did not trust them or want to listen to them! They were blocking access to my own guidance and I couldn't get any support. They even dared plant images in my mind, showing me the pair looking glossy and well groomed together, a 'beautiful couple'. They told me I was being selfish and I should step out of Steve's way. For a short while they undermined me and I was torn. Perhaps I wasn't meant to be his partner and I should step aside? Perhaps this was for his highest good and I was being selfish and blocking his happiness? It was a crack in my defences that they exploited until I got utterly sick of them bullying me and told them to, "Fuck right off and get out of my head!"

Painting that room has to have been one of the longest days of my life. It seemed to calm Steve, but it felt like his farewell gift to me and I felt so deeply sad I could hardly utter a word.

The manipulation of Steve went on. New Year's Eve was a huge pretence. All I wanted to do was sit alone and bawl my eyes out, but I put on a brave face for the kids. Then the New Year texts started to arrive. I felt intensely uncomfortable amongst all these jolly 'Happy New Year!' messages.

My sixth sense told me she'd been in touch. Steve looked uncomfortable and embarrassed when I asked him. He showed me his phone. There was half a text from her. One of those nauseating messages that people send round to all their friends. I've never liked them much, but this one felt like pure poison with its encouragement to kiss and make love slowly. I felt sick to the core.

Steve confessed then that the same text had already come through half a dozen times at least. Every time a new text message came through from someone else this same curtailed message would be delivered again from her. It just kept coming in, I would hear the phone bleep and there it was again. The bastards were bombarding him!

Light behind the Angels

I asked Steve if I could phone Semele and ask her to tune in. He agreed and I rang her explaining we were in some trouble without going into any details. I asked if she would read for me.

When Semele tuned in she felt her solar plexus churning and then saw White Buffalo Calf Woman. We knew she was on track as Steve had already seen a Native American marriage rite where a buffalo skin was being painted to symbolise the vows the couple were taking.

On the cards Semele picked up a big decision to be made. Something was tangled and needed sorting out. A situation had to be left behind. She felt Steve might leave me for a while but would be back as there were no cards to show the end of our relationship. Then she picked up a need to break an old vow, it wasn't current, but it was being called in and it needed releasing.

Semele felt that our relationship was about to 'go up a level' and this had activated the issue. She saw White Buffalo Calf Woman again, this time holding out legal documents and felt that the situation would be sorted out in six to nine months and this would be the ending of a pattern. She also picked up that there was something about the situation that we didn't know and got a strong, "No! Don't go with her!"

I felt heartened by the reading, but Steve was less persuaded than I was because Semele is my friend, however I felt that picking up on White Buffalo Calf Woman was a very good sign that she was reading along the right lines.

I went upstairs alone and sat down to channel with pen and paper. I'd been separated from my own guides for too long and I needed to know what they would advise. Here is what came through:

Be still and at peace for we desert you not. You are a special child of the Universe and shall be cared for. Do not despair of events that transpire. They serve to clarify your feelings and deepen your capacity for love. Already this changes and you notice the new waves of feeling that surge through you. Sometimes it is in our darkest hour that the brightest treasures come to light.

It was with great relief I made my connection with true loving wisdom again. My guides' intense love for me made me shed more tears, but these were tears of gratitude as I knew I would be supported through this drama. I asked for more specific help:

You are looked after and deserve to abide in love. We will ensure this for you but cannot promise that it will come from Steve. That is his free will and decision to make.

Steve's heart is being broken open. Inside he will find the colours of the world that he has been depriving himself of. It is a fresh start for both of you whatever he decides, and you must recognise this.

You have asked Steve to commit to you from the heart, yet his heart is not his to give at present. He still holds two sacred vows there which he has not been willing to release. One is to his wife in this time. Though he does not intend to rejoin her he made his vows before God, not believing in them, yet they are active and embedded in his heart.

His other vows were made to Deer Who Leaps in all sincerity and were eternal. These have been activated by your decision to commit fully to Steve. He cannot accept your love into his heart until these are revoked. He is being shown possible futures to bring the seriousness of his commitments to him. If he was simply told about her, but not shown the emotion he would dismiss the issue.

You cannot accept half measures now. You have renounced your love for (name of 'twin flame') *and you have cleared the vows you made to your ex husband. You deserve someone who is willing to do the same level of clearing for you and come to you with an open heart.*

Though this time hurts you it is necessary and important. You cannot deepen your relationship with Steve until his heart is clear. This is his decision to make and not yours so you must accept it.

He has held onto his marriage through guilt. He is sad that he let his wife down and caused her so much pain and suffering. When he fully admits this to himself he will be ready to release the marriage. These are the legal documents you were shown and the time span shows how long it will be before he is legally available to commit to you or anyone else.

His past life vows have been activated now as he was unaware of them and they would have interfered in your relationship together. You picked up on the vows accurately this year and we sent you the illness to underline its importance but he didn't recognise it then and misinterpreted your behaviour.

He must choose between you, but really there is no choice if he does not revoke the vow as it still binds him. He can play it out and he will find the truth of the matter through experience, or trust his love for you and let you heal the issue. You can only offer your services; you cannot force him to do this.

He can connect with you fully and authentically when his heart is free of these past commitments and he releases the fear he carries as a frightened child within himself. He will need to soften and show his vulnerability to do this healing as it is deep. This he will come to in his own time.

Steve was still unable to tell me what he was going to do. We needed to get out of the house and with snow on the ground we went for a long walk together on Hergest Ridge that New Year's Day. This

Light behind the Angels

long backed hill lies right on the border of England and Wales and is popular with walkers, but there weren't too many out to brave the cold weather.

I spelled out plainly to Steve that there was no room for a 'trial run' with this woman. If he went to see what passion he could find with her then everything would be over between us. I would not have him back and so if he'd been considering that as a possible option he'd better forget it. He had instilled far too much self worth in me over our time together to be allowed to mess me about. We walked and we talked

It seemed to me that I was being shown an 'extreme balancing'. I had turned my back on a fantasy dream of love with my 'twin flame', could he walk away from these promised scenes of passion and commit to a real and genuine loving relationship with me?

Back in the Celtic shop for the first time in 2009 I had a visit from our mutual friend June. I told her a potted version of what had been going on over Christmas and New Year. She surprised me with the vehemence of her reaction, "It is all wrong! A circle of confusion. Steve is where he is meant to be. Steve is what he is meant to be. Don't listen to lies! Feel the lies in your gut. You and Steve are One." She was quite overcome by the power of the message and I knew it was her own guide talking through her.

Steve journeyed back to his Native American life as Black Wolf. He had to see the promises he'd made to his squaw and he wanted to look at what had happened to them. He saw that the marriage ceremony was held in the name of White Buffalo Calf Woman and a buffalo hide had been painted with their sacred symbols to join each of them forever. The same symbols had been painted on their tipi.

Things got more twisted as he looked into the life. He saw himself as a young, but powerful medicine man. In his tribe there was a very pretty younger woman who wanted him to teach her his craft. He refused as his knowledge was only for the men. She tried to seduce him with her beauty, but he loved his wife who was now pregnant and pushed her aside.

It seems she had a temper. As a woman scorned she rushed him with a knife wounding his leg and then ran away from the tribe. She found the cavalry and betrayed the whereabouts of the tribe to them. Her reward was to be raped and killed by the soldiers. The camp was then rushed by soldiers on horseback with guns and swords. They spared no-one. Black Wolf fought but couldn't save his beautiful pregnant squaw from being slaughtered and then he was shot himself.

He recognised the traitor. It was Glenda, the very woman I had called in the depths of despair when Steve had left me. It explained why I'd phoned her rather than one of my closest friends and why she'd been acting strangely around Steve. In her last teaching session with me she'd complained about his energies being too powerful for her, so he kept right out of her way and stayed upstairs in our bedroom practising his drumming. During a meditation she said she'd found herself floating up the stairs, feeling he was 'calling her with his drumbeat'. Now we knew of the past life entanglement things made much more sense, especially her comment over the phone, "You don't think it's me do you?"

Discussing Glenda's role in his downfall another scene came spontaneously to Steve. We were back in Egypt. Yes the little temple boy had indeed been one of my favourites, but he had also been someone else's pet. The Assistant High Priestess had made a special fuss of him. Steve saw that she had persuaded him to follow me, find out where I was going and inform her of what I was up to. He hadn't known the trouble he'd cause and he'd only been doing her bidding. Glenda's hatred of the High Priest had come from seeing my execution as all inhabitants of the temple, even the children, were forced to watch.

It seemed Glenda had betrayed us both, once unwittingly and then again deliberately. No wonder her relationship with both of us had got a bit blurred. I was concerned that we would have cords with Glenda.

I lay on my treatment couch and drew my customary golden circles. Yes there was something linking us, but it wasn't a cord as I'd ever seen one before. This was a moving stream of black dots going to and fro between our heads. I focussed in and was amazed to see the dots were bees. It was as though they were collecting my thoughts and flying them back to her. I put the kind of neon blue fly zapper you find in all the best chip shops around my head and the bees dropped into an increasing pile around my feet. Gradually the stream of insects thinned out and then there were none. From out of nowhere a plump anteater appeared and feasted on the insects. It seems Nature doesn't like waste, even on the astral plane!

We checked Steve out next. What he saw shocked me and confirmed the feeling of foul play that I'd had about all of this. Glenda was sitting in her golden circle unresisting and blank, but behind her stood a large and ugly demon. He announced that he held her soul and would keep it unless Steve won it back in battle. Despite all of the trouble this woman had caused us in past lives she was clearly a member of our soul group and in need of help.

Light behind the Angels

Steve readied himself with sword and shield for a fight on the astral. I sat by to offer all of the help I could, but was limited to calling out encouragement from the sidelines. I was reminded of the gladiatorial battles Captain Kirk would have in Star Trek.

At first things didn't look so good. Although Steve managed to land a few blows, the demon had managed more, taunting Steve that he was immortal, whereas Steve could die. Steve was sweating and wincing in pain each time he was hit. I could see he was in trouble and I asked my guides what I could do to help.

I felt Archangel Michael's presence standing by me and was reminded of his armour. I called into the arena, "Ask for help!" and immediately I could see it had made a difference. Steve reported that as soon as he asked for help he was clothed in golden armour from head to toe. The blows of the demon's sword made no impact on it and he complained, "Unfair!" but the battle had turned. Although the demon wasn't killed it was driven off and Glenda was released.

The battle had been a good reminder to Steve that help is available if you ask and that he doesn't have to fight his battles all on his own. I placed Glenda in a protective crystal layout, but felt it would be unwise to telephone and explain all that had happened. We needed to stay detached from her; at least until the past life issues threatening our relationship had been resolved. As it was she stayed away, but we knew from her friends that she was okay.

Steve had made his decision. After all we'd invested in our relationship he wanted to stay. He visited the beings in their lightship and told them bluntly and firmly to stay out of his love life. They expressed their displeasure but they backed off and at last Steve's regular, more earthly guides could come through.

We had to undo the past life promises as we knew that while they were still valid fate would intervene and confront him again with his past love. Although Steve was no longer part of the coven it seemed probable that whatever power could engineer all those New Year text messages could easily set up a 'chance' meeting. It was also clear from my channelling that their past life vows would stop us moving forward in our own relationship this lifetime.

Journeying once more Steve was taken to meet Standing Bear again. He was shown what had to be done. We needed to appeal to White Buffalo Calf Woman to release him from his eternal promise. We would need to conduct a sacred peace pipe ceremony in her honour and then he could make his appeal explaining our love for each other this lifetime.

June had sorted out a stack of Native American books for background research and we went round to pick them up. Again her guide seemed to speak through her. Rather than just thinking of us she came through with, "He would destroy her," meaning the other woman. I could well believe it. Steve's energies were always challenging. His mother had told him regularly as a child, "You'd make a saint swear!" Adulthood hadn't mellowed him. June passed on the message her Aboriginal Guide had given her for us the night before:

In many, many lives past you have been connected. Steve has caused Lauren great hurt, not always by him, but by life situations. Lauren has betrayed Steve, once only, but it was very painful. You have both suffered for these lives; this is the life to end the suffering and separations. (We felt this was a reference to Egypt and the workings of the curse.)

You are needed as a united power, but you still have several lives to clear first. You will know what they are and what to do about them. This is a hard time but it will make you stronger. You are One. Your combined strengths, power and knowledge will be something to contend with.

Your journey will be filled with awe, but it won't be easy. You both have the strength, ability and love to do this. Go back time and time again until you know. Sever useless bonds to make you stronger. Each time you succeed you grow.

Back home Steve got busy making a peace pipe in the shed. Meanwhile my contribution to the process was to decorate the pipe, so I sat and strung beads and feathers together ready. When the pipe was complete and assembled it looked beautiful and we hoped that the care that had gone into its making would underline our devotion to each other.

That evening we set up the lounge and created a stone medicine wheel, marking each of the four directions with crystals. We called in the quarters by rattling and using a Native American chant. We offered the peace pipe to each quarter and then smoked it together. We had been guided to smoke a mixture of sage, lemon grass and meadowsweet. I wouldn't recommend this blend for pleasure and I found pipe smoking a bit strong, but I did my best with it.

It was time for Steve to commune with White Buffalo Calf Woman. He hid his face and I knew he was shedding some tears for his lost love. He told me White Buffalo Calf Woman had taken the ceremonial buffalo skin and cut it into two, separating his symbol from that of Deer Who Leaps and so the vows were cleared.

Steve's mood was sombre. I knew he had genuinely loved his squaw in that life and it was very painful to let her go. He didn't want to talk about it and I had to let him grieve the loss in his way.

Light behind the Angels

Not long after Steve went through letting go of the marriage vows he'd taken with his wife and started divorce proceedings. He hadn't thought that still being married to her mattered, but it mattered to me. I didn't want to be living with another woman's husband. After my channelling I knew the vows were still binding on him. He didn't believe in a God at the time he'd taken them, but he'd said them in church so they were spiritually valid however lightly he'd meant them. Fortunately having been apart for nearly seven years and with property left to divide, their divorce went through smoothly and he was truly free.

Having cleared Steve's past life vows we entered into a new phase of our relationship. We felt the sort of delight in each other that you would expect right at the start of a relationship, not two years in. Neither of us had realised how much the old vows had been restricting the level of affection we could express for each other. Suddenly our relationship was flourishing on every level and I was at last feeling truly happy and in love with my soul mate.

The Three Nuns

'To have courage for whatever comes in life - everything lies in that.'
St. Teresa of Avila

The clearing of Steve's vows seemed to precipitate a need to clear anything and everything that was still holding us back. June's guide was still coming through with messages for us. I had known with a certainty for some years that I'd been a nun and I remembered in a healing that sore knees had come up. The healer felt I'd spent a lot of time kneeling on a hard stone floor praying, either as a monk or a nun. I do find kneeling on hard floors excruciatingly uncomfortable and this interpretation made sense to me, but I'd done nothing about clearing the energies as I hadn't been aware they were much of a problem. June channelled that I had to dissolve vows I'd made in three lifetimes I'd spent as a nun:

"Rescind the vows that are outdated, useless, such as vows of POVERTY, CHASTITY, OBEDIENCE and any that are not relevant in this time, it matters not if you know or remember them or the making of them. Just ask that all outdated vows and promises made in all of your past lives are taken from you so that you are clear in this life to live as you should. Any burdens you have shouldered knowingly or unknowingly, willing or not, should be removed. Ask that you be thoroughly cleansed and purified. FORGIVE most especially yourself."

I found that I had pledged all of these vows and that Chastity, Poverty, Silence, Obedience and Penitence had been quietly operating in the background of this life. They'd made me feel uncomfortable and guilty in the areas where I'd broken them and had been restricting me on a subconscious level.

Steve offered to help me through the process of releasing the vows from three lifetimes I spent as nuns. Fortunately at the start I was ignorant of how painful the process would be or I might have lacked the courage to see it through.

For the first lifetime I dowsed that a shamanic journey would be appropriate. Waiting for one of my usual power animals to lead me I was surprised by the arrival of a beautiful white dove. I followed it and I arrived in a monastery garden and heard the word *Carmelite*. I saw myself as a nun, dressed very much like nuns today, feeding doves from her hands at the dovecote. She showed me to her simple cell,

Light behind the Angels

which was clean, but utterly bare and she showed me the plain food she ate. She felt like a lovely lady and her energy was very serene. I explained that her religious vows were still binding on me in this lifetime. Four white doves arrived and lifted four silken banners from her shoulders bearing the words *Chastity, Poverty, Silence* and *Obedience*. They were flown away into the heavens.

Working on releasing her vows brought me unexpected gifts. I saw a life of deep inner peace and contentment with nothing to distract her from communion with God. That was a beautiful, simple life and by linking into it I can feel the peace wrapping around me.

After each set of vows had been released June had channelled that I would need cleansing with Epsom salts, salt and water and finishing with a sage water rinse. She provided a bag of dried sage for me that she'd picked from her own garden. I made a watering can full of sage tea and Steve took me off to the shower and scrubbed me with handfuls of salt. He then poured the watering can of sage water over my head. It was rather stinging on the skin, but I did feel cleansed.

We went out to lunch to celebrate and I felt glowing with health and very light. I knew I was looking at my most radiant and saw people's heads turn. People that knew me asked what I'd been doing to look so good. Now you know my beauty secret!

The next day I journeyed to the second nun's life. I found myself as an Abbess. It seemed to be a much older Medieval lifetime. I saw my hands first, fine white fingers on which I wore a gold signet ring. I was writing. Looking down I had a beautiful azure blue habit with a white head covering. She was a mature woman, perhaps in her forties. I could see that she lived a very privileged life and was used to the choicest cuts of meat. It was a life of comfort and riches.

The scene changed and I saw very briefly that she'd broken her vow of chastity and experienced a night of passion with a man. I recognised him as the Roman again, a visitor to the abbey. She had broken a vow she held sacred and from this time on she cast herself down as the lowest of the low. I saw she was given an option to leave the Abbey, but instead she became a penitent nun and lived on the floor of the kitchens, scrubbing and doing the most dirty and menial of jobs. I saw her eating scraps and stale crusts from the floor. Her knees were raw and she was filthy, wearing sackcloth and ashes. I couldn't persuade her to release her vows. She felt deeply ashamed of herself. In her mind Chastity and Obedience had already gone, she'd broken them by sinning, but she was punishing herself through her vows of Penitence and Poverty.

I returned from this journey and asked for support from Steve. I knew that even with my experience I wasn't going to be able to release these vows by myself. We set up a variation on the cord cutting. This time we used three golden circles of light which just touched each other. I stood in the centre of one, she stood in the centre of another and in the third we placed a heavy wooden casket.

One by one we looked for items that symbolised the vows and when we found them we threw them into the casket together. Heavy iron chains symbolised Penitence and they linked us together. I cut them away into short lengths and in they went. For Poverty she held out the stale crusts of bread she'd been surviving on and I found I was holding a plate heaped with food. I wondered if I'd been eating larger than necessary portions this lifetime to compensate for her near starvation. She threw her crusts into the casket and I passed her half of my food. It was interesting to see that my plate included meat, despite the fact that I'd been a vegetarian for over 25 years.

The filthy, rough, sackcloth garb had to go. I realised this was similar to the garment I'd worn in the cord cutting with my father. Once the clothes were inside the lid of the casket was shut and locked. I asked angels to come and take the chest away, letting them know I didn't want to see the contents again in this life or any other. I saw them fly it right into the heart of the Sun. My penitent Abbess was gently bathed and dressed back in her fine clothes. She still felt undeserving and didn't want to accept her former comforts, but Jesus himself came to reassure her that she was forgiven. Forgiveness done we hugged each other and I found I was sobbing with relief. Both the vows and the shame were released.

Whenever you shift something that has been in your energy for a long time there can be residue left in your auric field. It is like putting a stick in the bottom of a pool to hook out debris. The silt that gets stirred up muddies the water for a while. I could see and sense a grey smog around me on the morning after this healing, I looked and felt awful! Steve scrubbed me down again and finished with the rinse of sage water. It helped a great deal and I felt more like myself again.

Steve began to see glimpses of the third nun's life as I was working on the life of the Abbess. He knew it would be harrowing for me to look at. I already felt anxious about it. There was a sense that my guides had started with the easiest life and were building up from there. The Abbess had been tough to face, now what would I have to look at? In preparation for the last nun's life I dowsed that I needed the Australian Bush Flower Essences 'Woman' Essence, a combination essence which includes Billy Goat Plum, alleviating feelings of shame in the body.

I felt so fearful I asked Steve to journey for me first. He looked troubled when he returned. He reported that the time was shortly after

Light behind the Angels

the Norman Conquest and I was a fair haired Saxon peasant girl, only just past puberty when I'd gone into the nunnery. There was a sense that I'd come from a poor background and my parents would have given me to holy orders willingly as that would mean one less mouth to feed.

On my arrival as a novice a dark haired bearded Norman priest took a special interest in me. On the pretext of teaching me he took me aside and raped me repeatedly. The abuse was continuous and went on for months. After he raped me he would beat me and tell me I was wicked for leading him into sin, that it was my fault he was doing this because I was pretty.

I was a devout Catholic and I was very scared. I punished myself for the sin, taking my own wooden crucifix and beating my breastbone with it until my chest was covered with bruises. My periods stopped and I knew I was pregnant. I went to the priest and he cast me aside, no longer wanting me. No-one would believe me if I told the truth, it would be my word against the priest.

I could see no way out of my torment and the disgrace my pregnancy would bring to me and my family. In the end I hanged myself in my own cell. When my body was found I was taken down and given a pauper's burial outside of hallowed ground as I'd committed suicide.

It was harrowing enough just to hear the story. In my mind's eye the pictures were being played out and I could feel how terrified I was of the Catholic priest. I also knew him in this life and had been instinctively fearful of him. Now I had to connect with the girl and help her release her vows and the burden of pain and shame she had carried.

We set up three golden circles so that Steve could stand in one to give me support. My little nun was terrified and pitiful. She was sure she would be punished for what she believed she had tempted the priest to do. She hadn't crossed over properly as she was a devout Catholic and believed she had committed a mortal sin by taking her own life. We had to release her spirit so that this soul fragment could be taken into the Light for healing. Angels came and took her gently away.

Looking at this life left me feeling wretched. I bathed and was cleansed as before, but this time I was woken in the night with an acute bout of cystitis and there was a sense that I was feeling just some of the pain my little nun had experienced. After a couple of hours I wondered if I really had to go through this pain. I said the Divine Decree aloud three times and the pain subsided.

The Bush Flower Essence was still needed. Billy Goat Plum alleviates the suffering of rape victims who have a sense of the body feeling dirty and this poor girl had taken all of the blame for the attacks upon herself. I knew it would take a while to get the imprint of this life out of my physical and emotional bodies.

I was glad to have worked through all three nun's lives before the weekend as I was hosting a sound healing workshop. I hoped it would help me complete the healing process. I warned the friend who was facilitating that I might be a bit more emotional than usual. She told me that it was interesting that I and many others had been led to do deep levels of clearing in the first few months of 2009 as there had been several important astrological alignments that were ushering in the Age of Aquarius. She'd been told that the previous day the alignment was just as sung in the hit 70's musical Hair, *'When the Moon is in its seventh house and Jupiter aligns with Mars.'*

Over the workshop we were led through a range of exercises. One of the first involved using sound and movement as paired work and I teamed up with Steve. Fortunately we went into another room to do this as we dissolved into fits of giggles, which I think was a welcome release of the heaviness of the last past life.

Later we worked on singing our names. This felt intensely liberating and I used my magical name as it felt right within this small and trusted group. It was interesting that our songs all started off a little weak or shaky, but grew in strength as we worked on them. This was an exercise that brought lots of tears as we let go of old blocks and began to call our power back. As I declared through song my desire to be free, floods of tears streamed down my face. The scale of my grief surprised me, but I worked through it and I began to call out my magical name clear and strong, as if calling this other me down from the surrounding hills.

I felt it was important to do one last action to acknowledge the nuns, the last little nun in particular. I found the crucifix necklace that Fiona had given me and went with a trowel to an old church that has a Norman porch. By a lovely yew tree I buried the crucifix in consecrated ground for her and shed some more tears. Under the yew there were some crow feathers and I picked up one for each of the nuns and brought them home.

Not long after I found a little tin tobacco box in a flea market printed 'Three Nuns Tobacco', with the slogan 'None Nicer'. I bought it and remember the three when I look at it, though not with pain anymore. I am reminded most often of my Carmelite nun and her beautiful spiritual energy.

Light behind the Angels

The Cursed Lives

'Faith is the bird that feels the light when the dawn is still dark.'
Rabindranath Tagore

The release of my nuns' vows and acknowledgement and healing of their lives seemed to trigger a spontaneous download of past lives that had been blighted by the Egyptian curse.

June called me, she had been thinking of nothing much when she found she was seeing my life as a delicately built Japanese courtesan with flowing long black hair. She grabbed pen and paper and wrote down everything she was shown.

'There is a huge stone building, fields full of corn surround it. It is a busy place, but off quietly on their own a pair of lovers. He is a Samurai; she is the Lord's courtesan. They are committing a serious crime, their passion for each other is too strong and they take a terrible chance. They are lying in the grass a long way from anyone or anything, his horse grazes nearby. (I don't really want to see this.) Their passion knows no bounds. He has a scar on his bum. He is powerfully built but is so gentle with her, she is tiny, all over tiny, but perfect, she has only one flaw, a birth mark on her bum (they match). They know they are doing wrong but they can't stop it.

This has been happening for many months, but this time they are caught, someone has been spying on them and informed their Lord, a powerful and usually fair man, but he is possessed with a rage beyond belief. They are dragged naked back to him. He has all her beautiful waist length hair cut off. She is beaten and thrown out and banished. He is beaten, tortured and beheaded. Oh my God please clear this, your love for each other was so pure and beautiful.'

June confessed that she felt she had been the one to have spied on us and betrayed us to the Lord. She had expected praise for her actions and not the terrible punishments that she witnessed. Now she felt incredibly guilty. At least I could set her mind to rest. I'd discovered I'd been spied on and betrayed by my closest friends and family in so many other lifetimes that it was easy to forgive her. She had felt that my lover was Steve. Possibly he had been caught up in his own curse at last, but more likely it was the Roman again. Whichever one it was had suffered.

As a gift she had her daughter in law paint me a Japanese scene with a courtesan and her samurai warrior.

Light behind the Angels

Steve was shown a life where I was a beautiful Indian princess. He saw her running through the corridors of the palace in tears. When we went back to look at what had happened we found that her father had hired the services of a sculptor to immortalise her beauty in stone. Posing for the artist the two had fallen in love. Again they were found out and her father was furious as he was far beneath her station. Her father ordered his guards to seize the man and his daughter and she was forced to watch as her lover was taken to a bridge across a high river gorge and hurled over the edge to his death.

Her father swiftly arranged a marriage to a wealthy nobleman, older, ugly and fat, but a good match for her in his eyes. She begged him not to make her go through with the union, but he was adamant. In the next scene she was running along the corridors crying until she got to a tall open window high above the ground. She simply continued to run on and out into the air and fall to her death as her lover had done.

Not long after we were shown my lifetime as the daughter of a wealthy Italian merchant in the Renaissance. Yet again she was lovely to look at and yet again she fell for someone far beneath her, this time he was a handsome stable boy. They would roll in the hay and were passionate for each other. When she fell pregnant she had to tell her father.

The next time she met her love her father had hired an assassin. He stepped out from behind the boy and slit his throat as she moved towards him to embrace him. Horrified, she knew this was her father's doing and she was a spirited girl. She ran in fury to her father, shouting and raging at him. He pinned her against the wall and she yelled at him and beat him with her fists. When she wouldn't shut up he shook her, becoming more enraged. She started screaming and he held her by the throat to stop her. We don't think he meant to strangle her, but he did and her body fell limp. She was thrown into a canal.

Watching this life unfold I recognised that the Italian merchant was my father now. It may have explained some of the difficult energies we'd had between us that seemed out of all proportion to anything that had happened in this life. Following that regression I had a large red angry mark on my neck, just like a pressure mark, that took months to vanish. On the plus side my relationship with my father became easier still and the last of the habitual tension seemed to have evaporated between us.

I cried some tears for each of these lives in turn, but they didn't shock me or wrack me with grief like the earlier revelations. It felt like it was enough to see them, acknowledge each of them and feel a little sadness for the fates these girls had suffered. I felt I was being cleansed of all of my past life sorrow swiftly so that it would no longer lay as a heavy pattern on me and I could move on.

Light behind the Angels

Phoenix Rising

> *My will shall shape my future*
> *Whether I fail or succeed shall be no man's doing but my own.*
> *I am the force;*
> *I can clear any obstacle before me or I can be lost in the maze.*
> *My choice, my responsibility;*
> *Win or lose, only I hold the key to my destiny.*
> Elaine Maxwell

Phoenix guidance and messages about birds and wings were still coming through on a very regular basis. At a Rock and Gem show a woman I had never met before insisted on fetching her boyfriend, drawing him over to the stall she introduced him as 'Phoenix.' Later the same day I was approached by a man who had chatted to me for a while at the stall, left the building to go home, then felt compelled to turn back and pass on the guidance he'd had for me. He took me aside and apologised, asking me if I was happy to hear an unsolicited message. I liked his manners and nodded, "Go ahead with what you have been contemplating. It is time to spread your wings."

Several friends and students picked up on the phoenix around me. Semele even saw it flying ahead of her car as she drove to visit me one day. I wondered whether I'd been missing the point as repeated messages like this normally mean you haven't acted on or integrated important guidance. I'd never had such frequent and sustained messages before.

In meditation Steve saw my Eagle dive on the Phoenix and grab it with its talons. The Phoenix exploded into flames and when it hit the ground a tiger leapt from the ashes. Interpreting the images he suggested that I might be self-sabotaging my own progress as it was one of my power animals that had brought the Phoenix to the ground.

I journeyed and Steve drummed. I went to the Lower World first and met up with Raven who had a gift of a protective cloak for me made out of his feathers. I put it on and instantly felt calmer. The new animal ally, a huge tiger, came to greet me and licked my face with her massive tongue. This was a fresh experience. My personal animal guides had tended to be winged or scaly, although several of Steve's animals had appeared and helped me in the past. I love all of my helpers, but it was comforting to sink my hands into warm fur. I felt my tiger was there to give me the courage to move forwards.

She let me ride on her back and we bounded off, arriving at a cliff with a magnificent view over a winding river valley. I felt she was showing me broader horizons.

I remembered a journey from a year before. It was similar. My guide had been stern with me then, "Know thyself, see the light around you. Stop giving power away, keep your power, contain it." He had then taken me to a doorway high on a mountain top and shown me the world at my feet, before pushing me down the mountain, my hands full of gold light.

At the time I realised I had a lifelong pattern of giving my power away, passing it like a hot potato. I would have a revelation or an insight and find the closest person to give it to, instead of keeping it to nourish or empower myself. A bad habit cloaked in the guise of helping others.

I still felt I'd like more clarity, so Steve journeyed for me whilst I drummed. First he met with his own power animal who took him to see a small girl of 5 or 6 who was very sad. She was holding a little brightly coloured bird in her hands, but it was dead. He asked her name and he heard, "L-L-Lorraine," between her sobs. Steve stopped the journey and came back to me, describing the scene. "Does this mean anything to you?" He mimicked the little girl's hiccupping breaths and at once I recognised the peculiar way I used to cry as a child. I would get so upset I couldn't speak and my breath would come in little gasping sobs. I'd forgotten all about that. I grew out of it as I got older and I sound pretty much like anyone else if I cry these days. The little girl was me and she'd said her name was Lauren, but had difficulty getting the word out.

Steve journeyed back and found little Lauren again. He gave her a ride through the stars on a flying horse, to cheer her up. That stopped the sobbing, though she was still very sad and hadn't forgotten the dead bird she was holding. When they landed Phoenix was standing in front of them on the path and Tiger was there too. Little Lauren held her hands out with the bird cupped in them and the Phoenix burst into flame. First the flames lapped over the left side of her hands, then over the front, then the right side and finally over the back so the flames had come from all four quarters. When all the flames died down the little bird was standing on Lauren's outstretched palms, it gave a tiny 'cheep' and flew off.

Returning from the journey Steve recounted what he'd learned and blew back the little girl fragment of me into my heart and my crown. I felt very tender towards her. I'd forgotten what a sensitive little thing she was and just how much she would get upset if anything had suffered or died.

Light behind the Angels

Earlier in the day we'd walked the dog and Steve had pointed out a tiny wren lying dead on the pavement. I stopped and picked it up. It was still bright eyed and must have only just died, probably hit by a car. I'd placed it gently in the hedgerow.

Steve commented that it might not be so great to be able to bring things back from the dead. I reassured him that my healing powers weren't up to raising Lazarus just yet, whereupon Steve revealed he'd been thinking more of zombies. I think that exchange neatly illustrates the difference between us!

That weekend I was teaching my students to journey shamanically for guidance for each other. Steve joined in. As I was drumming he undertook two journeys for me. First he met with his power animal who took both of us along a pathway lined by my parents. There were multiples of my father on one side and multiples of my mother on the other. They didn't stop us and at the top of the path at a cliff face the rainbow bridge rose taking us to a meadow filled with flowers, each of which had a bee on it. Cows were grazing there. I interpreted this as my parents were still there, but not hindering my progress.

The image reminded me of the Fool in the Arthurian tarot deck, who must take a step out into 'thin air' but there is a rainbow bridge ready to support his feet. I remembered that the tiger had taken me to a cliff edge too; it seemed that I needed the trust to take that first step into the unknown. Steve laughed, he'd worked out that the symbolism of the cows and the bees stood for the Land of Milk and Honey!

Steve journeyed again, this time to the Upper World. He was met by an Eagleman who cried at him, raised his wings and took flight from a cliff edge. Here he hovered and morphed into me. I was surrounded by birds of all kinds and as each flew past they donated a feather to a pile growing at Steve's feet. Then I flew back in as an Eaglewoman and alighted on a marble altar. As I stood there the altar became water and reflective, then it became a fire that engulfed me and in the fire I was transformed into the Phoenix and rose in flight.

Here was another beautiful and powerful journey starting with a leap into thin air from a cliff. I took the donation of feathers as a confirmation that the bird energies I had been working with in my healing had been understood correctly. I had been writing a course to help others connect with the amazing healing and transformative energies of the bird kingdom and we would be using feathers I had been collecting ethically from different species. There was also a representation of each of the elements: Air, in the flight of the Eagle,

Earth in the marble altar, becoming Water and finally transforming Fire at the end.

I'd always observed that some of my students undergo a transformation and access amazing psychic gifts, often beyond my own abilities. I don't want to turn out duplicates of myself and I glow with pride when I see a student take off and find his or her own truth, it is the best reward a teacher could ask for. Rapid change may be in store in their personal lives too; difficult relationships, unrewarding jobs and draining friendships tend to improve or are swept away.

Years before Semele had summed my role up as a 'catalyst' and Steve suggested my site should carry a warning, "This woman may seriously change your life." Now I realise that by allowing myself to be 'put through the fire' I have been able to recognise and acknowledge the power of the Phoenix. I have risen from the ashes of my former selves and the transformative energies of the Phoenix helps me to assist those that are ready to burn away their karma, transmute their blocks and step into their true power.

Epilogue

> *'Keep me away from the wisdom which does not cry, the philosophy which does not laugh and the greatness which does not bow before children.'*
> Kahlil Gibran

Delving into past lives I have healed old wounds, released outworn pledges, removed curses, shackles, bonds and recovered shattered fragments of my psyche. Why put myself through such pain, such angst? Through the process of deep cleansing, stripping away layer after layer of past life grief, I have uncovered more of my true self.

It was time; time for me to wake up, time to self-realise. To bring my consciousness more strongly into the present I've had to work through my past. Whilst so much of my energy was stuck I was very limited in my perception of myself. I had a belief in my eternal soul but I didn't *know* it. Now I know that I have existed from the start of time and will continue to exist after my physical body is dust. Such knowledge cannot be found with the mind, it has to be experienced and when you touch the truth everything changes.

It would be a mistake to think that past lives are a way to escape from the mundane world and find a more diverting version of yourself. You need to look for the patterns, learn the lessons, heal the wounds and bring the knowledge into your life now. Do not get caught up in glamour. Past life healing is not about saying, "I was so high, so beautiful, so powerful and so rich." To look back wistfully is of no earthly use, although it may prop up the fragile ego.

Do you think we walk around dressed up and role playing our Egyptian selves? Of course not! I get on with my healing, teaching and writing and Steve has now retired as a mechanic and follows his true calling, as a Shaman who can relieve people of unpleasant entity attachments. We are still Lauren and Steve, but we carry greater power within us because we have been acknowledging and healing our past.

Are we enlightened beings? We can be. Sometimes. The journey for both of us continues as it does for all those who live on this planet.

Work through your own past lives to reveal more of who you really are, to be ever more present, to be more conscious in the now. You may find that you too have been dreaming awake, moving through habitual patterns, restricted by unconscious bonds.

As the New Age dawns on Earth we must all awaken to the truth of ourselves. I believe that each of us that awakens makes the path a little wider and less precipitous for those who follow. I asked my Guides for a message to help all who struggle with the pain of the human condition. I leave you with their wisdom:

Let us lift the last veils of deception from you. In the One moment all that has occurred is but a dream and you are the dreamer.

Wave after endless wave. Your troubles are all on the surface. On the waves you will ever be tossed and in turmoil. The surface only is disturbed, the deeps are still and quiet. Dive beneath the surface of yourself now and connect with the changeless depths of you. There you will find the treasure, the pearls, not tossed around on the wave tops. The pearl is hidden deep within and to reach it you must dive into your innermost being and not be distracted by the surface drama.

Such supreme beauty awaits mankind when he awakes from his dream of himself and looks to the treasure of his soul. You must go deeper and deeper into the mysteries of the eternal you. It is the only journey worth taking and its price is forgiveness, forgiveness of others, but especially of yourself. For who can blame the dreamer for their actions? It is only when you are truly awake that you can take full responsibility for what befalls you, for now your eyes are opened and you can see.

About the Author

Lauren still lives and works in Mid Wales with Steve, her son, dog, cat, and chickens. If you feel ready for the Lauren D'Silva approach to self empowerment you can contact her through her website to request healing or tuition on Crystal Therapy, Past Lives or Bird Spirit Healing. Lauren is also available for spiritual guidance sessions. Be prepared to let go of who you thought you were and get to know who you really are.
www.touchstones-therapies.co.uk

As New Age Editor for Bellaonline, Lauren has written on a wide range of topics including past lives, twin flames and soul mates, crystals, spirit guides and spiritual development. You can browse several hundred of her articles on the site for free.
www.bellaonline.com/site/newage

Bothered by unpleasant energies? You can request a free initial consultation from Steve Deeks-D'Silva.
www.entity-removal.co.uk

As High Priestess and High Priest and Lauren and Steve preside over Handfasting ceremonies and other rites of passage. Contact Lauren through her site for more information.

Printed in Great Britain
by Amazon.co.uk, Ltd.,
Marston Gate.